s? How d
ur ma
e beginning'
as it? How di
ing about it?
ules? Are yo
Do you have
ogether? Do
sex with you

ASK ME HOW IT WORKS

For Mom, Ate, Nanay and Dima

Contents

1	*What's it like?*	1
2	*How did it start?*	17
3	*Was your marriage open from the beginning?*	39
4	*Whose idea was it?*	59
5	*How did you start talking about it?*	89
6	*What are the rules?*	109
7	*Are you ever jealous?*	139
8	*Do you have adventures together?*	165
9	*Do you still have sex with your husband?*	197
10	*How much do you tell each other?*	225
11	*Aren't you afraid of feelings?*	249
12	*What happens if you fall in love?*	279
13	*So does it really work?*	313
14	*What do you tell your daughter?*	347

Epilogue: *Are you happier this way?*	371
Resources	385
Acknowledgements	387

I

What's it like?

The alarm woke me from a short, shallow slumber. The first stealthy sliver of pale morning light crept in through the blinds, falling on Robert asleep beside me, the sound of his teeth grinding in my ear. Had he popped his mouth guard in before we passed out? I couldn't remember. Everything was a blur so early in the morning, after so long a night.

Reluctant to leave the heat of our bodies under the duvet, I reached out and grasped for my phone, finding it on the nightstand between my spare asthma inhaler and a pump jar of lube. Battery almost depleted, it blinked the time: 5 a.m. For a moment I was tempted to hit snooze, but I knew better. It was too easy to surrender to the lure of five more minutes and wake five hours later, in the harsh unforgiving glare of morning. And that wouldn't do.

If I hurry, I can beat reality before it wakes up for breakfast, I thought.

Summoning my willpower, I eased myself from Robert's arms and slid out of bed. I fished my discarded bra and panties off the leather easy chair, peeled my tights off the nubbly red pouffe, and scooped up my dress, a puddle of black on the living-room rug. In the dim light I slipped on last night's clothing like a ninja: practised, silent, quick. I could do this with my eyes closed.

From the debris of our Friday night — Robert's empty beer cans; the ends of our stubbed-out joints, which he always rolled so deftly; and my single glass of whisky, which he always poured for me Irish style, with a drop of water – I plucked a few things to tuck into my bag: the half-empty bottle of Nikka from the Barrel, a lacy white thong with fake pearls strung along an open slit, a purple double-ended dildo.

You said you would never! Robert had said last night, after we collapsed against each other in bed, panting and exhausted. *Do you remember you told me that on our second date?*

I did? That feels like ages ago.

We were in the basement at Radion, he reminded me. *You asked me what my deepest, darkest fantasy was. When I told you, you said, 'Sorry, but that's never going to be me!'*

Oh, right. I remember. I didn't see the point in pretending to have a dick.

He had laughed. *You sure didn't* look *like you were pretending.*

Yeah, well . . . this thing turned out to be plenty of fun for everyone.

Feeling under the covers for our new purple friend, I had found its smooth silicone heft and pulled it out for both of us to contemplate. *I didn't expect that.*

Now, dressed and packed, all possessions accounted for, I tiptoed into the bedroom and perched on the edge of the bed. 'I'm going,' I whispered with a gentle nudge, though Robert hardly even registered my departure.

'Come back soon,' he murmured, more asleep than awake, eyes still closed.

'I will.' My lips grazed the dark stubble on his cheek before I slipped out the door into a chilly Amsterdam dawn. I had chosen to slither home at the right time: sunrise painted the clouds with a luminous jumble of pink and orange, a hint of brightness gleaming through the grey.

Whizzing past the old windmill, down the length of the Westerpark, I coasted home on my last legs as the rush of exhilaration faded, the smoky tendrils of pleasure dissipated into the damp morning air, and the final bright-hot glimmers of intensity cooled to the dull red pulsing embers of fatigue.

Cycling home through my adopted city at daybreak was a balm and a pleasure, the hush of its streets and the mirror stillness of its canals a release. On mornings like this, after nights like the one I'd just had, the wind on my face felt like pure freedom.

There had been many nights, and many lovers.

On any other night, my ride home might have been the last train back to Amsterdam, stuffed with drunken Carnaval revellers in ludicrous costumes, from Charlie's apartment in Nijmegen. It might have been the 6 a.m. Uber from Rick's, a text message sent from the back seat to acknowledge my safe arrival and thank him for the night, or Massimo's white van loaded up with Sicilian produce, blaring classic rock all the way back to West from Noord.

It might have been, as it most often was, a bicycle ride home on autopilot in last night's clothing, a walk of shame minus the shame, past the neighbours sitting down to breakfast with their kids by the window, not more than a fleeting thought given to wondering what they have seen, what they think, what they know.

The ride home was never just a journey from point A to point B. It was a transition from one space to another, from one me to another: from sexual freedom to domestic bliss, from the elusive thrill of the new and other to the bone-deep comfort of the beloved and mundane, a thin slipstream of time in which I shed the skin of libertine and lover, and reassumed that of mother and wife. After alternating between both for this long, I hardly felt any friction coming home to my husband and child.

No matter the point of departure or mode of transport, the final destination was always the same.

The house was quiet. I headed straight for the shower to slough off my night, allowing my mind to go blank under the hot water. There would be time to replay the highlights later. All I could think of was sleep. Scrubbed clean and hair wet, I crept into the still-dark bedroom, lifted a corner of the duvet, and slid into bed beside my husband.

Marcus's back was turned, but when I reached for him he rolled towards me, more asleep than awake, eyes still closed. He pulled the curve of my body to his, enveloping me in his familiar warmth. The solid weight of his leg over mine, an anchor in the deep. I was floating, but now I was tethered: to him, to us, to my life and ours.

A warm welcome hadn't always been waiting for me. There was a time when Marcus kept his back to me, pretending to be asleep even though I knew he was awake. These morning embraces were hard-won, as were the carefree bicycle rides that carried me home to them.

In a few hours, my half-closed eyes would open to find our daughter snuggled in between us, a starburst of black hair and slender limbs wrapped in a purple-and-green fleece mermaid tail, before I fell asleep again. When I woke fully, it would be to mid-morning sunshine streaming in through white-painted shutters, chirpy cartoon chatter from the living room, and the aroma of fresh coffee from the kitchen.

Marcus would bring in breakfast for three on a wooden tray table: bacon, cinnamon rolls, pancakes with powdered sugar and *hagelslag*, the chocolate sprinkles that are a Dutch breakfast staple. Spotting the purple double dildo peeking out from the top of my bag, he would say, 'Huh. Well, how was *that*?'

I would give him a look that said, *Shh, later*, as little feet thudded towards us, drawn by the smell of bacon and the promise of morning cuddles in Mama and Papa's bed.

And he would understand. *Later.*

For now, there was only us, and sleep. The last thing I heard before the world faded out was the sound of his teeth grinding in my ear.

Home, I thought. *I am home.*

*

On my Tinder profile, a careful selection of words describes who I am and what I'm looking for.

Tropical girl in Amsterdam. 1.56, my height in metres – I live in a country populated by the world's tallest human beings, so this is significant information. *Cocktails, conversation, dancing, kissing* – a shortlist of preferences and activities meant to attract the attention of those who enjoy the same, and filter out those who don't. Yes, there are people who don't enjoy kissing. I've met them and don't care to meet more.

Best keep it short. Brevity is power. Do men even read these things? I wind it up with a casual bomb drop. *Oh, and my man knows I'm here.* I'm being purposely ambiguous; *man* also happens to be the Dutch word for husband, hinting at commitment while sidestepping the thorny morality of marriage. I finish with a trick out of my copywriting toolbox: the call to action.

Go on, ask me how it works.

Apparently, men do read. Nine out of ten times, the first message I receive from a new match says: *So how does it work?*

In the eight years since my husband and I first threw open the windows of our seventeen-year marriage to the wild winds of consensual non-monogamy, *How does it work?* has been the first question I've received from people I've met, considered, rejected or enjoyed as sexual partners. It has been the opening salvo to multiple flirtations, conversations and interrogations over the years, both scout and sensor, the advance party of a line of questioning that has grown familiar, even predictable.

Curiosity is one of the qualities I like best in myself and admire in others, so I don't shy away from questions. New ones arise all the time; responses change over time. Questions worth asking are always worth answering. But a question like *How does it work?* leaves too much to tell.

Maybe it's better if I just show you.

*

Another Saturday. Alone at last.

The two of us had only an hour, maybe an hour and a half at most. Exchanging glances with the giddy anticipation of lovers on an illicit dalliance, with a squeeze of gloved hands, Marcus and I set off towards the Vondelpark on a crisp, sunny, late-autumn afternoon.

We had just deposited our daughter, violin strapped to her back and scores in a canvas tote, at her weekly orchestra rehearsal. Our shy girl would have preferred one or both of us to sit outside the rehearsal room, door open for the occasional reassuring peek, but parents were not allowed to linger in the building and had been asked to collect our children at the appointed end time. This gave us a glorious child-free hour with no errands to run, nothing to do except enjoy our city and each other.

Our meandering trajectory towards the Vondelpark was a stroll down memory lane: past the shops along the Overtoom, which Marcus and I had scoured for furniture when we first moved to Amsterdam; past thick tangles of wisteria clinging to painted balconies, waiting for the spring; past the Lunchroom Wilhelmina, a tiny sandwich shop crowded with rickety tables and mismatched chairs, where we liked to come when we were childless and carefree.

Alongside the memories we shared, the things we discovered drew us closer together. Peering into an open archway, we followed our curiosity into a hospital complex built in 1891, whose brick walls now housed artists and architects, therapists and start-ups. Dry autumn leaves made a satisfying rustle in our wake as we wandered through the courtyard, marvelling at how Amsterdam still held so many surprises for us after all this time.

At the Blue Teahouse in the park, we fell in line for mulled wine and coffee and took our paper cups to a bench by the water. I nudged Marcus at the sight of an elderly couple strolling arm in arm: *It'll be us, someday*. What lives had they lived together? What stories might they tell? He said the old man with the sleek felt hat and suede elbow patches looked a little too dapper to be future him, but the dame with the voluminous cobalt-blue coat could definitely be future me.

The minutiae of a shared life filled our conversation: household, schedules, work, tasks. Like most parents granted a window of freedom from their child, we spent a sizeable chunk of our time talking about that child. We listened and laughed, planned and aligned. All too soon, it was time to return to the music school, to our daughter, and to parenthood.

If this had been any other Saturday, we would have headed straight home after orchestra rehearsal. But today wasn't quite an ordinary day.

To make the most of the rare dry weather, on the way home we stopped by the Westerpark, our green backyard. Released into the wild, our daughter spied a knot of schoolfriends at play and ran towards them. We smiled and nodded at their parents, huddled together with glühwein and coffee as we had been an hour ago, locked in a battle of wills: would the parents get cold or the children tire first? The kids almost always won.

At three o'clock, Marcus squeezed my hand: it was time.

He gave me a tight hug. 'Have fun,' I told him. 'I got this.'

'You sure?' he asked. He always asked.

'Of course,' I said firmly. 'Enjoy yourself. We're all good.'

He strode over to the wooden jungle gym and held out his arms to our giggling, upside-down child, who dropped on to the sand for a hug.

'Mama will take you home,' I heard him say. 'I love you.'

'Love you,' she replied breathlessly, eager to return to her games. 'See you later!'

Tomorrow, I thought. *See you tomorrow.*

He glanced back at me for a moment. Like a mother bidding her child goodbye on the first day of school, I smiled back, arranging my face into an expression of enthusiasm and encouragement.

WHAT'S IT LIKE?

It's going to be fine. You're going to have so much fun! You'll forget all about me. You'll see.

The look worked. My husband walked off in the direction of the hotel in the middle of the Westerpark, hoisting his backpack over his shoulders. In it were a portable Bluetooth speaker, four lengths of jute rope 8 metres long, condoms, lube, and probably a few other things I didn't know about, that were nobody's business but his own. He took his phone out of his pocket, checking to see if his rendezvous was waiting.

See you tomorrow.

My frozen feet soon forced me to give up my ground in the parent–child battle of endurance. I disentangled my daughter from her troop of dangling monkeys, shepherded her home, and ran her a hot bath while I ordered sushi. I sang along with *The Prince of Egypt*, DreamWorks's animated hit from the 1990s, as she slurped steaming spoonfuls of miso soup and popped translucent bubbles of roe in her mouth. The Red Sea parted as I rubbed jasmine-scented argan oil into her long, wet hair, brushing it until it was shiny and smooth. Bedtime was easy and sweet; she was out at eight on the dot.

That left my evening all mine to enjoy. Though I had chosen different pleasures – lace and satin soaking in the sink, an ambergris candle on the windowsill, a nibble of dark chocolate and a few puffs of hash – I fell asleep with my book spread open on his empty pillow, knowing that Marcus was enjoying his.

My husband came home in phases. First, a WhatsApp message time-stamped 2:33 a.m., seen through squinting eyes blurry with sleep. *By myself now. I'd like some alone time to decompress. Can I sleep here, grab brekkie and be home around 9?*

Then the hiss of the shower, shadows in the bedroom doorway, backlit by the bulb in the hall, the creak of closet doors, the damp weight of him sinking into bed. At last, the thigh thrown over mine, the arm around my ribcage, the hand at my breast.

Sundays in our home begin late and unfurl at a slow pace. Blessed with my genetic capacity for deep slumber, my daughter is that rare species most parents would kill for: a good sleeper and late riser. The next morning was just like any other: she and I dawdled on the couch in our pyjamas, books in our hands, fleece mermaid tail cocooning her legs as the cat hopped up and curled into a furry black loaf on mine, all of us quiet, unhurried, content.

Papa, the king of Sunday morning pancakes, needed his sleep. Grabbing a mixing bowl and wooden spoon, I stepped up to the stove, forgetting what spelled the essential difference between fluffy American pancakes and thin Dutch ones. Halfway through the first batch I remembered: baking powder. To disguise my lack of culinary finesse with a teachable moment, I presented my lumpen creations to my daughter as clouds: cumulus, stratus, nimbus. Given free rein to dispense powdered sugar and *hagelslag*, she was both gleeful and entertained.

Marcus padded into the kitchen at half past ten, present in body but hazy in spirit. I recognized the floaty expression, slow reflexes and wandering gaze as signs of recovery from an intense night. He needed time to process his experiences, to take it slow and easy. From experience, I knew he would coalesce over the day. By evening, he would be solid, attentive, fully reintegrated as husband and father. It would take an early bedtime, a full night's sleep and several cups of coffee to restore him to the alertness and productivity his corporate job demanded, to be sharp and decisive as his work required. But that could wait until tomorrow.

Right now – as with most of our time, except for the hours when we agreed otherwise – family came first. In the meantime, he would coast on the ebb and flow of our lazy Sunday, hauling himself back to shore after being temporarily unmoored from responsibility. Until then, I was captain of the ship.

He would do the same for me.

*

On another weekend, you might overhear the quiet murmur of conversation elsewhere in the house while our child revels in her allotted hour on the Nintendo Switch, a present from Santa Claus and Sinterklaas – the American and Dutch incarnations of Saint Nicholas, one a throwback to our childhoods and the other a centrepiece of hers – who joined forces last year for a big gift.

Whatever you imagine goes on in this house, talking outstrips it by far. Morning-after check-ins over coffee on the balcony, when we think (or hope) the neighbours aren't listening. Commitments restated, new agreements drawn up in the bedroom, door closed but not locked. A litany of sins in the shower, one of us the penitent behind a curtain of condensation, the other a wet, naked priest in a steamy confessional booth. A snort of laughter here, a raised eyebrow there. And always, the option to say, *I've heard enough, thanks*, trusting it will be understood and respected.

As a family, our daily lives are grounded in a comfortable ease that the demands of our open marriage rarely disrupt. After all this time, we're more or less a well-oiled machine. Sometimes I'm still surprised by how normal this all feels. When everything works, which is most days, I go about my business with a light heart, a sense of balance, and a confidence that comes from knowing that everyone in my life is happy, loved and growing – myself included.

It wasn't always like this. Not at the beginning. This was the work of years: of countless conversations, multiple mistakes, and as many attempts to learn from them.

Which brings us to the first and most obvious question. *How did it start?*

Everyone asks, but not everyone wants to hear the real answer. What I say depends on who's asking, and how they're listening. If I sense a casual interest – a date eager to move on quickly to other things; a new acquaintance at a party, drink in hand and ready to flee at the first sign of awkwardness – I give the standard response. 'It took a long time, but we talked about it a lot and decided to give it a try. We agreed we could always close the marriage again if it wasn't working. But it is, so here we are.'

The standard response serves me well. It's a box to tick, a quick release: short and neat, a compact version of a complicated truth, easy to inject with wit and punctuate with a wink. But you're probably not interested in the standard response. I can tell – something in the eyes, the posture, a lingering quality in the pause that follows the question, a deepening of the attention when I begin to speak. A genuine interest might persuade me to provide an answer that matches the depth of your curiosity.

WHAT'S IT LIKE?

I might say it started when my husband and I moved to Amsterdam. With its reputation for liberalism and tolerance, permissiveness and sex, Europe's Sin City as the starting point of an open marriage seems to fit. If you met a couple from Amsterdam who told you they were in an open marriage, you might not be surprised. It might even make sense.

But if I'm honest, and if you're willing to listen, I would say it started long before Amsterdam, in the unlikeliest of places. I would say it started in the Philippines – a staunchly conservative, fiercely Catholic South East Asian nation of 115 million people and 7,641 islands, one of the last two countries on earth where divorce is illegal – where I was born.

2

How did it start?

He was broke and ambitious, an awkward engineering graduate from Kolkata with a scraggly moustache and a full scholarship at the Asian Institute of Management in the Philippines, which, in the 1970s was considered the Harvard Business School of Asia.

Having recently arrived in Manila, his plan was to return to India as a highly eligible bachelor with a prestigious international MBA, command a hefty dowry, marry a nice Bengali girl from a respectable Bengali family, and lift his entire clan – whose hopes for a better life had been pinned on him since childhood – out of poverty and into prosperity. A certified nerd, dutiful son, and bearer of his family's dreams, he studied hard and kept his head buried in books and business cases.

He never saw her coming.

She was tiny and proud, a deep-dimpled firebrand from Santa Cruz, Laguna, with a heart-shaped face, quick tongue and mercurial temper. Breadwinner since the age of seventeen, she worked to support her mother and sister while putting herself through college, danced with a folk troupe, and picketed outside the Malacañang Palace gates with other long-haired hippy leftists before realizing that being an idealist didn't mean she wanted to be a Communist. On the night they met, she had planned to turn up at a boarding house in Pasay for an AIM student party she'd been invited to by friends from her office. It turned out to be a set-up; a blind date was *not* part of the plan.

She disliked him at first sight. Her sole objective was to prevent him from getting into her pants, which she did by refusing to sit beside him and keeping the door to his dorm room open all night. No funny business. Not on her watch.

He was on to her. At the end of the evening, he collapsed in bed with his bottle of San Miguel, laughing. She was funny, but he liked her. He was amused; she was not.

He was my father; she was my mother.

My parents may have met on a blind date, but this was the Philippines. No romance could prosper without courtship: an age-old ritual where man and woman are locked into the roles of pursuer and pursued, drawn out for months or even years, clearly marked by formal milestones along a timeline somewhere in between heartbreak and happily ever after.

In the Philippines, courtship begins with a man's announcement of his intent to woo, preferably with a declaration, verbally or in writing, of his beloved's beauty and virtue. A woman may then allow him to pursue her or tell him he doesn't have a hope in hell of winning her heart. She may also let him down gently with an offer of friendship; these days, we call this friendzoning.

It starts young. Boys write love letters, sing love songs, and perform acts of service for the girl and her parents, putting their best foot forward to demonstrate what a perfect boyfriend (and later, son-in-law) they would be. Girls devise ways to keep boys at a distance, their perceived virtue and market value heightened by the lengths to which their suitors go to woo them, and how long they can withstand the full force of such romantic persistence.

Determined to win her over, my father borrowed a scooter to begin courting my mother at home, at the tiny apartment she shared with Nanay and Tita R., my grandmother and aunt, in the smog-choked alleys of Sampaloc, Manila. Nosy neighbours heralded his arrival, shouting, '*Ayan na yung Bumbay!*' ('The Indian is here!'), giving her enough time to close the wooden shutters and pretend she wasn't home. He waited outside until my soft-hearted Nanay intervened on his behalf – '*Kawawa naman!*' ('That poor boy!') – and invited him in.

Determined to shake him off, my mother decided to hit him where it hurt – in his pocket – by becoming too high-maintenance to sustain. After a birthday spending spree that included fabric *and* tailoring for two new dresses, plus lunch and *halo-halo* for her and two of her closest girlfriends, he came to her the next day with his bank passbook. Balance: 0. She had cleaned him out.

My father knew what she was doing, but he had wanted her to have a happy birthday. He had wired an aunt in India for help, but until he received the money, he could no longer afford to see her. He could barely afford to feed himself.

She should have been triumphant. Instead, she was overcome with guilt. She had only wanted to discourage him, not starve him to death. 'When . . . when will the money arrive?' she stammered. 'How will you eat until then?'

'I don't know,' he said, mild and unassuming. 'I'm from India. I'll find a way.'

In that moment, my mother's heart began to beat for him, for she had effectively turned him into the one thing she could never resist: an underdog. Chastised and contrite, she began to make sandwiches and bring them to his dorm.

My parents were married ten months later.

Everything I learned about marriage, I learned from my

parents. Theirs was my favourite love story, and they were my favourite characters: two scrappy kids in love who dared to buck tradition, did things their way – and against all odds, came out on top. To me they were Mom and Dad, but in my mother's stories, she always called them Mommy and Daddy. She never tired of telling those stories, as I never tired of hearing them.

Mommy and Daddy taking off from the office to get married at Makati City Hall on their lunch break, with only 50 pesos between them and a witness they had pulled off the street into the courtroom. Mommy and Daddy bringing home fried chicken from Max's to break the news of their wedding to my grandmother. 'When I saw the fried chicken, I said to myself: "*Naku!* Something is going on,"' Nanay once said. She refused to let him return to his dorm room that night. 'You are husband and wife now. You should no longer be apart,' she insisted. He never left, and my sister was born nine months later.

Mommy and Daddy returning to Kolkata with the new baby and a slew of gifts including the first colour TV on the block, on a shock-and-awe mission to dazzle my grandparents into accepting their Filipina daughter-in-law. They left the baby with Dima and Dadu to travel around India, a period Mom describes as 'that time your sister had to do sales'. With her luminous hazel eyes and wispy fine brown hair, my one-year-old sister sold the marriage spectacularly. Mom and Dad returned to find my grandparents madly in love with their first grandchild, the lost dowry forgotten.

Mommy and Daddy's first car, a Mercedes-Benz his wealthy boss promised to give him for free if he managed to drive it home. Having never driven in his life, Daddy chugged, sputtered and snaked through Manila's smog and traffic until he arrived triumphant and soaked in sweat, presenting Mommy with the shiny new prize he'd won through sheer pluck and determination.

Long before I attended weddings where priests preached of love as sacrifice, I understood that marriage was an adventure. Seeing Mom's eyes sparkle, her dimples deepen and her smile flash with every retelling, I understood that the adventure made you come alive, and that the best thing about it was finding someone who wanted to go on that adventure with you.

I understood that life was a game played by a team of two. As husband and wife, only the two of you decided the rules of the game; and, together, only the two of you decided what it meant to win. 'No one understood Daddy and me the way we understood each other,' Mom would say. 'As long as you understand each other, who the hell cares?'

By all Manila middle-class indicators of success, my parents were winning. By their early thirties, the dirt-poor scholar from Kolkata and the feisty working student from Santa Cruz had two adorable little girls, a two-storey home in a private gated community, his and hers sports cars, the luxury of travel around Asia and Europe. They started out with nothing but achieved more together than they would have alone, in a society that neither encourages nor rewards deviations from the norm.

Filipinos are many wonderful things – joyful, hard-working, fiercely familial – but as a people we are not inclined to unconventional decisions, feats of daring or displays of individual uniqueness. Life in a poor, tumultuous, disaster-battered country like the Philippines is hard enough as it is; why make it harder?

Among hundreds of millions of people, opportunities are few; the vast majority who cannot afford to pay for them must be prepared to fight for them. Day-to-day survival is the national goal, its pursuit wired into our collective DNA. Laughter is the national coping mechanism. Survival depends on sticking to what works – which is what everyone around you is doing, and most likely what your parents, their parents, and their parents' parents have always done. This doesn't make it easy for those who are different – as my parents clearly were, and as I would realize I was, too.

Thanks to over three centuries of Spanish colonial rule – ended by the Treaty of Paris, which sold the Philippines to the United States in a package deal with Puerto Rico and Guam, and ushered in three decades under an American governor-general – the Philippines is one of the last remaining strongholds of the Roman Catholic Church. It is also one of only two remaining states in the world where divorce is forbidden. The other is Vatican City, population 825.

Three hundred years in a Spanish convent and thirty years in America's Hollywood, as we say in the Philippines, left devastating scars in our history, identity and culture, and screwed with our psyches big time. Nowhere is this more evident than in Filipino attitudes towards sex, love, marriage and commitment, which are shaped by Catholic guilt and American puritanism. As I write, a divorce bill languishes in Congress, while lawmakers squabble over the endless renaming of roads and the covert reallocation of government funds to their own pockets. It may very well stay there forever.

Instead of divorce, the Family Code of the Philippines provides three legal options for couples who might be driven to end their marriages.

In a declaration of nullity, a court declares the marriage contract null and void – in fact, that it was *never valid* at the time it was made, based on twelve distinct grounds including age of consent, fraud, incest, bigamy and same-sex marriage.

In an annulment, another set of conditions renders the marriage *voidable* if one party is proven to have concealed, at the time of the marriage, an unsound mind, conviction for a crime or 'moral turpitude', drug addiction, alcoholism, sexually transmitted disease or homosexuality. Take note: the development of any of these conditions *during* the marriage is not considered sufficient legal reason for a marriage to be annulled. They must have been present at the time you were wed, and you'd better have proof.

Neither of these first two options mandates financial support, parenting plans or shared custody; they are simply terminations of a contract, releasing both parties from any obligation to one another – a complete negation, as if the marriage never happened.

Finally, there's legal separation, the only option that considers adultery or abuse as acceptable grounds for parting ways. However, couples who are legally separated are not allowed to divide their assets or to remarry, as they are still considered married under Philippine law.

If you're having a hard time keeping all this straight in your head, believe me: you're not alone. All three legal exits from marriage are torturous and convoluted, and they can take anywhere from two years, for the wealthy and well connected, to five to ten years for the rest of the general populace. In the corrupt labyrinth of the Philippine legal system, husband and wife become adversaries, locked in an acrimonious courtroom battle for up to a decade, decimating their life savings, ripping each other to shreds so that in the end not only their marriage is left in tatters but also any civility or goodwill towards one another.

Designed to protect the nuclear family, all three routes are nuclear options, leaving only scorched earth from which to rebuild new lives. The goal may be noble: to compel couples to reconsider any impulse to leave a marriage, either at the first or five-hundredth sign of trouble. The reality is that the vast majority of Filipinos live one illness or disaster away from destitution and can't afford to buy their way out of an abusive or dysfunctional marriage. My parents' and grandparents' generation still scoff at divorce as the easy way out, the cowards' exit for flighty millionaires and American pop stars who have money to burn and assets to divide, but not the tenacity or grit to make it work. Perhaps this is shifting, but the lawmakers don't care – it might very well profit them not to.

Once you're married in the Philippines, you're bound for life regardless of the health or happiness of the union. The only acceptable path is clear. Social pressure reinforces it; the law mandates it. Life is made for two; marriage is for life. Anything less than forever is a failure. The state of the relationship when it crosses the finish line is less crucial than reaching the end together. Make it work at all costs, or face financial ruin, societal shame and lifelong loneliness.

In the Philippines, fiftieth wedding anniversaries are routinely celebrated in gold-trimmed hotel ballrooms by hundreds of relatives who queue up for buffet dinners; adorable grandchildren and great-grandchildren dressed to match for their choreographed dance numbers; and homemade slideshows set to love songs about grey hair and eternal fidelity. As I grew up, I saw adults around me, almost without exception, get married and stay married. For the most part, it's a beautiful thing. I grew up seeing the extent of what's possible in a marriage, and what people who love each other are willing to do for each other to make it work.

There were Tito C. and Tita P., the parents of my childhood best friend. In the Philippines, you call your parents' friends and friends' parents *Tito* and *Tita*, uncle and aunt, as a sign of respect. They were the first real marriage I grew up seeing, a flesh-and-blood husband and wife who weren't characters in one of Mom's stories. For the first eleven years of my life I was embedded in their family, witness to their utter adoration for, and unyielding patience with, one another.

There were the countless weddings, anniversaries and renewals of wedding vows I sang for as a soprano in a choir for over a decade of my life. Much later, seeing my friends in their own happy marriages renewed my belief that a marriage works as long as you want to make it work.

Each time I witnessed a newly minted marriage or golden wedding anniversary, I saw a vision of a deep, persistent, long-lasting love that I was certain would be mine someday. To this day, I hold no bitterness towards the kind of commitment I grew up seeing, nor am I trying to convince anyone that monogamy is a sham we've all been sold – not when the lives of many of those closest to me are a testament to how beautiful marriage can be.

Longevity as the sole measure of the health and success of a relationship has its dark side. Is it romantic? Yes. Is it toxic? Also yes.

The pursuit of longevity at any cost, without a dignified or easy legal exit, has produced a nation not only of incurable romantics but also of philandering husbands, martyr wives and maligned mistresses, the latter two referred to in whispers as *legal wife* and *kept woman* or *querida*, a euphemism borrowed from the Spanish; scores of illegitimate children, without legal recognition or rights; second, sometimes third and even fourth families, both hidden and flaunted; and plenty of juicy gossip. Secrets are preferred to scandal, but sweeping indiscretions under the rug never stopped anyone from dishing on them after Sunday Mass or over a late-night game of mahjong.

As I grew older and my view broadened beyond my immediate vicinity, I began to sense that secrecy was one of the unspoken underpinnings of marriages that society deemed successful. Beneath the oft-quoted biblical passages and loudly professed exhortations to *make Jesus the centre of your marriage* and *never underestimate the power of a praying wife*, every marriage seemed to be supported by its own small web of things better left unsaid.

The secret savings account you keep in case your husband turns out to be abusive and you need to take the kids and run. The online shopping deliveries squirrelled away before the husband comes home from the office. The hidden budget you never show your wife, and the code of silence that protects your night out with the boys.

Growing up, I heard enough sly jokes among husbands and saw enough silent suffering among wives to understand that, in many ways, the success of a marriage depends on what one can get away with, and how much the other can bear. I've lost count of the number of times I've heard 'as long as they come home' or 'as long as they are a good provider' or 'for the sake of the children' to justify marriages that are intact on paper but rotting in secret.

I began to wonder why the sacrifice (mostly on the part of the wives) and secrecy that seemed to underpin marriage were so far removed from the sermons I heard at all those weddings and anniversaries, and from the kind of love my parents had. Secrecy might have been crucial to other marriages, but not theirs.

Not that my father didn't try. I was already married when my mother asked me, 'Did you know I found out that Daddy once had a girlfriend?' It was early in their marriage: Mom was in the final months of her pregnancy with my sister, Dad well into his metamorphosis from a broke graduate student from India with zero style into a young finance hotshot who sipped Johnnie Walker and wore slim-cut suits to the bank. He was suddenly desirable and aspirational, the English-speaking boss who made the local office girls giggle. In Mom's eyes, the secretary made a play for him and he fell for it.

Perhaps Dad thought it was a harmless flirtation, that Mom would never find out, or that it was part of the success he deserved. But convinced she was in love, the girl began calling him at home, begging him to leave his pregnant wife. Wringing his hands, desperate to avert disaster, and all out of solutions, he came clean with the whole story.

'Mommy, help me. What do I do?' he said. With my sister on the way, they had become accustomed to calling each other Mommy and Daddy in private.

'Don't worry, Daddy,' she said. 'I'll take care of it.'

The next day on her lunch break, she marched into his office and confronted the secretary. By the time she was through, the girl's reputation was irreparable, while my father's star continued to rise.

I grew up hearing much about Mom's famous temper,

but she never spoke of this episode with bitterness or resentment, only that familiar gleam in her eye. If there was any anger, it was directed not at him, but at their common enemy. It wasn't a deal-breaker; if anything, it was a triumph. Loyalty to each other transcended all else. One of them had bungled a play, but the other had swooped in to save the day. They had each other's backs no matter what, and their team was still ahead.

Sundays were for family, Saturdays for each other, but Friday nights were theirs to enjoy apart, with a *don't ask, don't tell* policy.

While Mom went to movies at the Quad or listened to records at a girlfriend's house, Dad would put on his red polo shirt – 'his fighting gear' she called it, smiling at the memory – and join the boys for smokes and Scotch at a 'girlie bar', one of the strip joints along the neon-lit stretch of P. Burgos in Makati. 'No questions asked,' she said, 'and see you at home.'

One Friday, curiosity got the better of her. Breaking protocol, she wanted to know where he went on their nights apart. Dad gave her a long, deep look as he considered her request. 'Do you want to see?' he said at last. Mom showed up at the girlie bar with him that night, cementing her status as the 'cool' wife among the gang. Her retelling never betrayed a hint of jealousy or judgement, only a wide-eyed fascination with the naked female bodies on display, and surprise at her own appreciation of their beauty in the play of shadows and strobe lights. 'Like sculptures or nude paintings,' she murmured.

The rebellious allure of *don't ask, don't tell* Friday nights faded into a comforting familiarity. Dad wore his red polo shirt less often after that, and Mom's movie nights with her girlfriends didn't seem as important. 'It was nicer to be together,' she says, 'even if we were only reading or watching TV.'

Their team was still ahead, but the game was getting harder.

My father, a vice-president at an international bank, was caught between the final machinations of a Filipino dictator clinging to power and the profligate spending of an Indonesian tycoon who would cause the collapse of the bank where he was employed. A casualty of Asian tigers playing fast and loose with money, falling into the cracks that their games caused in the South East Asian financial system, Dad lost his job.

The owner of the bank reassigned my father to mergers and acquisitions, redeploying him to Hong Kong as the company hatchet man. Every day for the next three months, he retrenched dozens of employees, bracing himself for their desperation and vitriol; every night, he drank to numb himself and forget.

The sparkle in my mother's eyes would disappear, her gaze turning flat and steely as she told me about the long-distance calls, my father in tears, begging her to take him home. The weekly flights between Manila and Hong Kong, bleeding their savings dry. The dingy apartment, the empty whisky bottles under the bed, the shattered husband.

Their playbook was clear. She swept in and bailed him out as she had before. 'It will be okay, Daddy,' she told him. 'I'll work for the two of us, you'll find another job soon. We can do it together.' She brought him home in October 1984, in time for my third birthday. After three months of unemployment, depression, anxiety, and borderline paranoid schizophrenia, refusing in-patient psychiatric care, he took his own life in January.

All my life I believed my father had died of a heart attack. I had been too young to know the truth. My mother only revealed the true cause of his death when I was thirty-five, almost the same age as my father was when he died by suicide. It was only then I understood that silence could be a shield, and that some secrets were permissible, even necessary, to protect the ones you loved.

Perhaps sometimes love needed secrecy after all.

*

My mother concealed the truth of my father's suicide within the unassailable fortress of her love, surrounded it with the tenderness of her stories, and veiled it with the radiance of her joy. Throughout my growing-up years, she never showed the slightest hint of anger, bitterness or resentment, despite being thrust into a life of hardship as a widow at the age of thirty-six. She raised me to adore Dad as much as she did. The sparkle in her eyes when she spoke of him lasted a lifetime.

While other mothers cooked, cleaned, and gossiped together at the school gates, Mom called the tough shots, made bold decisions, and absorbed all the risk of a single mother fighting for our survival. She ran our household like a manager, with a staff of three or four – driver, maids, live-in nanny – to whom she delegated the mundane tasks of domestic servitude that broke other mothers' backs, trapped them and, in my eyes, kept them small.

Yet Mom continued to pursue adventure whenever she could, savouring the small delights our life afforded us, and taking us along for the ride. On weekends she would pack us into her tiny Ford Laser, along with Tito T. and Tito G., her flamboyant gay sidekicks, and drive us all to the beach. At the peak of her Princess Diana obsession, we would dress up in hats and Laura Ashley sundresses and hold tea parties in our garden. She is seared into my childhood memories as fun and joyful, brown and barefoot, laughing and lithe.

As a beautiful young widow, Mom had no shortage of suitors. But Dad's death placed him high on a pedestal no other man could ever hope to reach. The closest Mom ever came to remarrying was to H., a divorced American private-portfolio manager who jetted around the world from his home base in Europe, and whose business she came to represent in Asia. Because we couldn't imagine ourselves calling him anything but Tito ('But he's American, so make it English'), by a quirk of translation my sister and I called him Uncle H. But he was the next best thing to a father we ever had after Dad.

Uncle H. shuttled between Europe and Asia, sustaining a cross-continental relationship and two households with long-distance calls and frequent-flyer miles. Our families grew close in the decade that he and Mom were together: his children spent summer in the tropics; my sister and I flew to enjoy summers in Europe. Plans were made, a house bought, places at an international school secured, but our families never became one.

Mom and Uncle H. broke up when I was eleven, and I don't think he ever really got over it. For years, postcards covered in his illegible scrawl arrived every few days, sent from tax conferences and gourmet excursions. Eventually, these were replaced by lengthy BlackBerry missives, Facebook posts peppered with exclamation points, and WhatsApp voice notes with 'Happy Birthday' sung in a jolly baritone, not a single birthday missed. He and Mom stayed friends, and our families remained entwined into adulthood. But she never remarried.

Before my early teens, then, I understood that circumstances could allow for more than one love in your life. But the place that your husband and the father of your children occupied in your heart was untouchable. Love could be felt for many, but lifelong loyalty belonged only to one.

By the time Mom and Uncle H. parted ways, I was deep in the private Catholic school system, where respectable middle-class Filipinos send their children for a decent education. In exchange for the shaping of my mind, I submitted myself to the Church's policing of my body, carried out by the nuns, the Prefect of Discipline, and the class sergeants-at-arms – the measurement of hems, the control over the length and colour of hair, the obliteration of any physical expression of uniqueness.

And I learned what it meant to be good.

Every day for thirteen years, I put on my school uniform, which consisted of a pristine white blouse with a pointed collar, knife-edge pleats and stiff string tie knotted at the throat, always with a white cotton undershirt (because a bra is a temptation that should never be seen); a black-and-grey plaid pleated skirt, never shorter than two handspans below the knee (because decent girls are modest); white knitted ankle socks, no fancy embroidery or trendy designer logos (because respectable girls never attract attention); and plain black leather shoes, no flashy side-stitching or chunky heels (because good girls never show off).

I learned that my body was an instrument of sin and must be hidden; and that good girls must obey by becoming less loud, less colourful, less troublesome – simply *less*.

The rosary prayed at the top of each hour, the Angelus broadcast over the speaker system at noon, and the Masses celebrated every first Friday of the month, in addition to religious days of obligation, were all meant to mould us into the paragons of obedience, modesty and simplicity.

At morning worship each day, my classmates and I would sing praise songs, hear the Gospel read out loud, then be called upon to 'reflect' by 'sharing' how the Word of God illuminated our personal experiences. I listened as girls in my class wept over what they called 'family problems': womanizing fathers, long-suffering mothers, hateful mistresses, and the heart-wrenching discovery of hidden homes, secret half-siblings or gambling debts. I felt sorry for these girls, their mothers, and our teachers – many of whom were either green and provincial, or jaded and weary – who were clearly not equipped to deal with any of this.

I thought of my parents, of my sister and I, and I said to myself, *We're so lucky. We're different.*

The Catholic private-school system was rigged to keep boys and girls apart until we graduated from high school. This was meant to preserve our purity, prevent temptation and keep us away from the clutches of sin. Sin was what they said when they couldn't say the word 'sex' out loud.

Pregnancy – that destroyer of reputations, families and futures – was all we knew about sex. The comic strips buried deep inside cheap tabloids, the battered copy of *The Joy of Sex* stolen from unsuspecting parents, the lewd jokes we parroted without knowing why they were funny – none of these told us anything about what sex was really like. Neither did the adults, not knowing that innocence is dangerous in itself.

As girls, our value seemed to rest in our virtue, which had to be protected at all cost. That meant no boys. Our theatre productions featured male roles played by the most boyish girls. In my junior year I became the standard bearer of a petition for a school dance. The principal relented – as long as no boys were invited.

Boys who weren't family members didn't exist or were suitors, kept at arm's length by the formal rules of courtship that everyone but me seemed to know so well. Girls were proud of how they kept boys in limbo, forcing them to send love notes through networks of classmates and cousins for months, even years.

I couldn't understand it. 'But do you *love* him?' I kept asking. 'If you love him, shouldn't you just tell him?' My puzzlement was met with pity. Clearly, I was a clueless amateur.

With boys and girls so strictly segregated, the typical 'boy meets girl' love story was a foreign concept that existed only in the canned TV series, Hollywood movies and *Sweet Valley High* paperbacks we all devoured. No matter how different old-fashioned Filipino courtship was from airbrushed American fantasy, both seemed to share the same goal: to find, marry and live happily ever after with the mythical, elusive other we all thought of as The One.

As loud and constant as our prayers or lessons were, they couldn't drown out our girlish prattle about sex and romance, a mix of curiosity, wild speculation and dubious hearsay that buzzed around me in a constant hum. Everyone in my teenage world, from my girlfriends to Jerry Maguire, was obsessed with The One who would complete you, make you happy forever, fulfil all your dreams, hopes and ambitions, and become the Forever Love of Your Life.

Every racy paperback, every box-office blockbuster, every sliver of girlhood gossip was clear: these Ones were so magical and rare that only One was allotted to you in a lifetime. If you were unable to find them, or found them and somehow botched it up, you were banished to a lifetime of unhappiness, either as a spinster or in a failed marriage without so much as the option of a dignified, socially acceptable exit. You were basically screwed.

I couldn't reconcile this elaborate subterfuge with my mother's stories or how she had loved, even flourished, after my father's death, even if she had never married again. Did everyone really get just one shot? What about Mom? If there was only The One, what if, through no fault of your own, you lost your One early in life? If they died, did your chances of happiness and love die with them? Were you doomed to be unhappy for the rest of your life and die alone, worthless and unloved? Was that it?

No, I thought, *that's impossible. There must be another way.* I secretly decided that there was no such thing as The One. I kept this to myself; I didn't think the world would take very kindly to it. All throughout my teen years, I thought I was on to something that no one else knew about.

Then I met Marcus.

3

Was your marriage open from the beginning?

Hidden in the shadows behind the School of Economics, in an old forest-green Mitsubishi Space Wagon with a rosary twined around the rear-view mirror, four years of pent-up collegiate sexual frustration exploded in a flurry of flesh, sweat and Hawaiian print.

A perspiring, bespectacled Management Engineering major rubbed the steam from his glasses and pulled down the bikini top I'd swiped from my older sister to wear as a bra under my pink patterned slip dress, while I fumbled with the buttons on his yellow Hawaiian-print shirt and yanked the zip of his denim cargo shorts open.

If you had told me that the guy applying himself to my breasts at that moment was my future husband, I would have said you were crazy.

This guy? Marcus? Marcus Ibarra? No way.

That was how I thought of my husband the first time we got down and dirty in his parents' car – first name attached to his last, as you tend to think of acquaintances or peripheral characters, rather than friends or flesh-and-blood human beings. After all, he was just a guy who sat in the front row of Merit English on Mondays, Wednesdays and Friday mornings, sorted into the same advanced-placement class by our university entrance exam scores, thrown together by numbers and fate.

Three times a week, from 7.30 to 9.30 a.m., I sat in the back row with my new best friend Tin, watching the boys with the raging hormones and rabid curiosity of two eighteen-year-olds from all-girls' Catholic schools, now thrown in with the boys we'd long been denied. How were we expected to focus on learning? Doodling in our mimeographed copies of the great essays of Filipino literature, we whispered to each other about this guy's smooth calves or that guy's lickable nape.

And we would marvel at Marcus Ibarra's hair. Pin-straight, chin-length, and parted down the middle in late-1990s boy-band style, his hair would swoop forward in a glossy black curtain whenever he bent down to take notes. Sometimes he pushed it back with a headband clearly snatched from a girl (who she was, we never knew), but most of the time he left it free to dazzle us with its enviable sheen.

It was Tin who nicknamed him Mr Purple Hair for the way his black locks glinted with deep eggplant highlights in the morning sun. It was an accurate observation and a cuddly nickname; we agreed that, with his stocky build and baggy jorts, Marcus was a cuddly kind of guy.

'There goes Mr Purple Hair,' Tin would say, nudging me as he shuffled across the college cafeteria, never without a couple of thick Advanced Calculus and Operations Management textbooks tucked under his arm. 'I think Mr Purple Hair is getting a bit *fut-fut* around the middle,' she pointed out in our third year, but not unkindly, softening the word 'fat' with the cutified voice we reserved for kittens, babies and chocolate. 'How's Mr Purple Hair?' she asked me in our senior year, when Marcus ended up seated behind me in my final Filipino history class before graduation.

Marcus Ibarra remained a peripheral character on the fringes of my college life until the night of Blue Roast, the annual bonfire for graduating seniors. Named for the school colour and the *lechong baboy* and *lechong baka* (whole pig and whole cow) spit-roasted over open bonfires on the grassy square in the centre of the campus, Blue Roast that year was luau-themed, which explains all the Hawaiian print that was later torn off in the car.

I had just arrived at Blue Roast straight from the salon, fidgeting in my stolen bikini and feeling self-conscious about the freshly cut bangs that my hairdresser had convinced me were a good idea, when I bumped into Marcus – alone, beer in hand, affable and unassuming as always – and we started chatting.

Maybe it was the dry heat of the bonfires, or the celebratory thrill of a thousand fresh graduates buzzing in the heavy, humid summer air. Maybe it was seeing Marcus's ex-girlfriend onstage with her new boyfriend, receiving some silly award for Most Public Display of Affection and snogging each other's faces off. Maybe it was the second bottle of San Miguel beer that I grabbed with a giddy recklessness, pushing my abysmal alcohol tolerance to its utter limit. Maybe we were just two sex-starved 22-year-olds sensing freedom and possibility. Maybe it was the bangs.

The last thing I remember before Marcus slung his arm around my shoulder in a friendly, almost big-brotherly way, and before I turned my face to his as if it was the most natural thing in the world, was me telling him: 'I've been single all throughout college.'

'I find that hard to believe,' was his reply. 'So have I.'

Then we were kissing – a real, open-mouthed, passionate kiss, veiled by the soft purple-black curtain of his hair.

'Let's get out of here,' he said, taking my hand.

Escaping Blue Roast, we sped off towards the University of the Philippines just minutes away, where no one would recognize our faces, to the secluded parking lot he'd stashed in his top-secret mental file of prime make-out spots for moments such as these. There, next to naked in his parents' car, ignoring the silent judgement of Jesus as he dangled from the rear-view mirror, I got to know Marcus Ibarra – his warm brown skin and pillowy lips, his gentle hands and powerful thighs, a revelation that had been in plain sight all this time.

I had my period, so we stopped short of sex that night. But after we caught our breath and decided to go home, Marcus regarded my face in the dim golden yellow of a distant lamp post as though it was the first time he was really seeing me. In a way, it was. And for the first time, I was really seeing him too.

'You're so beautiful,' he said, reaching out to stroke the side of my cheek.

Trying to play it cool, I failed. Instead, I burst into tears.

After so many years of my feeling invisible and incapable of attracting anybody's attention, someone finally saw me. I wanted to believe he meant it, but it all seemed too much to hope for in the moment. Marcus was kind and seemed unshaken by my tears, but I remember kicking myself inside, thinking: *The first guy to kiss you in years and now you've just scared him away.*

Marcus pulled up at my front gate well after midnight, killed the engine, and asked for my number. 'You don't have to call me,' I said, attempting the breezy air of someone who was worldly-wise to how these things worked, who understood that beer-soaked blowjobs meant nothing to horny college boys. It didn't even qualify as a one-night stand! Why should he care, and why should I?

But I did give him my number. And he did call the next day.

*

It wasn't exactly courtship, but it wasn't just sex, either.

What Marcus and I shared in those earliest days was a kind of nomadic horniness. When we weren't sequestering the family phone behind locked bedroom doors, to the agitation of everyone else in the household, we rattled around in the Space Wagon in a semi-permanent state of mobile arousal, searching for discreet places to park, one or both of us on the lookout for roving security guards and passers-by.

The biggest challenge of our budding relationship was finding pockets of privacy where we could explore each other's bodies without getting caught. In the Philippines, privacy is a rare luxury. College students don't move out, spread their wings and fly away to freedom; even in our comfortable, urban middle-class bubble, no one could afford to live on their own. Independence might be won by moving from a provincial town to a big city for college, in which case you were likely to end up in a strictly supervised, gender-segregated dormitory named after a hero or a saint.

Fresh out of college, Marcus and I didn't have years of partying under our belts, nor were we poised on the brink of sexual liberation and carefree exploration, as many of our peers in developed countries with social safety nets might have been. Our twenties were not a time to date, sleep around, or blow our brains out on Ecstasy at music festivals.

No, we studied hard, got good grades, and pulled all-nighters off to graduate early, proving we were worthy of the investment in our education, whether by our parents, a well-off relative or, in my case, private donors to a scholarship fund. After a solid run as responsible students, we were expected to become reliable income streams: land steady jobs, contribute to our families' survival, and ease our parents' financial burdens, giving them a chance to breathe a little easier after a lifetime of working themselves to the bone.

Somehow, in between our first office jobs and torturous daily commutes, Marcus and I squeezed every available peso from our entry-level salaries to find outlets for our barely contained frenzy for each other. They were far between and meticulously planned: a room in a business hotel on Ortigas Avenue; a stolen afternoon in one of the notorious drive-in motels with tacky fantasy theme rooms and bookings by the hour; a tiny *nipa*-thatched hut on White Beach in Puerto Galera, our first trip out of the city together. The hut had no electricity or hot water, but the sheer white mosquito net above the bed and the tea lights I packed and lit on our first night filled it with a romantic glow.

Our quickest, most convenient and cheapest escape was to the movies. In the dark, Marcus would ease his arm around me and I would snuggle into his embrace. Then, with a surreptitious glance behind us, he would slip his fingers beneath my neckline, seeking, rubbing, teasing, until an entire universe of sensation became concentrated in the sensitive nub between his thumb and forefinger. His expression impassive, profile lit by the flickering screen, he would work me up into one toe-curling climax after another as I shuddered against his shoulder, struggled to contain my involuntary writhing, and buried my whimpers in his chest.

At near-empty matinees and last full shows, I developed the secret superpower of nipple orgasms almost by necessity. To this day, I still don't know what *Gangs of New York* was about, apart from what the title suggests, and it took me three screenings to confirm that Nemo was indeed found.

So we took our pleasure at the movies, and in dining out together afterwards. We might have looked like we were dating, but the old-world romance of Filipino courtship and the desire to prove himself as a worthy suitor was hard-wired into Marcus. Acts of service were his love language. He would pick me up from choir rehearsals on campus or, after I started working as a copy-editor for a trade magazine, from my office in the Makati central business district. Then he would drive me home, relieving me of the misery and danger of late-night commuting in chaotic, sprawling, unpredictable Manila. This was how he won my mother's trust, too: if Marcus was driving me home, I was safe.

In between cinematic orgasms, being mired in Manila traffic, and managing hasty, furtive sex on the fly, Marcus and I were falling in love. Our first phone conversation after Blue Roast had lasted for hours, leaving me to wonder why I'd never talked to him before. Marcus was so smart, so interesting, and so *different* from the other guys our age who were obsessed with cars, video games and basketball.

'Isn't he a little . . . *serious* for you?' asked one of my choir mates. I didn't care. He drew, painted and cooked. He was a national debating champion, well read and argumentative like his pious and principled lawyer mother; he loved martial arts like tae kwon do, *arnis de mano*, kung fu and karate, which he and his brothers had been taught by his salt-of-the-earth, black-belt father.

Both of us had been single throughout college, having lost our virginity to our high-school sweethearts only to be dumped by them. We were both middle-class kids at an elite private university, brought up by self-made, working-class parents; he tutored high-school math, I was on scholarship and wrote for *Seventeen*. We had both ventured outside the confines of our sheltered Catholic school life doing things we excelled at: he had travelled to South Africa, Thailand and Canada for international debating championships, while I had toured Europe as a soprano with my college choir.

Both of us had tasted life out there, in the wide world beyond home and university – and both of us wanted more.

More came when Marcus landed a job with a large multinational company with its Asian headquarters in Singapore. We'd been dating for less than four months, but the prestige of the offer, the allure of independence and the prospect of earning dollars was hard to resist. Though we were already in love, I insisted our relationship shouldn't hold him back from a golden opportunity. *Let's see where this goes*, I told him.

I cried all the way to the airport on the day he left.

*

Our first months in a long-distance relationship were also our first steps into adulthood. Marcus savoured his newfound independence, with a new city to explore and a job that sent him on all-expenses-paid trips around Asia. Meanwhile, I left publishing to work in television, a high-prestige, high-stress writing gig in a company that never slept, alongside young creatives fuelled by buzz, hustle and coffee. In exchange for frequent all-nighters, my job in TV gave me the flexibility to squeeze in a few rounds at the boxing gym, run off to choir practice and have a late dinner with my friends, all before heading back to the network to dash off scripts slated to air at 5 a.m.

Life was full and rich, but I missed Marcus. In a frustrating twist of weirdness typical of life in Manila, the roots of an ancient mango tree behind my house prevented the local phone company from installing an internet connection at home. Forced to spend on long-distance phone calls and dial-up internet cards, we talked late into the night, the intensity of our longing burning up the lines until Marcus's next visit, or until I could save up enough to join him on a business trip.

From his parents' humble Space Wagon, we graduated to hotel rooms in Bangkok, Mumbai and Hong Kong. I loved Marcus's work trips home most of all. From the office, I would race to the Manila Peninsula, a five-star hotel with a decadent breakfast and a swanky lobby, where Manila's socialites gossiped over *halo-halo*, buttery *ensaymada* and Spanish-style hot chocolate.

A hotel room, a knock on the door, and there was Marcus, standing in front of me.

Sometimes we didn't even make it past the door, falling on each other on the cream hallway carpet or the marble bathroom floor. We took long hot baths with bubble bars I picked up at the mall days before in delicious anticipation. (To this day, walking past a Lush store still makes me think of sex.) We ordered in pizza from Yellow Cab or Chinese from North Park, which we ate in matching fluffy white bathrobes before falling asleep in each other's arms. Intimacy, comfort and luxury grew intertwined on those nights, which became my escape from the relentless grind of Manila and Marcus's relief from the impersonal coldness of Singapore. Those nights powered us through the next round of tearful goodbyes until the next time we could be together again.

It's easy to look back now and say that those early years set us up well. Our long-distance love developed our communication and trust, and a healthy tension between distance and desire, independence and space, longing and self-reliance. I wasn't aware of it then, but the freedom to live a life of many different textures, together with the security of knowing I was loved, desired and cherished, was a potent combination that enabled me to flourish.

Before I knew it, we were three years in.

*

I had agreed to our long-distance relationship with a light heart and no expectations. But I was the one who was left behind, scraping by on a full-time job and two side hustles, slogging through the indifferent chaos of Manila, day after day, while he jetted around Asia on the company dime. Tired and frustrated, I wanted out of this endless loop of separations and reunions. My job wasn't as cushy, my pay cheque not as fat, but my life was all I had and I loved it. I couldn't make him give up his career for me, but I couldn't give mine up for him, either.

Now that I knew what this relationship *really* required, I wanted to choose anew, with my eyes open. 'I'm not sure I want to do this any more,' I told Marcus over the phone.

The silence on the other end of the line was heavy with sadness. He told me he understood, and that he loved me.

Our break was short and aimless. I didn't quite know what to do with my freedom but go on with life as usual: work, choir, boxing. After I poured my feelings out to a high-school friend, she said something that put it all into perspective. I'll never forget her words.

'Life is hard,' she said, 'so choose the things that are worth the work.'

Marcus made my choice easy. He was worth the work.

Shortly after we reunited, during one of our usual Friday night calls, I was especially weepy and frustrated about the distance. Before we hung up, Marcus said, 'All right, then. Flight's booked. See you in three hours.' I thought he was joking. He wasn't.

He had scored a seat on the last flight out from Singapore as we were on the phone. 'Meet me at the Pen,' he said, ringing me from the airport. He turned up three hours later, just as he had said. The sight of Marcus at the front desk, sweet-talking his way into a last-minute hotel room just shy of midnight, overwhelmed me with relief and joy.

It was then that I thought: *Maybe I've been wrong*. Maybe rejecting the whole concept of The One had been nothing but a childish rebellion: small, secret and foolish. Maybe all I needed was to find my One. Now that I had, I finally understood what the songs and movies, the romance novels and wedding sermons were all about.

Several months later I joined my choir on a tour of France and Spain; Marcus met me there. He proposed to me at the Palais-Royal in Paris just two days before my twenty-fifth birthday. We placed tearful calls to my mother and sister from the Sacré-Coeur in Montmartre, to his parents from the top of the Arc de Triomphe. The diamond on my finger marked the end of longing and uncertainty, and held the sparkling promise of a beautiful future together.

A year after the proposal, Marcus and I were married in a little round chapel on a hill in Batulao, Batangas, on 29 December 2007, with almost 150 of our nearest and dearest in attendance. There were no tears when he went back to work in Singapore a week after our wedding; after four years apart, longer than we ever expected, we knew this would be our final airport farewell. I flew to join Marcus several days later, leaving my family, friends and career behind to begin our new life as husband and wife.

*

With the sharp gleaming opulence of its luxury high-rises and the rubber-stamp sameness of its government housing blocks, its sweltering heat and inescapable malls, its regimented pastel order and relentless determination to erase every last vestige of its past as a backwater fishing village, Singapore felt less like real life than an endless holiday in a Disneyfied version of Asia's sprawling megacities, with appropriate touches of local colour but none of the grit or chaos.

Our life as newly-weds felt like playing house. Marcus and I furnished our three-bedroom condo in Yio Chu Kang with IKEA's finest, ate our way through food courts and hawker markets, and resolved to burn off the chicken rice and *nasi lemak* with laps in the pool on weekends, but never did. I slotted into the circle of friends Marcus had made at work, mostly expat newly-weds in the first flush of cohabited bliss. While looking for a job, I was the perfect portable spouse, passport and suitcase always ready for the next trip to Seoul or Shanghai.

Without work or friends of my own, my once-full life

now revolved around Marcus: tagging along on his business trips and barbecues with his friends, making plans for our next long weekend in Hong Kong or Hanoi, dependent on his approval and funded by his pay cheque. It didn't seem fair for me to have fun while he was at work, so I self-limited my exploration of Singapore to after office hours or weekends, and only when he was with me.

After so much time spent apart, melding my identity with my husband's felt natural and expected, romantic and blissful. Wasn't this what married life was all about?

I found work as a writer and producer for a creative agency with teammates from all over Asia, in a quirky Singaporean shophouse with a big grey tomcat. We adopted a kitten at home, a skittish rescue with white eyebrows, a black coat and a crooked tail, whose adoption papers named her as Charcoal.

Even as I floated on the honeymoon high, newly-wed life came with unexpected adjustments. Acutely aware of everything I'd given up to be with him, Marcus was attentive and caring, if a little eager to please. He was quick to freak out at any hint that I might have regretted my decision to move to Singapore. Our first arguments were petty – a forgotten wallet in Seoul, nearly passing out from hunger on the Great Wall of China – but they rattled him. I had to reassure him that disagreements didn't mean I was unhappy with my choice or would pack my bags at the first sign of conflict.

I missed my mother and sister, and the familiar comfort of an all-female household. The adjustment to Marcus's maleness, his constant physical proximity, his unspoken but palpable expectation of non-stop sex and 24/7 access to my body, came as a shock. 'I just want to get dressed without you grabbing my boobs!' I cried during one of our early fights. Undressing in our own home began to feel like putting on the red light, an invitation to sex, except it wasn't.

Was it *okay* to feel like this? Wasn't it my *duty* to give my husband sex whenever he wanted it? Was I being a bad wife? Squelching these thoughts, I decided I would focus on everything that was great about our life together: our friends and travel, our easy compatibility and abundant laughter. After all, Marcus had surrendered his expectation of round-the-clock sex soon after I brought it up, and I never had to push back again. Whatever unease I still felt was all in my head, I reasoned to myself.

Within a year, I quit my agency job and went freelance, taking my clients with me. At the same time, digital nomad culture was starting to take off. I devoured *The 4-Hour Work Week* by Timothy Ferriss and marvelled as blogger Chris Guillebeau hacked air miles and credit cards to finance his spectacular trip around the world. I began to feel alienated from the work-hard, shop-hard ethos of Singapore. Status-conscious, money-driven and regimented, it felt less like home and more like a launchpad – and I was ready to bounce.

Liberated from my desk job, flush with cash and confidence, I envisioned us setting off on a new adventure: I would freelance on the road, Marcus would take an unpaid sabbatical, and we would travel the world as a last hurrah before starting a family.

I was wild about the plan. Marcus was not.

As hungry young graduates in Manila, we had both longed for adventure, opportunity and progress, an undefined yet beckoning *more*. Moving to Singapore had ticked that box for Marcus; our life together here was adventure enough.

Gaining momentum in his career, thriving on the stability of a corporate nine-to-five, and lulled by the comfort of a hefty salary, he was loath to interrupt his trajectory for a few months of travel. A new experience was a great idea . . . but did it have to come with so much *risk*?

'I would rather look for a new job than take a sabbatical,' he countered when we reached an impasse. 'At least that wouldn't be a pause for my career.'

That was it! We would leave Singapore and find work somewhere new. A round-the-world trip would inevitably have to end; if we found jobs and relocated under our own steam, our grand adventure could continue ad infinitum. It was just a matter of finding the right job in the right place. How hard could that be?

Marcus still wasn't sold on the plan when Amsterdam showed up on the cards. A friend working at a Dutch multinational had offered to put him in touch with a vice-president at their Amsterdam headquarters. Marcus shared the draft of his cold email with me, spelling out what he thought the company needed, what he could do for them, and why they should hire him. It was bold, direct, and maybe a bit much.

I baulked. 'Do you think you really ought to say this? Why not tone it down a little?'

'Trust me,' he said, and hit send.

As it turns out, the Dutch are a bold and direct culture. Within three months, the cold email became a job offer. What felt like a long shot was now a major life decision. I was jubilant, gaining instant credit among my fellow creative types who were excited to live their weed-scented dreams vicariously through me. My British creative director had lived in Amsterdam and waxed lyrical about eating croquettes 'out of the wall' and watching live gigs at the Paradiso, assuring me these were integral to the Amsterdam experience.

Meanwhile, Marcus struggled with corporate separation anxiety. 'Why would you want to move to Europe?' his boss asked, incredulous. 'Europe is dead. Nothing is happening there.' His company offered to move us back home to Manila or to their global HQ in the conservative American Midwest. Perhaps stock options would change his mind?

No, thank you. I had no idea what croquettes or the Paradiso were, but they sounded way better than super-size steaks and stock options, and seemed to promise a life that was so enchantingly unknown, so completely *other*.

Marcus and I came to our final decision at the end of a sunset swim in our condo pool, our raisin-wrinkled fingers entwined below the surface of the water as pink-streaked clouds and tropic humidity hung heavy above our heads. After weeks of weighing pros and cons, it felt as though we had reached a compromise between my appetite for adventure and Marcus's aversion to risk: a place that felt sure and certain, from which we could leap into the unknown together.

'You moved here for me,' Marcus said. 'This is my chance to do the same for you.'

*

Amsterdam was a go. Overnight, we had visas to secure, resignations to tender, and a three-bedroom condo with furniture that had to be shipped or sold. Through friends who'd relocated abroad, I learned the quickest way to sell furniture was online, either on Lonely Planet's Gumtree forum or an

American website called Craigslist. I decided to check out Craigslist first.

Figuring out how to post an ad for our furniture was easy enough. Afterwards, I hopped idly from one section of the site to another, browsing items for sale, jobs, and community posts, until my eyes fell on a bold heading that read: *Personals.* Beneath it were five links. *Strictly platonic. Miscellaneous romance. Casual encounters. Missed connections. Rants and raves.*

What did it all mean? I didn't know, but it looked more exciting than furniture.

I sat frozen in front of my laptop like a contestant on a game show, tantalized by choice, tickled by what riches might await behind each door. I just had to pick one.

I think I'll go with Door Number Three, Bob.

Casual encounters it is!

Click.

Where was my prize? What I found instead was a string of indecipherable codes, combinations of letters and numbers that made no sense, each one a clickable link.

$M4M - M4W - W4W - W4M - MM4M - MM4MM - MW4W - MW4M - MW4MW - W4T - M4T - T4T.$

Sheer curiosity and good user-experience design made me do it.

I clicked.

I fell into an internet rabbit hole and discovered the Craigslist personals, where men, women and everything in between posted ads searching for men, women and everything in between – in every possible combination and configuration. My curiosity, which had up to that point been a gentle simmer, hit a rolling boil.

Each link led to page after page filled with rows of

personal ads. Some were written with a clear effort towards wit and style, others in fits and stutters that could barely be called sentences. Some were timid and unsure; others florid and romantic, shocking and explicit. Some came with pictures of headless torsos, others with photos that could have belonged on a company ID card. I scrolled past them, taking it all in, too startled by their variety to fixate on any particular one.

Here, in the Craigslist personals, was humanity: in search of wives, blowjobs and used nylon stockings, chasing sex, thrills and love, hoping for answers, longing for connection. Each ad was an expression of a secret yearning, a human being naked in their need but safe in their anonymity. They were fascinating in their range and randomness, private desires bared in public for my curious eyes and reading pleasure.

One by one, the pieces I put up on Craigslist were sold – the IKEA Billy bookcase, the floral-print two-seater. But I continued to return to the personals to check for new confessions. Updates were few and far between – Singaporeans seemed to keep their illicit desires tightly under wraps, or maybe they just didn't have any.

It was probably just as well, I thought. I didn't have time to waste: there were farewell barbecues to plan, cat vaccinations to sort out, a walk-in closet and condo unit to pack up. Soon, Craigslist confessionals were all but forgotten in the whirlwind of activity that accelerated as our moving date drew closer.

Besides, nothing on a laptop screen could compare to the adventure that awaited on another continent, where our new life in Amsterdam was about to begin.

4

Whose idea was it?

Amsterdam was a world of change hurtling towards us. I charged forward to meet it.

Every experience was novel, every sensation foreign: winter's frigid kiss on my cheeks, the soft scratchy embrace of wool on my skin, and the fluctuations of temperature between outside and in, which I could never seem to get right; the abundance of cut flowers at corner shops and markets, luminous in their freshness and breathtaking in their variety; the rippling symmetry of centuries-old buildings reflected on the canals as we whizzed past on our shiny new bicycles – low-slung beach cruisers with fat wheels, which we'd brought with us and turned out to be all wrong for Amsterdam; the cool delicate press of a tiny *biertje* on my lips in the cosy warmth of packed *bruin* bars, where I was dwarfed by a towering forest of blonde heads.

On weekends Marcus and I explored our new city together, united in our delights and discoveries. Sharing it all with him was everything I pictured in my dreams of a life elsewhere. I embraced the joy and excitement of starting a new life on a new continent. What I hadn't anticipated was the insidious sense of displacement and isolation that crept in with it.

On Monday mornings Marcus would get on his bike and cycle to his new office along the IJ, leaving me alone in our rental apartment for most of the week. Then I discovered the paradox of the new: that it can be both thrilling and unsettling, bringing you to life when it flares, and leaving you achingly lonely after it fades.

I joined expat groups online and spent the little I earned from my occasional freelance writing gigs on coffee and brunch with other trailing spouses like me, who had swathes of time to kill while their husbands and boyfriends were at work. I watched them knit scarves, compare sewing patterns, and scramble to get dinner on the table before the menfolk came home. I wondered: *Is this what good wives and girlfriends do?* I had never seen my mother do any of these things. I decided that I wanted not only to belong, but to prove – to my husband, my new friends, and to myself most of all – that I could be a good wife, too. I took up knitting and told myself, *These are your friends now. This is your life now.*

Our home was never so clean, or Marcus's shirts so meticulously pressed, as in our first year in Amsterdam. When I wasn't cleaning, watching mindless reality TV, folding laundry or ironing, I was online. I spent hours poring over blogs, writing about every tiny discovery, and fought to stay connected to home by clicking through Facebook albums of weddings and baptisms, watching my friends' lives go on without me.

Loneliness descended upon me like a stealthy grey cloud, and I didn't even notice.

It was only a matter of time until I found my way back to Craigslist.

Compared to Singapore, the Craigslist personals in Amsterdam sizzled with activity. Transient tourists, curious expats and kinky locals pumped out a salacious stream of anonymous cravings for my reading pleasure. From public sex to gang bangs, rope play to fetish parties, Amsterdam poured forth more colourful characters, more imaginative fantasies, more titillating sex – just *more*.

It was deep into our first winter in Amsterdam when I came across a Craigslist personal ad posted by Erik, a salesman from Sweden. He and his wife were 'open' and active in 'the scene', whatever that meant. He had her permission to visit a swingers' club while travelling for work, and he was looking for a woman to join him. The ad piqued my curiosity with its honest, matter-of-fact wording, its pleasant, friendly tone and the unusual relationship it hinted at.

Now that *is interesting*, I thought. Interesting enough for me to open a throwaway Gmail address and send a reply to a Craigslist personal ad for the first time.

It would not be the last.

Hi there! I'm afraid I won't be the woman who visits a swingers' club with you, but it sounds fascinating. I hope you find what you're looking for! I wrote.

After some thought, I signed the email Kali. The Hindu goddess of destruction and creation – with her midnight-black skin, many-armed warrior dance and defiant red tongue stuck out at the universe – seemed like a woman comfortable with the dark side of sex.

Hi! Thank you! came the reply. *Have you ever been to a swingers' club?*

No, but I have questions, I wrote back.

Erik answered them all with a refreshing openness that startled me. Was it this easy to pick people's brains about sex? It dawned on me that people *wanted* to share, to boast about their exploits to a captive audience, to feel that someone was listening – and I was riveted.

Lovers on the side. Three-, four-, and moresomes. Partner

swapping. It was the first time I had ever heard the words 'open marriage'. What impressed me the most was that Erik and his wife were in it together. They were a team: a cool, European, swinging team of sexual adventurers. They seemed to have it all: a solid union, a home and children, mature and honest communication, and a scandalously indecent amount of fun.

The Swedish swinger-salesman came and went. On the morning he was set to fly home, I woke up to my first snowfall. Marcus and I ran out into the street, giddy as children, playing with the scant few centimetres of snow as if they were great drifts. Lashes kissed by snowflakes, cheeks pink with cold, I felt starry-eyed and delirious at the dizzying array of possibilities that had burst open before me.

Marcus and I could be that couple. We were young, hot and childless. The world was our oyster! Now was the time to take risks and push boundaries. Cheese and tulips were nice, but *these* were the adventures we'd come to Europe for. We could totally rock this.

*

By the time I worked up the courage to bring any of this up with Marcus, the snow had long melted, and our first green and glorious spring in Amsterdam had given way to the moody reality of an unpredictable Dutch summer.

We were on a date at a barbecue pop-up in a garden, woodsmoke scenting the air while butterflies flitted around us. I sensed I was about to shake things up, but I was optimistic, tingling with excitement even as I tried to keep my tone casual and light. We were always on the same page about everything. This was a new adventure to experience together, like everything about our newly-wed life. Surely he would see that.

Nothing could have prepared me for Marcus's reaction.

'Go to a swingers' club? Have sex with other people?' he exploded. 'Why are you thinking about these things? We're *married*! Married people don't do that. *Decent* people don't do that.'

This was not the response I'd hoped for.

Thrown off by his vehemence, I scrambled for an appealing counter-offer. A threesome with two women? Wasn't that every man's fantasy?

'Never,' Marcus declared. Other men might fantasize about such things, but he would *never*. Good husbands never *looked* or even *thought* about other women. And he was a good husband. A good man. A *decent* one.

It took me a while to realize that Marcus's pointed insistence on his own goodness, decency and moral uprightness was a barb aimed at my apparent lack thereof. For the first time, the eyes that had only ever looked at me with adoration and affection were filled with disappointment and distaste. Was he – was my husband *judging* me?

Marcus shot down my every suggestion, from a joint visit to one of the famous red-light window girls, to swingers' clubs and sex parties. 'Do you want someone else? Is that it?' he accused me. 'Isn't sex with me enough for you?'

'No, that's not it!' I protested. 'Look, you and I are partners for life. We have, if we're lucky, forty or fifty years of sex ahead of us. Do you really want to have sex exactly the same way, every single night for the rest of our lives? What's wrong with changing it up every now and then?'

'What's wrong with the way we have sex now?' he countered. 'Is it so terrible?'

I tried to backtrack, to appease and pacify him. But everything I said only made him angrier. Everything was the wrong thing to say. By the time dessert was served I had sunk into silence, wiping away my tears, while he sat across the table, stony-faced and sullen.

To Marcus, it was either black or white, good or bad, right or wrong, and he knew on which side of the divide he stood. No matter how playful, casual or delicate I tried to be when bringing up the idea of exploring new sexual territory together, Marcus would explode, then stonewall me. Every attempt ended the same way: Marcus, the good husband, virtuous and loyal, left angry and bristling; and I, the bad wife and discontented troublemaker, reduced to tears.

The only thing that seemed to work was to say nothing.

Then Marcus's anger would subside, and he would become my warm, loving, affectionate husband once more. If I never brought it up again, we could cook together in the warm glow of our kitchen, filled with light and laughter. If I remained silent, we could ride our bikes to the park without argument or incident, and lie together in the sunshine with a bottle of wine. If I left all of this alone, we could enjoy the good things about us and our life in Amsterdam, of which there were many.

At the time, I struggled to understand him and the source of his animosity, his propensity for explosive anger and scathing judgement. This was a side of him I'd never seen or even considered possible in the early years of our courtship, long-distance love affair, and marriage.

I wish I'd understood then, as I do now, that he was simply afraid. He'd given up a promising career trajectory in

Singapore to move here because I wanted to. He was displaced and precarious, having forsaken the security of his old job to prove himself at a new company, in a foreign culture. And now the one thing he was most certain of – me, his wife – wanted to throw the most intimate parts of ourselves open to unpredictable new influences.

I wish I'd recognized his fear, and given it the time, tenderness and reassurance it needed. I wish I'd had the words to express myself better, the maturity to take it slow, and a deeper understanding of why he reacted the way he did.

Now I know I could have waited. Now I know many other things I could have said. *What about this do you find so upsetting? It means a lot to me that we try something like this together. Is there anything I can do, or we can do, to make it feel safer, easier, less overwhelming for you? Do you need more time to think about it? Should we park this conversation for another day?*

Above all, I wish I had said: *I understand.*

Instead, I chose silence.

It was just easier that way. No more fights. No more tears. No more peaceful evenings at home or romantic getaways ruined by my crazy ideas.

Hurt by the rejection of the person I loved most and so deeply wanted to experience everything with, I buried my desires. But in the fertile ground of my imagination, kept alive by my curiosity and fed by whispers from faceless strangers, desire took root and grew into shame.

*

They're just emails, I told myself, even as they began to stack up in my inbox in the dozens.

Each Craigslist reply led to the assumed names and ephemeral identities of men I would never meet – mostly lonely and sexually frustrated, all of us privately deviant in some way. None of them had access to my body, but through them I discovered that sex could unfold in the mind.

Those emails were the sexual education I never received in school, nor in any of the furtive sessions in the back of the Space Wagon. From anonymous instructors, I learned about the fundamentals of dominance and submission, teasing and edging, power play and aftercare. I learned that words and imagery were both powerful tools of pleasure and a virtual playground that somehow felt safe, or at least less risky. I asked for fantasies to be described to me in detail so I could picture myself in them. At least somewhere out there, some version of me dared to be sexual, even if only in a stranger's imagination.

The longest email threads were with a man who called himself Ken, who claimed to be an experienced Dominant. I never saw his face; he never asked to meet. Instead, he would email me detailed instructions, a notch more revealing every time.

Stroke your pussy 5 times. Email me when done.
Stroke your pussy 10 times. Email me when done.
Show me what you are wearing.
I want to hear you moan. Send me a recording.
I want to see your pussy. Send me a picture.

Then I would follow his orders, report back, and wait to be told that I was good.

That's fucking hot.
I'm hard for you on the tram.
Do you like hearing that, my slut?

Very good, my slut. What a good slut you are.

Perhaps obedience had been drilled into me by my Catholic schoolgirl education; perhaps the seeds of being a good girl had been sown in me even before that. Ken's approval was a compelling force; a delicious haze that slowed my brain, accelerated my heartbeat and compelled me to act. I became aware of my body's involuntary responses to the absence of physical stimuli; it was a dangerous and mind-opening revelation. It was like nothing I'd ever felt before; if I had, it had been buried deep in my psyche, and Ken knew how to awaken it.

In the meantime, I had gone off the pill and we'd begun trying for a baby. In an attempt to bring my virtual fantasy life into my real one, I shopped for new lingerie, bought sex toys, watched more porn, and tried harder at sex. In bed, I attempted to elicit fantasies from Marcus, who insisted he had none. When I finally managed to pry one out of him, I leapt to fulfil it.

One evening, Marcus came home from the office to find me cooking dinner in a black lace teddy. 'Cooking' might be a generous description; he maintains I had nothing more than a pot of boiling water on the stove. I didn't burn dinner, but the sex we had that night was on fire.

Two months later, I found out I was pregnant.

The pregnancy was magic. It brought me back to what was real, pulled Marcus and myself closer together, and wrapped us up in a cloud of bliss. We delighted in the reactions of our friends and family; we held hands at baby stores and ultrasound appointments; we started having more sex than ever. It wasn't the experimental sex I wanted or the teasing games that played out in my secret inbox, but it was intimate, loving and tender. With my sensitive breasts, burgeoning belly and widening hips, I felt hot in my pregnant body, and that made the sex hot.

Perhaps that's what made it easy for Marcus to dismiss the emails when he found them.

I was careless, leaving the email account I used for Craigslist open on my phone. Marcus had spotted the first few lines of an email thread with Ken, dove in, and followed the trail. We never discussed the fact that reading my emails had been a violation of my privacy; it was rendered irrelevant by my violation of his trust.

'Who is he?' he demanded. 'What does he know about us? Did you meet him? Do you like being called a slut? Is that what you want?'

I broke down and confessed. 'They were only emails,' I said, in tears. 'I never met him, I had no intention of ever meeting him.'

'It would have gotten there eventually!'

'No, it wasn't like that!'

Marcus grilled me for what seemed like hours. Then, when all his rage had burned itself out, he promised to forgive me if I promised I would never do it again.

I did, and deleted the email account on the spot.

For weeks after, Marcus smarted with anger. Everything I did was tinged with guilt and shame, driven by the desire to make it up to him and prove that I was worthy of his forgiveness. Years later, Marcus told me he often wondered if I'd set up another account and continued to email strangers on the sly.

'It was easier to dismiss them as "just emails", so I did,' he said. 'I didn't want to deal with what was under the surface. I just wanted to forget about it and move on.'

So did I. After all, we loved each other. We were going to have a baby together.

The easiest thing to do was let the joy and hope of the pregnancy sweep it all away.

*

As soon as Marcus and I walked into the apartment, I knew.

Three picture windows formed a triptych of the canal, letting in an abundance of natural light so precious in gloomy Amsterdam. Beneath a canopy of elm leaves tinged with autumn's first touch of gold, a pair of swans drifted past, and a black-hulled houseboat with a cheerful red stripe and gleaming portholes winked at us from across the water. The talc-white shutters inside the bedroom windows could have been lifted from a summer house in the south of France. Glass doors opened out to a wide, wood-planked balcony where wisteria twined its slender green arms up and around a trellis overhead.

Every detail welcomed me home. I could feel Marcus's excitement without even looking at him; I knew he felt it too.

A few things had to go: the solitary paperback-sized concrete shelf in the hallway, more gallery piece than functional storage. The concrete fruit bowl on the kitchen countertop, containing a single apple. The distressed beige sweater that I'm sure, if I had bothered to check, was hand-loomed from 100 per cent fair-trade wool, air drying in the closet. They belonged to the owners, a pair as minimalist and elegant as their home; fresh from a break-up, it seemed they couldn't wait to get rid of the apartment – and each other.

By the time the elms outside had shed their leaves, the

apartment was ours. The minimalists didn't even counter our offer.

The elms were spindly and bare when all our worldly possessions were hoisted on to the broad shoulders of the Student Verhuis Service, loaded on to a lift, and moved in through the window, Dutch style.

On our first night in our first home, Marcus and I fell asleep under a naked duvet on a bare mattress in the middle of the living room, surrounded by a total of 110 boxes – up from seventy-six when we first left Singapore – that we were both too tired to unpack. We awoke the next morning to find the world remade in white. The first snow of the year had fallen overnight, blanketing bicycle saddles and houseboat roofs, washing clean all that had gone before, granting us a blank slate from which to begin anew.

The baby wouldn't come for another eight weeks, but that morning stands out in my memory as the last time it was just the two of us. Before the final sprint of shopping, painting, assembly and installation; before Mom arrived from Manila; before twenty hours of labour in a rented birth pool at home and an emergency Caesarean section at the hospital; before our daughter was born on another snowy morning, another new beginning.

For a brief, shining moment, my world was just Marcus and I, holding each other under the duvet as the cat leapt up on to the windowsill, surveying her new domain. Just the two of us, sharing a peace so fragile that neither of us dared speak for fear of shattering it, in our freshly whitewashed cocoon of half-open boxes and gently falling snow.

*

It was almost midnight. I waited at the entrance of the Warschauer Straße S-Bahn station, on a temporary footbridge that linked two platforms: one for trains heading towards Berlin-Mitte, the other towards Ostkreuz and Lichtenberg.

On the opposite bank of the Spree was a hotel room with a baby, a sitter and a bottle of milk. Somewhere, lost in the city, was a husband. But this night was not for them. It was only for me.

Coming along on Marcus's business trip to Berlin had seemed like a good idea. It was the baby's first time on a plane. She was two months old: she could barely hold her head up for her first passport photo, but she no longer had to be nursed by the hour. While Marcus attended work meetings and events, I pushed a stroller around Kreuzberg, rushing out of shops and museums every time she began to cry. While he drank beer with colleagues, I spent nights cloistered in a dark hotel room, listening to her breathe.

After four days, he said: 'Take a night off. You deserve it.' A babysitter was found and instructed in the basics of feeding: time, measurement, temperature.

At first, I was at a loss for what to do with my unexpected liberty. In the sleep-deprived fog of new motherhood, I'd forgotten what time by myself was like. It had only been two months, but the old me, with idle hours and a hundred ideas and activities to fill them, felt like a lifetime ago. Feeling untethered and uncertain, I considered languishing in the hotel bar, but that would be a waste of precious freedom.

I found myself drifting online to Craigslist.

As I scrolled through the secret desires of Berlin, a headline leapt out at me, compelling and incomprehensible: *Very handsome man looking for big belly*.

Why would anyone find that sexy? I wondered. I skimmed through the ad, past combinations of letters I'd never read before: BBW, SSBBW. I would look up their meanings later: *big beautiful woman, super-sized big beautiful woman.*

My post-partum body was a mess, but if I had anything, it was a big belly.

I clicked reply, attached a photo, and reactivated the old alias. Kali the mother, Kali the destroyer, she who destroys the universe even as she births it.

His name was Thomas. It was a little last-minute and a bit too late, but would I like to meet him at midnight, at the entrance of the Warschauer Straße station?

It's only a drink, I told myself as I waited, shifting from one foot to another, clutching a diaper bag that I hoped would pass for a regular purse.

It doesn't have to go anywhere. I deserve a night off. I deserve this. It's only a drink. It's only a drink. It's only a drink.

'Kali?'

I turned towards the voice. A stranger – tall and lean, with light blue eyes, pouty lips and a strong, square jaw – stared back at me, his blonde curls backlit by the fluorescent signs of the late-night snack bars outside the station.

I had read his ad multiple times. Though it began with the words 'very handsome man', I had not been prepared for the description to be quite so accurate.

'Yes,' I said. 'Thomas?'

He reached out to shake my hand and together we crossed the bridge over the Spree into Friedrichshain.

He led me to a grimy student bar with taped-over windows and dim yellow light, where we sat on threadbare chairs with wobbly legs in the corner closest to the front door. I felt disoriented, as though I'd slipped through a crack in time into an East German living room before the fall of the Berlin Wall, where the spectre of nuclear doom lurked beneath the pretence of domestic comfort.

Two beers appeared, and small talk began. Thomas was amiable and easy to be with, with a barely discernible accent and a quiet confidence I found both appealing and unnerving. I had only taken a single sip of my beer when he kissed me.

Every illusion I had that this was *just a drink* disappeared when his lips touched mine. Did he pull me on to his knee, or did I slide into his lap? Did he guide my body towards his, or did I turn away from the bar, to hide from all the eyes I was certain were on us? I can't recall. Everything was happening all at once, and I was melting into his arms, light-headed with euphoria, hurtling towards oblivion.

I might have been able to let that night go, to bury it deep in the crevices of my memory, if he had not done what he did next.

If only he hadn't pulled down the front of my dress as if it was nothing at all, put his lips to my bare nipple, and found the quickest route to pleasure, as I knew from all those dark afternoons in the cinema; and if only my breasts, hyper-sensitive and engorged, hadn't betrayed me.

If only he hadn't looked up with wide blue eyes that caught the light, lips parted in surprise and glistening with milk that belonged to my baby, and said, 'You taste sweet.'

If only he hadn't done that, and if only I hadn't liked it.

I might have found the courage to get up, leave him in the bar, and run back to safety.

But I didn't.

Instead I followed him out of the bar to a concrete sprawl

covered with graffiti and littered with rubble. There, between shadows like gaping mouths and moonlight filtered through half-closed eyes of broken glass, Thomas lifted my dress, turned me around and looked at me all over.

I had been naked many times in front of my husband, but this felt like the first time a man was taking his time to really see me. His gaze made me feel as though my body hadn't just been laid to waste by pregnancy and childbirth. As though the folds of loose skin and raw red stripes on my belly, the broad flare of my hips and fleshy ridges of my scars, were all beautiful.

His pale strong hands squeezed my belly with an intensity that both paralysed and electrified me. When I reached for the zip of his jeans, he brushed my hand away and said, 'I'm not that kind of guy.' His words jarred me, tilting an already confusing night on a surreal axis. What kind of guy was he, then? And what did that make me?

Panic set in, and I said I had to go. As he walked me back to the bridge where we'd first met, he asked if we could meet the following day.

'I don't think that's a good idea,' I said.

'Why not?'

Instead of saying, 'I have a husband,' I replied: 'I have a baby.'

'Born?' he asked, eyebrows raised.

Of course, *born*! Did he think all women produced breast-milk at random?

He asked how old the baby was, and smiled when I answered, 'Two months.'

'Well, your baby won't judge,' he said.

If only he hadn't made it sound so easy or look so good. I

might have been able to walk away, let it end then and there, and never seen him again.

But I didn't.

*

They're just emails, I told myself after returning to Amsterdam, repeating a familiar refrain.

Sleep-deprived and isolated, I felt invisible, a ghost of my former self.

But Thomas saw me. Rather, I felt seen by him.

Google Hangouts became our meeting place, and the only place I could show up as someone other than a wife and mother. Conversations in my real life revolved around the minutiae of motherhood: diapers, feeding and nap times, baby-friendly cafés and all-inclusive holidays – never ranging too broadly or probing too deep. Perhaps the other mothers also longed to talk about other things, but we were bound to the million and one details that consumed us, interrupted by the cries of the infants who depended on us, and limited by the bone-deep exhaustion that unified us.

In our virtual space, Thomas and I talked about everything my rusting brain needed to stay alive: pop culture, music, books, art, history, politics, sex. We delved into our growing-up years – his in East Germany, mine in the Philippines – our early romances and heartbreaks, our interests and obsessions. In our chats, a tiny flicker of the me I used to be fought for survival, feeding on the attention he lavished upon me.

I knew there was no future with him, nor did I want one. He was set to move to New York the following summer, and his departure stamped an expiration date on our correspondence. This inevitable end made me feel safe enough to act recklessly.

The thought of starting anything with Thomas never once crossed my mind; the thought of leaving Marcus never entered it, either. In spite of everything that had happened, and I continued to let happen in secret, I was falling in love with my husband all over again.

For Marcus as a father was a revelation.

Our daughter's birth had been fraught with complications, ending in an emergency C-section. Though the Dutch were famous for discharging new mothers as soon as they could get up to shower and ride their bikes home, for seven days after the birth I was bed-bound with a catheter between my legs, daily morphine injections in my thigh, and an endless parade of doctors and interns for whom I lifted my hospital gown as they took notes on my ruined nether regions.

I couldn't walk for a week. For the first few days, I couldn't even get up to take my own baby in my arms when she cried. But Marcus was there.

He was literally hands-on from Day One: the first to hold our daughter while waiting for me to wake up from my sedated sleep; the first to bathe her, cradling her soft downy head and her wriggling pink body in his trembling hands; the first to feed her drops of formula from a syringe while I pumped furiously, staking my entire utility as a human being on my breasts' ability to produce milk.

Every time she cried in the middle of the night, hour on the hour, Marcus woke up and changed her, handed her to me to nurse, dozed while waiting for us to finish, then swaddled-swayed-rocked her back to sleep. Not only at the hospital, but long after we came home, throughout all the sweet hard months of her babyhood, until she no longer needed milk at night.

As a father, Marcus was perfect: tireless and tender, playful and patient, steady and gentle. I had somehow sensed this when I married him, but to witness it unfolding before me confirmed what I'd always known: I had chosen the right man. This man who helped bathe my weeping scars and change my bloody bandages; who squeezed my hands and wiped my tears when the doctors finally removed the catheter after nineteen days; who took to fatherhood as if he'd been born into it; who cared for both of us with a love that seemed inexhaustible. It was this man I wanted to be with for life.

It wasn't Marcus's fault that fatherhood left most of his life, career and friendships untouched, while motherhood decimated mine. It wasn't his fault that he continued to receive recognition from his work, while my self-esteem withered without it. It wasn't his fault that my life, my senses, my very self, shrank and moulded themselves around this fragile creature whose existence depended upon mine.

She was a marvel: entire universes in her translucent curled fingers, in the soft fine whorls of down on her back, in her every cry, gurgle and breath. I may have birthed her, but it was she who swallowed me whole. She became my whole world, consuming me as I had never been consumed before. In that tiny, all-encompassing world, there was only Marcus, myself, and our daughter.

She cemented us together from the day she was born, uniting us in rapture and exhaustion, unpredictability and wonder. No one else but Marcus and I will ever share the disgusted squeals over the geysers of liquid poop that shot up her back and into her hair, and the hysterical laughter that felled us after cleaning them up; the relief of finding our first babysitter and the giddiness of our first date after her birth ('Take my money!' we chorused, forking out an exorbitant €12 an hour to enjoy the simple pleasure of dinner and a movie); the first utterances that became our code words, and her first nicknames; and all the thousand unending discoveries and delights of being her mother and father.

Sex seemed irrelevant in this new world, distant and unreachable through the fog of our sleeplessness and fatigue. Passion faded into the background, incongruent with the demands of the round-the-clock care of a newborn. My body was repurposed into a source of nourishment and comfort, and there was nothing I could do about it.

Yet our daughter was the sweet infinite wellspring of our joy, the lifelong adventure I'd anticipated but never seen coming, the crucible in which the steel of our marriage was forged and remade. If our love had not grown deeper by becoming her parents, what happened next might have torn us apart.

*

I began to claw back my independence. I started travelling after my daughter turned a year old: a trip to Milan with friends, producing a shoot in Zurich, a blogging conference in Copenhagen. I relished the sanctioned selfishness of these trips. The plush hotel rooms, hefty freelance pay cheques and blissful solitude felt like a hard-earned reward for services rendered as a dutiful wife and mother.

It was easy to convince myself that I deserved all of it. Thomas included.

The alibi arose a year after we first met: friends from Manila travelling to Europe for a summer tour. Knowing how lonely I was, Marcus couldn't refuse me this trip.

A hotel room in Vienna, a knock on the door, and there was Thomas standing in front of me on the red hallway carpet.

There was a beauty in those stolen hours I can't deny or regret, nested as they were in the wrong decisions. I will never forget how Thomas brought me to stand in front of the mirrored closet doors and made me look upon my own nakedness. Then he caressed me from head to toe, describing each part of my body as he stroked it: *full breasts, juicy nipples, beautiful belly, fat ass.*

It was the first time I had ever heard the word 'fat' and understood, from the way he looked at me and touched me, that it wasn't being used to hurt or diminish me.

It was both curious and thrilling how taken he was with my post-partum belly, the part of myself I hated most and was desperate to conceal. He would grab it hard during sex, making me feel that even the bits that I believed were ugly deserved as much pleasure and attention as the rest of me. His hands squeezing the soft rolls of flesh, his fingers digging in until I gasped, seemed to say, *This part of you is beautiful, too. All of you belongs in this moment.*

As in the virtual space we had shared for months, Thomas allowed me to be as playful and sexual as I wished, both relishing my hunger and satisfying it. How could this side of me be worshipped by one man, and shamed by another? Why did I have to choose to be one or the other? Why couldn't I be both?

Leaving Thomas asleep in the hotel room, I caught my early-morning flight back to Amsterdam knowing I might never see him again. When he moved across the Atlantic in the autumn, the urgency of sexual attraction faded to the low, comfortable hum of platonic intimacy. Yet I was the first person he called when he landed, even before his own mother.

Somehow, over a year of stolen moments and hidden chats, Thomas had become my closest friend, more real and present to me than the other wives and mothers I met for playdates and tea, with whom I exchanged recipes and teething tips across swings and sandboxes. How had I let this happen? I was stuck. Marcus would never accept this friendship, not the way it had begun.

So I did the only thing I could think of: nothing.

It was easier to do nothing, until I could figure out something.

I wanted to bring the eroticism, playfulness and freedom I had found into my real life – a life that for the most part I loved and was happy with. I felt a universe of promise calling to me; worlds beyond and selves within I longed to explore. Craigslist would always supply new anonymous partners if I chose to continue on this path.

But I couldn't. The secrecy would wreck me and destroy my marriage. Already I was aware that something in me was becoming guarded and careful. I was afraid that one day, the myriad little joys of my everyday life with Marcus wouldn't reach deep into me as they used to, blocked by a hard, dull knot of guilt in my stomach. The fear of being found out and losing everything was a constant tension that I was growing accustomed to, even as I tried to desensitize myself to it.

I didn't want to wake up one day and feel nothing for

Marcus and our fledgling family — or worse, resentment for him and loathing for myself. I longed for my sexual self to be seen and accepted by the man I wanted to be with for life, not stashed away in a hotel room where I wasn't supposed to be, with someone who never should have been there in the first place.

But how? How could I bring my separate selves together without tearing my marriage apart?

As I would soon discover, there was no other way.

*

With Thomas gone, I needed to focus on what was right in front of me: my family and life in Amsterdam. I needed to make real friends. I channelled the hours I spent online into Facebook groups and Instagram, hoping to be asked to events and meet-ups. I seized each invite like a lifeline, a chance to wean myself from my dependence on Thomas and anchor myself more firmly to my new home. It was slow work, but I had to believe it was worth it.

It was two years later when, with autumn's lashing rain, sidewise winds and chilly grey mornings, there came an invitation to an Instagram community meet-up close to home. I had just arrived when my phone rang. It was Marcus.

'Don't come home or I will kill you.'

A deadly silence opened up between us, a yawning chasm. My stomach plummeted into it.

The inevitable, which I had refused to face, had come for me at last. This was the moment I had been denying, dreading, but hurtling towards ever since that night in Berlin, a lifetime of lies ago. Though I knew exactly what he meant, the shock obliterated my recollection of what Marcus or I actually said next.

I might have said, 'Marcus' or 'What?'

He might have said, 'I found your laptop' or 'I know everything' or 'How could you do this to me?' The words blur in my memory as my world began to spin.

'Marcus, wait. I'm coming home.'

'Don't,' he might have said, or 'We are over.'

I blurted out some vague excuse about a family emergency and ran for my bike. I flew home, panic hammering in my chest, and bounded up the stairs. Just as I inserted my key into the lock, I heard heavy footsteps on the oak floorboards. I pushed open the door and there was Marcus, a dark seething mass of rage, holding my open laptop in one hand and blocking the doorway with his free arm.

'No!' he snarled. 'This is no longer your home!'

He slammed his weight against the door, forcing it shut. I shoved back, throwing myself at him with everything I had.

'I don't want you here!' he roared.

Reduced to an incoherent stream of begging and babbling, I beat against the force of his rage behind the wooden door. *Please please please let me in please please get out fuck you you bitch you lying bitch –*

Without warning, the door swung open. My laptop flew out at me, skidding towards the edge of the landing, and I scrambled to catch it before it tumbled down the carpeted steps.

'There! That's what you want, isn't it? That's the only thing that's important to you!' he cried.

'Is everything okay, do you –' The neighbours, huddled on the stairs above us.

'Please leave us alone!' I cried, then dove for the door before he forced me out again.

I wedged myself in and followed Marcus to the living room, shaking with every step.

The laptop screen showed my Gmail account, left open in haste when I was running late yet again. A Google Hangout had popped up while I was out. Thomas, of course.

Marcus had opened it and backread through hundreds, if not thousands, of lines of chat. Through months of inane memes, shared links and uneventful electronic blather, until he found what he didn't know he was looking for.

My sexual relationship with Thomas had ended after that summer in Vienna, over two years ago. The sexual overtures, raunchy jokes, flirting and sexting of our early chats had dried up. We were careful to police the boundaries of our new platonic territory.

Except once. A breakdown in a moment of weakness. One minute we were chatting about everything and nothing, as we always did, and the next Thomas was describing what he wanted to do to me in explicit detail.

Just like I did that last night in Vienna, he typed.

Mmm, I loved that, I replied.

We never spoke of it again. But that one reference to Vienna was enough.

Marcus stormed into the bedroom. I followed in his wake. An empty suitcase lay on the bed, two passports in it. My heart went cold. He threw open the closet doors, pulled out clothes, tossed them into the case.

'Please, Marcus, stop,' I begged.

It was then that he gripped me by the shoulders. For an

instant I thought he was going to shake me. Instead he punched me in the gut.

I gasped, drowning in thin air. We both recoiled in shock.

In that moment I blamed myself for turning us into these unrecognizable, twisted versions of ourselves. All the shame I had made myself choke down for years overwhelmed me, visceral in its intensity, threatening to force its way up from my gut and expunge itself as bile.

For the first time in my life I knew what it felt like to be the object of my husband's hatred. I knew then that I would rather die than feel this way again, or cause him this kind of pain.

He abandoned the clothes and suitcase, tearing through the apartment back to the living room, where he drilled into every single detail of my betrayal. I stood there, shaking, and told him everything.

After what seemed like hours, the white-hot heat of his rage exhausted itself. Mercifully, he fell silent, his face dark.

Somewhere from deep within, I dredged up the wherewithal to ask him to stay.

'It's late,' I whispered, sounding as pathetic and small as I felt. 'Please. Stay here tonight.'

If I could get him to calm down long enough to stay the night, maybe we had a chance. Maybe we could make it through.

When he spoke after an eternity, his voice was low and tight. 'Fine. I don't know about tomorrow. But I'll sleep here tonight.'

One night. It was more than I hoped for, and more than I felt I deserved at the time, but it would be enough.

Marcus took the couch, leaving the bedroom to me. I

cried myself to a shallow sleep with the passports under my pillow, hyper-vigilant that he would wake up in the middle of the night and change his mind.

*

Every relationship comes to a moment of reckoning.

It looks different for everyone. Sometimes life, not your partner, is what brings that moment to your door. I had forced this moment upon us with my choice to betray Marcus's trust. He could have walked away; it would have been his right. Now I had to confront the terrifying reality that the damage I had dealt to him and to our marriage might be irreparable. I had to accept that there might be no discussion, only the end.

The next morning, I woke up from a fitful sleep feeling dead inside. But there was Marcus, still on the couch.

And there was our daughter. By some miracle, she had slept through the night, oblivious to everything. She was three; what she did not witness, she would not remember.

Saturday was a haze of pain, numbed by the routine of childcare. We switched into autopilot: breakfast, playtime, even a trip to the park, as if it was any regular Saturday, as if our marriage wasn't teetering on the brink of collapse.

The routine of parenting was the glue that held us together that first day, long enough for the worst of the shock and pain to subside. I don't know how we made it through, but we did. Without our daughter to care for, it might have all fallen apart.

That night, the sweet simple storybooks and lullabies of her bedtime were a balm. They felt precious and fragile, like treasures that could slip through my fingers at any moment and be lost to me forever.

After we had put her to bed, the brittle peace we had managed all day crumbled. We sat opposite each other in the gathering dark of our living room, staring at one another with dead eyes.

The first words out of Marcus's lips floored me.

'I will stay,' he said.

My eyes filled with tears and I opened my mouth to speak, but he silenced me with a shake of his head. 'All I can promise you is my presence. You have to do the work. You need to work on yourself. This is not a one-time incident. This is a pattern.

'You have to figure out why you keep *doing* this,' he went on, each word heavy. 'I don't care how you do it. Find a therapist. Figure it out. I'll be here. But you have to do the work.'

Marcus's words were the slimmest sliver of hope in the midst of the abyss I'd opened up and hurled us into. Grasping the final and only chance I would ever get, I threw myself at it and gave it everything I had.

I would not fuck this up.

5

How did you start talking about it?

She arrived on our doorstep with a smile on her kind, unlined face, her silver-streaked hair flecked with glints of October rain.

Was this the woman who would save our marriage?

Perhaps it was because 'non-violent communication' kept popping up in the Facebook groups and online forums I scoured in my frenzied, late-night searches for therapists, answers, and salvation. Perhaps it was the thread of glowing recommendations that led me to her, or her email signature, which read *Amanda Adams – Communication Coach*, followed by a hyperlinked invitation to *Download e-booklet – 'Easing Connection: From Conflict to Win-Win Outcomes'*.

Perhaps it was the way she listened to me – deeply, her expression open and clear, without judgement – as I confessed to my repeated infidelity in a fifteen-minute intake call over Skype, cringing with shame to say the words out loud to this strange woman. By then I had revealed far more to strangers on the internet: my desires, my fantasies, even my body. Laying bare my infidelity to Amanda felt like performing open-heart surgery by the blinking green light of a webcam.

Perhaps it was the gentle, unhurried way she spoke after my storm of tears had subsided. 'Patterns of behaviour often stem from unmet needs,' she began. 'NVC is a way of communicating, rather than a mode of therapy, that teaches us to speak and listen to each other with empathy, so that we feel we can express our needs fully, and feel heard and understood.'

Figure out why you keep doing this, Marcus had said. Was it really as simple as this woman made it sound?

Her job, she went on, was to empower us with tools, coach us in their use, and help us find creative ways to honour both our needs equally.

Perhaps it sounded too good to be true, or perhaps I was just desperate. I wanted to prove to Marcus that I was worthy of another chance, to convince him that we could be happy again, to show him that I wanted no life but our own. To reach him, to be forgiven, and to build anew.

In the end, I think what drew me to Amanda was her compassion. It radiated from her like warmth from the sun, beaming right through the screen into the black hole in my chest. In the darkest place in my life, I gravitated towards her light.

When Marcus moved back into the bedroom less than forty-eight hours after our marriage blew wide open, he was following a script that had been drilled into both of us by a culture without divorce. Leaving was not the answer; it was never an option to begin with.

In a way, we had been warned. This was Marriage 101, part of even the most basic and predictable of church sermons, in every wedding Mass I'd ever attended including our own. Problems – couched in such poetic metaphors as 'storms', 'tests' and 'challenges' – were inevitable. They were no reason to cut and run. Giving up is for the weak; resilience is hard-wired into Filipinos' collective psyche.

Our marriage vows were 'for better or worse'. We had clearly entered the zone of the worse. Now we had to tough it out, do what we had to do as individuals and as a unit, to weather the storm. This was a test of grit, and we were a pair of achievers accustomed to white-knuckling through adversity.

HOW DID YOU START TALKING ABOUT IT?

Neither of us wanted to be the first one to quit. Neither of us wanted to lose it for the team.

Now Amanda sat in our living room, hands cupped around a mug of tea, her presence as warm in person as it had been onscreen. On the coffee table between us, she had laid two sheets of paper, each printed with neat columns of words enclosed in a hand-sketched heart.

Marcus sat on the couch as far from me as possible, arms crossed over his chest, eyeing the two hearts with a stony expression somewhere between indifference and scepticism. He'd had his own fifteen-minute call with Amanda but said nothing about it except: 'If you think she's the right person, let's go for it.' It gave me the feeling that he expected her to fix me while he sat back and watched.

'As humans, we all have needs,' Amanda began. 'Physical needs – like oxygen, food, water and shelter – are universal and essential to our survival. But our behaviours are driven by a vast range of emotional, mental and spiritual needs.' She gestured to the heart labelled *Needs*, which was filled with words like 'belonging', 'affection', 'solitude', 'self-expression' and 'recognition'.

'Needs and longings vary widely from one person to another,' she went on. 'For example, Marcus might need more solitude or affection than Deepa, while Deepa's longing for adventure isn't as strong a driver for Marcus. The important thing to remember is that needs are inherently neither right nor wrong, good nor bad. They just *are*.'

Surprise rippled through me; I could sense Marcus felt it too. Weren't my sexual needs, the ones that had gotten me into trouble in the first place . . . *bad*? Wasn't having those needs . . . *wrong*? Weren't Marcus's needs *better*, more worthy than mine? Hadn't I gotten into this mess by failing to give up my needs for his? As the betrayed, didn't his needs deserve primacy over those of the betrayer?

Amanda's words were a departure from the script, except if you'd asked me to point to this script or tell you where I'd learned it, I couldn't have told you. I might have gestured vaguely in the direction of my Catholic schoolgirl past, where sex was bad and wanting anything to do with sex made you bad. Where obedience meant virtue, self-denial meant self-worth, and good girls grew up into wives who were subservient to their husbands. Where the base desires of the body were to be renounced, and the noble needs of the spirit were to be exalted.

Right out of the gate, Amanda put *both* of our needs, whatever they might be, on equal footing: valid, worthy of attention and consideration. We had already begun rewriting the script of everything we knew.

Before I could try to read what Marcus was making of Amanda's statement, she set a timer for our first exercise: speaking and listening to each other in turn.

Her instructions were easy enough. For the speaker: *Share anything that's in your heart. Try to be aware of your underlying needs. See if you can distinguish them from the feelings you have about those needs.* (Here she pointed to the heart labelled *Feelings*: 'angry', 'hopeful', 'frustrated', and so on.)

For the listener: *Try not to interrupt. Park your own thoughts – any opinions, questions, analysis, solutions you might have – until it's your turn. Then you'll be asked to repeat as much as you can of what you heard.*

I couldn't tell you exactly what either of us said in those first ten minutes, charged as they were with pain. Only fragments come back to me now, jagged splinters poking through scar tissue. Piecing the shards together is delicate work, even all these years later.

I remember that Marcus needed to know *why*. Why I went back to Craigslist. Why I went to meet Thomas in Berlin. Why I kept saying I didn't want to leave him for another man. Why he should trust me again.

He needed to know *how*. How I could have done this to him. How I could have lied to him for so long. How I could have disregarded his feelings so completely to get what I wanted. How I could have been so unhappy, when we'd just had our daughter, the most profound joy of our shared life.

I tried to make Marcus understand: the loneliness I felt at watching his life continue, rich and full, while my world shrank to the size of a tiny human being. The isolation of new motherhood, which was supposed to have been obliterated by its rapture. The hurt of his rejection and the shame of his judgement.

I tried to make him understand that I longed to explore new pleasures and adventures with him, and wanted a life with no one else but him. But everything I said sounded thin and weak against the impenetrable walls of his anger. He could barely contain himself.

'How can you have the *gall* to want *anything*, when you've already taken so much for yourself?' he exploded. 'Lied to me, gone behind my back –'

'Marcus –' Amanda broke in.

'– nothing but excuses, nothing but a selfish disregard for our marriage! *Your* wants? *Your* needs? What about *my* feelings? What about what *I* need?'

'Marcus, if you could please bracket your own thoughts while Deepa is speaking,' Amanda reminded him.

'I'm sorry, but this is just indulging the kind of self-centredness that led to this fucking mess in the first place!' he spat.

Amanda remained firm, in her gentle way, until Marcus backed down. For her to hold space for me to be heard, even though at the time, neither Marcus nor I believed that I deserved it, felt like the greatest kindness in the depths of my shame.

When asked to repeat what I'd said, it was as if he hadn't heard me at all. Hearing him replace my words with his own, I sank even deeper into hopelessness. How would I ever get through to him?

Amanda guided him through to the end. Then it was his turn to let me have it.

'You put your own needs above my feelings,' Marcus said. His voice had gone cold. 'You only cared about what *you* wanted. You blatantly disregarded my feelings to get your way. You made me feel like a fool by lying to me. You utterly disrespected me. You exposed just how selfish you can be. Now I know what you are capable of. How will I ever trust you again?'

Every word stung, yet it was only the truth.

The person I loved most in the world had seen the worst of me; there was nowhere left to hide. There was no defence or justification; there had never been. All that was left was to face the enormity of the hurt I had caused him, and to accept responsibility for it.

I have forgotten much of what we said to each other as we took turns speaking and listening, struggling to hear each other through the filters of our own judgements and feelings. But one decision stands out, sharp and searing in its clarity.

I remember thinking: *This is the man I love. I was responsible for making him feel this way.*

And I remember deciding: *I never want to make him feel this way again.*

After over an hour taking turns, Marcus and I were drained from the effort of excavating each other's needs from an emotional minefield. But this was the first time we had talked about the affair without tearing at each other, inching forward instead of going in circles. The tension between us had softened, creating a space that felt like the first breath after a deep sigh.

Amanda would later send me a summary of our needs, which I read over and over. Each word weighed heavily on me, precious as gold clawed from lava.

Marcus's needs: respect, stability, security.

To feel considered, to feel like the priority, to protect the marriage, to rebuild trust.

Deepa's needs: exploration, sexual variety, adventure, togetherness.

To satisfy curiosity, to express yourself fully, to not deny parts of yourself that you want to be alive.

When Amanda left, she was both enthusiastic and encouraging. We had made progress, she said, and would practise empathic listening again in coming sessions. Then we would work towards reaching new agreements that honoured both our needs – yes, all of them – equally.

All of them? Was that even possible?

Everything I had learned growing up, from Catholic school to our wedding sermon, spoke of love as sacrifice. Needs were sacrificial lambs to be laid down on the altar of love. The greater the sacrifice, the greater the love. As proof of my love, I give up my needs for yours – and you'd better as hell give up yours for mine.

I had tried to forget, hide or cut off the parts of me that

didn't seem to fit into the picture of an ideal wife, mother or marriage. But I had only succeeded in starving them until they ate me up from within.

To accommodate *all* our needs equally, Marcus and I would have to think bigger, in more radical and creative ways than we were used to. I had thought compromise meant making myself smaller. It had never occurred to me that another option existed: that we, as a relationship, could expand instead.

After closing the door behind Amanda, Marcus turned to me. For the first time in weeks, the hard flat edge of anger in his eyes had gone soft, replaced by a yearning, uncertain tenderness. I saw that he wanted this to work as much as I did, and that he missed and needed me as much as I missed and needed him. Without a word, he held his arms open and I melted into them, the relief of his affection enfolding me.

*

In between sessions with Amanda, Marcus and I plodded on, operating as a family as best we could. We clung to the routine of parenting, the only steady ground in the midst of treacherous terrain. Caring for our daughter felt safe; it held us together, even as everything was falling apart.

We continued to mark occasions – my birthday, a promotion for Marcus – with candlelit dinners and smiling selfies at our favourite restaurants. To our family and friends, we were doing all right. We closed ranks around the raw, gaping wound in our marriage, protecting it from voices and opinions that might have urged us in one direction or another.

We took it one day at a time. Some days felt hopeful, as when Marcus told me he had been considering his options.

'What does that mean?' I asked.

'Leaving you. Starting a new life with someone else,' he said.

A stab of panic in my chest. I held my breath, fighting back tears.

'I don't want that,' he said. 'I don't think it would be better than this – than what we have. What I want is the life I have with you.' He stopped. 'The life I *had* with you.'

Some days, Marcus's anger seemed to take up physical space in our home, a glowering, suffocating spectre I had dragged into our marriage that physically forced us apart. Some days his eyes were filled with hatred and anguish; other days he couldn't even look me in the eye, fixing his gaze only on our daughter. On those days I was desperate for Amanda's guidance, for that glimmer of closeness we felt after she had left, fearful that we would never again be able to find it on our own.

Some days were almost normal, the way it was before, until one of us remembered. Other days slid back and forth between survivable and terrible, like a horror-movie glissando on a violin string. Some days, our daughter would do something that made us laugh, and he would look at me with eyes that asked: *Why did you have to do this to us? Why couldn't you have just let us be happy?*

In those weeks in limbo, I learned that pain can coexist with joy; sadness and wonder can sit at the same breakfast table in the morning; regret and hope can sleep in the same bed at night. I learned that life has room for all of these and more, sometimes all at once, and we don't get to choose. I learned that the proximity of loss can tarnish bliss even as it intensifies it, just as grief colours life after we lose someone we love.

In a way, Marcus and I were in a state of grief, mourning our marriage without knowing a new one was about to be born.

*

Our first session with Amanda had been about needs. Our second session, several weeks later, was about strategies.

'Sometimes, we confuse the *need* as being good or bad, when it's actually the *strategy* we choose — the action we take to meet our need — that proves healthy or harmful,' Amanda began. 'For example, we need food. One strategy might be to grow our own vegetables. Or buy food at a market. Or steal groceries from a store.'

Learning to distinguish our needs from the strategies we used to fulfil them, she continued, could help us evaluate what worked and what didn't. Then we could 'get creative' and try to come up with healthier strategies to meet each of our needs — both equally valid, she reminded us.

In my head, puzzle pieces began to click into place. Assuming, as Amanda did, that my needs for sexual exploration, self-expression, variety and adventure were valid, it could not be clearer that the strategies I had chosen to meet them — having an affair, betraying my husband's trust — had been hurtful and wrong. I could choose differently.

When Amanda set the timer for ten minutes, I tried using our new vocabulary of needs and feelings to parse the relationship I had developed with Thomas. Was the affair really just about sex? If it was, I could have found someone more available — even local — to replace Thomas once our sexual relationship had ended. No, other needs had been at play: being heard with reliability, being seen as more than a mother.

HOW DID YOU START TALKING ABOUT IT?

'So many needs met by one person, in addition to sexual exploration and self-expression,' Amanda remarked after Marcus had played back my words, getting it more or less right this time. We were improving quickly. 'It sounds like this person became your favourite strategy.'

'That makes sense,' I admitted.

'When we grow too attached to a favourite strategy, it can cause conflict,' she added.

'I can see that, too,' I said.

'Did you ever express any of these needs to Marcus or try to satisfy them within your relationship?'

'Yes.'

'And how was that received?'

Marcus and I exchanged glances.

'Not well,' I said, remembering his explosive anger and judgement.

I could see from the way Marcus sank back against the couch, brow furrowed and face clouded, that this was landing on him. Something was beginning to shift.

'It's not that I don't want to explore sexually with Deepa,' he said. 'It's just that doing these things — what she wanted to explore — doesn't fit into my idea of what it means to be a good husband. Or my picture of a good marriage. Maybe I need to find some flexibility for myself in what that picture is.'

'First ask yourself if that's a need of hers that you *want* to fulfil,' Amanda said.

'*Of course* I do! Because if I don't, she'll just keep looking for it with other people!'

She smiled at the words 'of course'. 'Human needs are vast and varied. If you think about it, it would be virtually impossible for just one person to meet *all* the needs of another.'

'I can't meet all of her needs,' Marcus said, his words slow and thoughtful. 'That's true.'

'The point is, you don't *have* to satisfy her needs if you don't *want* to. And that means nothing about you! But if you truly want to, you can.'

'How do I know that our marriage won't suffer? How do I know I'll always come first?' he asked.

'You can make a request, which is different from an obligation or requirement.'

'Such as?'

'For example, you can ask Deepa to come up with new strategies to replace Thomas, her favourite strategy,' Amanda said.

'Shouldn't she just do that without me having to ask?'

'Learning to ask for what you need marks an important shift from unspoken expectation to clear, explicit communication,' she replied. 'It can be pretty powerful. So is learning to accept "no" as a valid answer.'

No was an answer Marcus and I weren't used to hearing from each other. Hadn't we been taught that love meant giving the person you love everything, no ifs or buts? Hadn't we been taught that love was sacrifice? Where did *no* fit into what we had been brought up to believe about love?

I had to learn to ask Marcus for what I needed, even if I was afraid he would say no. In taking what I'd wanted for myself, I had made unilateral decisions in our shared sexual and emotional life without his consent. To give Marcus a say would return some of the agency and power I'd robbed him of, treating him with the respect he asked for and deserved.

'Then – yes. Yes, I would like Deepa to come up with

new strategies for fulfilling the needs that Thomas fulfilled,' he said.

The clarity of Marcus's request was a relief, a solid touchstone in the flux of the last few weeks. I was only too happy to say yes.

At the end of the session, Amanda congratulated us on our progress and asked if I would like to make any requests of Marcus in return.

I took a deep breath. 'I would like to ask Marcus if it's okay to have one last conversation . . . to say goodbye to my favourite strategy.'

To my surprise, he agreed.

In the aftermath of childbirth and the seismic identity shift of new motherhood, I could barely tell which was up or down, much less articulate my needs or choose healthy strategies to meet them. I had taken the easy way out: Thomas, attractive and stimulating, reliable and ever-present, always available yet too distant to pose a real threat to my marriage.

Building a life in Amsterdam was the slower, harder, longer endeavour: making the kinds of friendships I needed, finding new sources for the mental stimulation, growth and recognition I'd once derived from the career I left behind. The incremental effort I'd put into building my freelance network and circle of friends was only just starting to pay off, drip-feeding me with everything I'd relied on Thomas to supply.

It had taken almost six years for me to set down roots in my adopted city. I had to trust that those roots had made me strong enough to stand on my own.

It was clear that I couldn't continue with my favourite strategy. But perhaps I no longer needed to.

At first Thomas didn't understand. Couldn't we just go

on? Couldn't I make Marcus see that we were just friends, and had been for over two years now? But there was no changing how our friendship had begun.

'Thomas, he knows about Vienna.'

His silence was inscrutable. I was always the sentimental one, he the stoic. When he spoke, he pretended to be flip. 'Well then, talk to you never.'

'Don't be like that!' I dissolved into tears for the thousandth time in weeks. 'Please, please understand.'

'It's pointless crying over this,' he said. 'Pointless to ask for more, to wish things were different, to ask if I understand or not. What I think or feel doesn't matter.'

'It does,' I said. 'This is the last time we'll ever speak to each other.'

On the other end of the line, his silence thickened, taking on an unfamiliar quality. It took me a few beats to realize: was he crying?

'I do understand. It's simple and clear. Family comes first,' he said at last, his voice muffled. 'Do you think . . . do you think it's possible we might ever have a friendship that your husband knows about?'

It was beyond hope, but I couldn't bring myself to say that. Instead I said, 'I need to fix this, Thomas. I need to do it the right way.'

'Do it, then. Don't make any promises.'

'I'm not making any.'

'Should I say something tragic?' he said. 'Then: this is it.'

'I'll miss you.'

'I will miss you, too. Farewell.'

When it was over, I felt completely, utterly alone. I had to believe it was better this way, as it should have been from the start. This was the only way out: one difficult thing at a time.

*

Marcus and I didn't expect it, but our third session with Amanda would be our last.

I know this sounds hard to believe. Three sessions alone didn't magic away all our problems. As promised, Amanda had given us new tools: the vocabulary of needs and strategies, the method she called empathic listening, and making requests and agreements. Becoming adept at using these tools was our responsibility, and to be achieved over time, with practice and intention.

Something had been gathering inside me for weeks: a wordless longing hidden in the dark. It was set in motion the moment Amanda had given both our needs equal weight and validity, tiptoeing out of the shadows, into a space where it sensed it was safe. It tugged at me for the courage to give it a voice, and was willing to risk being told no for the chance to be heard. It whispered: *What if this is part of me, and not some temporary insanity to be fixed or cured? What if I could understand this, and myself, better? What if this deserves room to grow, out in the open, beyond hidden chats or secret hotel rooms? And what if that could happen in a way that respects Marcus's needs and protects our marriage?*

It was in our third session that this unnamed longing coalesced into a request. It became the request that changed everything.

'You shouldn't have to change what you believe makes you a good man,' I said to Marcus. 'You shouldn't have to do that for me, because being a good man is so important to you, and I love you for that. It's okay if you don't want to explore sexually with me. But would it be okay with you if I explored my sexuality on my own? If you knew everything, with full honesty, transparency and your consent?'

Years later, Marcus told me that when it came down to choosing between an ideal of a perfect marriage and the person he married, he chose me. As real and imperfect as I was, after having seen the worst of me.

'No,' he said. 'I would rather be with you. If you're going to do this, I want us to do it together.'

In that moment, I heard: *I can see this is important to you. I'm willing to do this with you.*

And it was all I wanted. For us to be all in *together*, as we had been when we'd set out on every other adventure: Singapore, Amsterdam, parenthood. I didn't want to force him into something he didn't want, nor to sacrifice his needs for mine. I knew where that road led, and I didn't want us to end up there again.

When we first bought our home in Amsterdam, one of the requirements for the sale was a report on the structural integrity of our building, which was built on soft, shifting ground reclaimed from marshland. Weaknesses in the foundations could cause a building to lean, walls to crack and basements to cave in, rendering even the most beautifully renovated homes unliveable.

The affair had exposed the weaknesses in our foundations. Seeking Amanda's help was like hiring an expert to work on them, peeling back layers to repair the structural issues, and learning how to use the right tools to address them before reconstruction could begin. Without this deep work, any improvements we made now would only be superficial; time would reveal the cracks. Whether it took months, years, possibly even a lifetime, we had decided that we were in it together for as long as it would take.

I didn't set out to have an open marriage, and I certainly didn't plan on cheating my way into one. It didn't present itself as the obvious solution, and even when it became apparent, the choice was no less confronting.

In all our sessions with Amanda, neither of us had ever mentioned the words 'open marriage', or the other terms we would learn much later: 'ethical non-monogamy', 'polyamory'. This agreement was the form our marriage took that would allow us to explore new sexual terrain together; it was a container that we hoped might fit the needs we had uncovered.

An open marriage is not a magic wand that disappears the past, nor a free pass that excuses problematic behaviour. It cannot bridge fundamental divides or save a dying love. It is a new way of thinking, communicating, being and loving that requires a strong relationship to take it on, the way only climbers at the peak of their physical and mental fitness attempt to reach the summit of Mount Everest.

As a team, Marcus and I were far from the top of our game. My infidelity had broken his trust, undermining the foundation that a relationship needs to meet the demands of an open marriage. Guilt would neither restore that foundation nor strengthen it; only consistent, incremental effort over time would do that.

Building an open relationship on shattered trust would be like constructing a skyscraper from rubble. Neither of us had a blueprint for what we were about to do. But we were willing to try something different and knew we could try something else if it didn't work. We loved each other and didn't want to lose each other. That would have to be enough.

With the choice made, Marcus and I tried to imagine what it might look like. How would we meet new people? How would we find new sexual partners and experiences to share? We were parents of a toddler, with no family close by to help us out and a fourteen-year-old babysitter who had to be home before midnight! Without the luxury of time to cruise bars, swingers' clubs or sex parties, how could we make this work?

The night we agreed to instal Tinder on our phones, there was something new in the air. The tension of the bygone weeks disappeared, replaced by the tingle of nervous excitement and the buzz of possibility. Even if we were about to charge into the unknown, we were about to do it together. We felt like a team again.

'We should probably put some rules in place,' Marcus said.

I agreed. So we did.

6

What are the rules?

When I was a little girl, my grandmother taught me words that she learned from her grandfather, words that she believed would protect me. She called them prayers, except they weren't like the prayers I learned in school: not like the rosary, with its murmuring repetition that could be hypnotic or tiresome depending on the time of day; nor like the Lord's Prayer, with its simple supplications for the essentials of life.

No, Nanay's prayers were special. On humid golden afternoons in the kitchen, with *Lovingly Yours, Helen* crackling from the radio and her devoted Spanish poodle a ball of cream fuzz at her feet, she taught me the ten names of Jesus Christ, which she insisted, when invoked, would call to my aid He who existed in all dimensions, in multiple incarnations, from the furthest reaches of the universe. Instead of the Sign of the Cross, in which our fingertips grazed the head, heart and shoulders as we chimed *Father, Son and Holy Spirit*, she taught me a different sign. Her wrinkled fingers sketched a map where God dwelt in our bodies; touching the belly with gentle reverence, she taught me to bless *Diyos Ina*, God the Mother.

Her words were different from everything I had learned. Their power rested in her faith, which was unwavering and absolute: she believed these words protected her, and so they would protect me. I never dared utter them out loud in school, where the nuns might hear, or around other people who might not understand, but whenever I felt most afraid, ill or lost, it was Nanay's prayers I whispered to myself. I learned early in life that what is different has its own power.

Perhaps it seems strange to bring up prayer in a book that is so clearly profane. But it is my grandmother's prayers that come to mind when I think of the agreements Marcus and I made at the start of our journey. An invisible map which sketched the areas that were sacred to us, marking the vulnerable places in our marriage that we wanted to protect. They diverged from the words everyone else said, the promises everyone else made, so we said them to no one else but each other.

They were agreements, but in the beginning we called them rules.

We held fast to them, believing they would protect us, or at least make the unknown safer as we navigated it.

And up to a point, they did.

*

The most obvious was the easiest rule to put in place.

Safer sex, always.

As kids of the 1990s, Marcus and I had grown up accustomed to the phrase 'safe sex', and figured that was all it was. Upon our re-entry into the arena of dating and casual sex as adults, we discovered that the conversation had changed. The innocent 'safe sex' of our youth had given way to 'safer sex', underscoring awareness of the fact that no sex with another person is ever 100 per cent risk-free. Accepting this risk was implicit in our agreement.

What we did explicitly agree upon was to always use condoms with other partners, without exception, and to get tested regularly, every three to six months. We also agreed to reserve unprotected sex only for each other.

Always let me know about your dates in advance.

In the beginning, Marcus and I fantasized about embarking on sexual adventures together. Reality fell short of fantasy as we ended up taking turns dating solo instead.

We would talk about a date first; then, once agreed upon, schedule it in a shared Google calendar along with dentist appointments, school holidays and kiddie birthday parties. Giving each other advance notice of our dates was simply practical: someone always had to be home with our child. It was also considerate and respectful of each other's time and energy. Planning allowed us to be aware of how much time we spent apart and together – and, if needed, to shift the balance towards the latter.

Later, for reasons of personal safety, this rule would include: *Always let me know where you are, and with whom.* As a woman – a short-legged, uncoordinated, unathletic one at that, for whom any kind of physical activity is pure suffering and who would be the first to be gobbled up in a zombie apocalypse – I was more at risk than Marcus. In case of a dodgy date or hook-up gone sour, my husband would be the first to come to my rescue.

A WhatsApp message with an address and a first name would suffice. We would also add a performative aspect to this rule, making a point of informing our dates that we were sending their name and address to our spouse. *My husband knows where you live* seems to be a useful deterrent to shady business, especially for men – or at least it has been so far.

You can ask me to change my plans or cancel a date. I can also say no.

We agreed that we would always consider each other's feelings and wishes over and above plans made with strangers. But any requests to change plans would simply be that: a request, not an order, requirement or ultimatum. *No* was still a valid answer.

No sexual partners in our home.

To protect our daughter and preserve the boundaries between family life and dating life, we agreed we would not bring sexual partners home. On the rare occasion when we happened to date other people in open marriages or living with children, who often had the same rule, we would accumulate an encyclopedic knowledge of the sexiest hotels for trysting in Amsterdam, in every neighbourhood, at every price point, with the bill split by both consenting adults. Those that could be rented during the daytime became some of my favourites. Bonus points for those with a cocktail bar and bathtub.

No coworkers.

We agreed that the subtitle to this rule was: *Don't shit where you eat*. Marcus worked in a conservative multinational corporation; this was simply self-preservation. For the most part, it was easy for him to steer clear of coworkers, although he panic-swiped more than once when he spotted someone from the office on Tinder.

It was more complicated for me. Since I was a freelancer, I didn't have bosses, teammates or colleagues, but could potentially end up working with anyone in the city. We set out on our open marriage at about the same time I resolved to buckle down and get serious about establishing roots in Amsterdam, by making real friends and building my professional network. Putting myself out there, in more ways than one, I would discover just how small and incestuous

Amsterdam was, especially among creatives. Later on, I would have lovers who wanted to hire me (and some did) and would end up sleeping with several people I had met through freelance projects.

Only after the projects wrapped, but not always before the client's cheque had cleared.

No friends.

Marcus and I agreed that we could sleep with our own friends, but that sleeping with each other's friends would only invite trouble. I've since had only one lover who started out as a friend; I still prefer to let platonic relationships remain platonic. It just seems less complicated that way. Real friends are too important, too rare; I don't need to ravage friendships for sex, which can be found elsewhere.

No sleeping over.

The intimacy of waking up next to each other was something we agreed to reserve for our marriage. It would take a global pandemic to shift this rule, but I'm getting ahead of myself.

No explicit sexual details, unless requested.

Marcus had a visceral aversion to specifics. For a long time, I believed he would rather pretend that I wasn't dating anyone and would prefer not to hear anything that wasn't absolutely necessary. By not volunteering particulars, we could be respectful of each other's moods and feelings; whoever asked could control the flow of information and stop when they'd had too much.

So we agreed: only tell me what I need to know, unless I ask.

Me? I *liked* to ask. Sometimes in the middle of sex with Marcus, which often made him squirm. Hearing details fed visuals into my imagination in real time, which was exactly what Marcus wanted to avoid. Details fanned the flames of my lust, but extinguished his. For me, it was exciting stimuli, and part of the pleasure of discovering a new aspect of my husband that some other lover had uncovered.

One date a week, max.

We argued about the frequency with which I dated. At the time I wasn't aware — and I don't think many people are — how easy it is for women to find dates online. It's a numbers game: there are simply far more men than women on dating apps, and the gender imbalance is especially high on Tinder. If I was less discriminating, I could have filled my calendar with a date every night of the week just for the sake of it. This could cause friction and drive us apart if I wasn't careful, so we agreed to cap dates at one a week.

These were the rules we started out with. Some would shift and relax over time, others falling away altogether, as we grew in confidence, trust and experience.

Looking back now, I find myself surprised by how much we never thought to cover with explicit agreements. Our wedding vows were made much in the same way; there's a lot of fine print that *to have and to hold* doesn't cover.

For example, we never actually came to an explicit agreement that we would never fall in love with anyone else, although some rules were designed to prevent that from happening by cutting emotional intimacy off at the pass. I suppose at the time it seemed like such a remote prospect that it didn't even occur to us to promise the obvious: that we loved and would only love each other, and that, despite giving up the privilege of sexual exclusivity, our first and only emotional loyalty was to each other.

We never discussed finances, either. It was implicitly assumed that we would each spend for our own dates from the bit of personal pocket money we allowed ourselves after the shared expenses of family, household and savings. We treated the expense of dating just like any other discretionary purchase, such as buying a pair of shoes or earrings, or going out for drinks with friends. In this respect, Marcus had the leg-up on me, the freelancer without a steady pay cheque. If I wanted to date (and spend) more, I simply had to hustle more.

I also find it ironic that neither of us ever promised not to keep secrets, although honesty was a fundamental condition of the whole exercise. Instead, we defined boundaries around what we *didn't* have to tell each other, based on our comfort level around sexual details. For all the rest, it was a given: we would be fully transparent.

Otherwise none of this would work.

*

Like moving to another continent or having a child, opening our marriage was a major life decision that Marcus and I signed up for with only the vaguest idea of how it might play out. We were heading into uncharted territory with not much more than a finger in the air, the rules we'd cobbled together the equivalent of a map sketched in spit. Whatever else we needed, we would have to learn as we progressed.

We weren't ready to announce our experiment to the world just yet. Since all our friends in Amsterdam were couples with young children, we thought it safe to assume that none of them would be on Tinder, otherwise they'd have at least as much explaining to do as we did.

We drew up the rules quickly the night we first went on Tinder. We read no books, consulted no experts, googled no search terms. In laying down these ground rules, our only guides were our gut instinct and each other. We would have to find our way by staying close to both.

We spent that first evening snuggled up on the couch, swiping through Tinder profiles and laughing over the ones that made us cringe while *Game of Thrones* clanged and screeched in the background. To be able to laugh together again after the schism of the affair was a spark of hope and healing, a signpost along the road that I prayed would lead us out of the worse, back to the better.

Plunging headfirst into the vast waters of Tinder, I was dazzled by the sheer number and variety of the options now available to me. I wanted to meet everyone, try everything. But it was the Dominant–submissive dynamic, which I was already familiar with from Craigslist, that I was most curious to explore.

Starting out on my journey of sexual discovery, I wanted someone with experience to lead the way. I was often surprised, even impressed, by the creativity and detail in the imaginary scenarios that Ken, the Dom I had met online when I first moved to Amsterdam, crafted for me. I admired that probing, restless mental agility; I wanted someone to think for me, so I could observe, follow and learn. As a good Catholic girl, obedience had been drilled into me. I was a natural at taking orders.

What I found most seductive about playing submissive to a Dominant was being granted permission to be sexual. To be absolved of guilt with explicit instructions and generous verbal approval. To be rewarded, instead of shamed, for being open about what I wanted and what turned me on.

The first man I hooked up with on Tinder understood this intuitively. He was a real Daddy-Dom type, an older man in his late forties. His profile photos showed bright, deep-set eyes, close-cropped hair that matched his salt-and-pepper stubble, and a subtle smoulder that seemed both mysterious and inviting. The abbreviation 'D/s' in his profile told me that he had what I was looking for. I was instantly intrigued.

From the moment we took our seats in a crowded taco bar off the Albert Cuypmarkt, I was struck by how charismatic he was, with an intense gaze and a restless energy radiating from his compact, wiry frame.

What made Daddy Dom extra appealing was how clearly he wanted me. He didn't try to hide it. I could tell from the way his gaze grew deep and piercing, searching my face as I twittered nervously; how he hung on my every word but ignored the nachos and margaritas on the table.

'You're very, very sexy. I'm incredibly turned on by the idea of . . . of meeting a married woman whose husband knows and agrees to it,' he said, leaning in so close that stubble almost brushed my cheek.

I sensed he meant *fucking* but decided to say *meeting* instead. Would it be like this from now on? This brazen honesty, this naked want out in the open?

It was the first time I'd experienced what it was like to be someone's fetish – an object not only of desire, but of a particular, hard-to-satisfy kink now so tantalizingly within reach. The effect on Daddy Dom was fascinating to observe. Only after many years and many lovers would I fully grasp what it meant to be fetishized, then choose to reject it. But caught in the first stirrings of something new, powerful and erotic, I was unable to resist.

It would be the last time Daddy Dom minced words. Suddenly everything was happening all at once: his hand on mine on the table, his voice murmuring in my ear. 'Is this all right?' to 'Will you let me kiss you?' to 'Did you come by bike or tram? I can leave my bike here.'

Daddy Dom knew exactly what he wanted and threw the full force of his intensity into it. Now I had the green light to let it sweep me away without guilt, shame or consequences — or so I thought.

'Let's get the check,' I replied. 'And call an Uber.'

When I stepped out on to the street to wait for the car, it was like stepping out into another planet. In this strange new world, where I had my husband's permission to share my body with a stranger, every sound was amplified, every millisecond stretched, every sensation inflamed by novelty.

The slow, deliberate pressure of his hand squeezing mine on the back seat made my heart beat louder. The thud of my boots on the stairs of his building echoed in my ears. His apartment was all curled shadows and dark edges, his bed a soft hungry animal that swallowed me up, his stubble a gentle, insistent rasp that felt electric on my cold cheeks.

Yet he did not undress me immediately.

I was still fully clothed when he nudged a knee between my legs to spread them apart; when he pushed his knee higher, pressing it hard into me, tightening his hand against my throat, crushing me deep into the bed; when he made me orgasm for the first time, with nothing but hungry kisses, a well-placed knee, and the sheer thrill of newness.

WHAT ARE THE RULES?

That was the first time he called me a good girl.

'Very good, Deepa,' he breathed, excitement vibrating in every word. 'Very, very good.'

It would not be the last.

*

I came home that evening to find Marcus heading out for a drink with mates from work. We were ships passing in the narrow hallway; this was how he had wanted it.

Of course, he knew about my date with Daddy Dom. The rules we had agreed upon stipulated that either of us could request the other to change or cancel their plans if we felt vulnerable, lonely or otherwise ill-equipped to handle the emotional load of a new date.

But Marcus hadn't asked me to. All he wanted was to be out of the house right after I returned, delaying the moment when he would have to face me after I had slept with another man for the first time with his full knowledge and consent. It had seemed wise to let him handle it however felt best for him.

Besides, I needed to calm down. With our child sound asleep, I was left with the quiet and solitude I needed to process the evening. I felt like a live wire, raw and exposed, senses buzzing. But live wires can start fires, and the electricity that was still rippling through me felt incendiary, safer hidden than flaunted. The replays in my head were so vivid, they might as well have been blazing in neon.

Someday, Marcus and I would come to call this period of respite 'buffer time': time alone to rest and reintegrate, to sift through new sensations and feelings, to hang up the identity of lover and adventurer and embrace that of parent and spouse. We would learn how to plan for it so that whoever was returning felt welcome and missed, without being shoved into domestic responsibility. We would come to appreciate this time as a gift we could give each other, one that put the recipient in a grateful, loving mood towards the giver. To return energized, in gratitude and love, is the best way to come home from any escapade, no matter how wild or exciting it may have been.

But that first time wasn't because Marcus felt particularly loving or charitable towards me. All he wanted was to avoid the source of all these new, difficult emotions: me.

I stirred when Marcus crept into bed late that night, and reached for him half-asleep as I always did. He refused to acknowledge me and hugged the edge of the bed instead, the broad curve of his back as rigid as a shield, until I turned away.

In the morning, he avoided my gaze when we woke. His replies to none but the most necessary practical questions of the day were brusque. He made breakfast, taking pains to ensure our bodies didn't touch as we moved around the kitchen in a silent, strained version of our usual morning rush. Then, without so much as a squeeze on the shoulder or a kiss goodbye, he was off to work, leaving me at home with our daughter.

By now she was three, and starting to smear together Dutch, English and Filipino in her childish chatter. But even her sweetest, funniest made-up songs could not drown out the roar of anxiety in my head. The exhilarating rush of Daddy Dom's approval was quickly fading, overpowered by my panic at the withdrawal of Marcus's affection.

Marcus and I have always been, and still are, physically

affectionate. We thrive on each other's hugs and kisses, always touching even in our sleep. But now, the distance between us was almost palpable. It was his reassurance I needed most, his presence that underpinned my entire sense of security and well-being, and to feel him pull away from me so completely sent me into a spiral of panic.

Marcus was clearly in pain, and I felt personally responsible for his misery. The thrill of the night before had been replaced by guilt, fear of Marcus's anger – less than three months had passed since the revelation of the affair, and the memory of his rage was still fresh – and a clinging desperation to know that we were still in this together.

Hadn't we *both* said yes to this? So why did it feel like I was being punished for something we had both, in principle, agreed on as a team?

Our shiny new tools from Amanda – the vocabulary of needs and feelings, how to listen and play back each other's words – felt far away and hard to reach. By the end of the day I was twisted with anxiety and dread, ready to do anything to make him feel better. If he had asked me that same day to walk away from the whole endeavour, I would have thrown myself at his feet and done it. Anything just to make him look at me, talk to me, and hold me again.

But Marcus was too stubborn to quit. We were locked into a challenge now; he was bent on proving he was the tougher of us two, and would never be the first to give up. I wondered if he was intent on freezing me out until I did.

Thump. Thump. Thump. Dishwasher filled and churning, daughter tucked into bed. The wet thud of suds against metal – something stuck? loaded the wrong way? – was the only sound that dared break the maddening silence.

I squirmed on the edge of the couch as Marcus busied himself wiping down the kitchen counter, which surely had never been any cleaner.

Thump. How long was he going to give me the cold shoulder? *Thump*. I couldn't stand it any longer. *Thump*. I had to say something or I would go crazy. I took a deep breath.

'How are you?' was a weak opening, but with the roar of anxiety in my ears, it was the best I could manage.

Marcus paused, wet dishcloth in hand. He looked at me with weighted eyes, but said nothing. *Thump*.

'Want to talk?' I said, patting the couch.

'I guess,' he sighed. With a heavy exhale, he wrung out the dirty cloth and draped it on the radiator, dragged himself to the couch and sank down next to me.

'How are you?' I repeated.

'I'm . . . I'm not good.' Trying to decipher the silence that followed — was he accusing? Angry? Jealous? Hurt? Lonely? — was like trying to extract emotions from concrete. He was unreadable.

'I'm sorry,' I said. I wanted to burst into a million questions, but tried to keep my tone soothing and even. 'Do you want to tell me about it?'

He shrugged. 'I'll be fine.'

'Please?' I reached for his hand. He flinched. 'You don't want to touch me?' I cringed at the panic I heard rising in my own voice. 'You won't even look at me?'

An age elapsed, in which the jammed dishwasher strained to fill in the gaps. *Thump. Thump. Thump.*

Eyes averted, he began: 'When I look at you, all I can think is how . . . some other man made you dirty.'

Dirty. The word was a slap in the face. Stung, I jerked my hand away.

But now the silence was broken. 'While you were out, all I could think about was what he could be doing to you at that moment. Another man's hands all over you. His mouth all over you. For all I know, his cum all over you. That's all I can see now when I look at you. Someone dirtying my wife.'

There it was again. *Dirty*. I had expected to hear *jealous*, *lonely* or *sad*, but *dirty*? My first impulse was to jump to my own defence: *I took a shower after! You said yes to this!*

But this was what I had asked for, wasn't it? I had to sit there and take it, didn't I? Even if his judgement cut me. Even if his disgust hurt.

'I don't blame him. I bet it's fucking kinky to fuck another man's wife!' he said. 'He's just taking what's free for the taking. But you . . .'

He let the words hang. I snatched them out of the air.

'So he's off the hook. And *I'm* the one to blame? *I'm* the dirty one?' Pitch rising, pulse racing, I felt my attempt to be patient, to listen, to resist being defensive, start to careen off the rails. I struggled to hold on.

'I'm sorry,' I said again. 'I'm sorry it's so hard. Is there anything I can do to make it easier?'

I held my breath, bracing for the answer: *Stop seeing him. Stop doing this. This was a mistake. I don't want to do this any more.*

'No. Maybe. I don't know.'

I didn't, either. The only thing I could think of was to tell him that I loved him.

'I love you and I want to make this easier,' I said, but he'd already checked out of our conversation, his expression solidifying into a mask, his gaze averted and opaque. He'd taken a front-row seat to the smutty movie in his mind, the defilement of his woman by another man, and it was drowning out all else.

Seeing him withdraw right before my eyes sent me into a swift spiral from loving and reassuring to shrill and sobbing. I hated how frantic I was for his reaction, any reaction, and I hated how he was stonewalling me. Each of us was locked into our own misery, until at last I crumbled, wrung out and drained.

Finally he looked up with a small jolt, taking in my puffy eyes and red, tear-stained face as if I'd just materialized next to him on the couch.

'I'm sorry,' he said. 'This is . . . hard for me.'

'I know,' I said. 'I'm sorry.'

'I have to think about what you can do to make it easier,' he said. 'I think it's just . . . it's just better if I have some space.'

In my desperation, I scrabbled in the crowded disarray of my mind for Amanda's toolbox – anything to make this feel less awful, anything for us to get somewhere.

Request. I could make a request.

'I understand that you . . . you need space to figure things out for yourself,' I began, playing back what he'd just said. 'Can I . . . can I make a request?'

'Go on.'

'Will you let me know when you're ready to talk to me?'

He frowned. 'Like, now? Or after a date?'

'Both,' I said. 'So I know to respect your space until you're ready to be with me again.'

'Yeah, sure. That's easy,' he said. 'I can do that.'

His *yes* was a pinprick that punctured the tight-stretched drum of my anxiety. Relief seeped in through the tiniest of openings. 'Great. Thank you. Thank you! That's all I need to hear.'

Now it was his turn to reach for my hand. I had gotten through.

'I'm here. You have me again. I love you,' I said.

'I love you, too,' he replied.

This time he squeezed my hand, and I squeezed back.

*

It turned out that respecting Marcus's need to withdraw – learning to trust that we would find each other again, and that I would receive the reassurance I needed, when he was ready to give it – was one of the few things I did right in those early days. But it wasn't always easy.

Sometimes I had to wonder if my pleasure was worth risking his displeasure, and if it would ever get better. Sometimes I had to remind myself that what was exciting for me was threatening to him. Sometimes I couldn't wait for him to signal his readiness, and ended up pressing him for more ways I could 'help' him get over his difficult feelings.

'I don't know, okay? I don't know!' he would say.

'*I don't know* is a smokescreen!' I would shout, frustrated. 'Why don't you want to look into what's behind *I don't know?* Give me something to work with here!'

It tore me up that seismic shifts were taking place in my life, and I couldn't talk to him – or anyone else – about them.

Marcus was clear about not wanting to know any of the

details. Having that rule in place – broad strokes only, unless asked – helped me respect his space and feelings. I felt it was the least I could do when I was already asking so much of him.

It seemed to make a difference. When it was time for the next date, the cycle of avoidance and anxiety would start all over again. Yet each new cycle seemed to be less volatile, a tiny bit better than the last. The oscillations between withdrawal and reconnection began to get shorter, less dramatic, more predictable.

Each new conversation widened the cracks in his dam, until feelings began to trickle out like water. Each admission of a need, and each strategy that I proposed or that we came up with together to address it, felt like a small triumph. I began to feel less like the guilty perpetrator, Marcus less like the victim, as responsibility for his feelings – and the power to influence their outcome – shifted into his sphere of control.

If he was feeling lonely at home, why not invite a friend over for dinner? To deal with the emotional labour of dates, we capped them at a manageable number a month. If one or both of us was tired of processing feelings, then we made sure to plan lots of time doing nothing together, vegging out on the couch, no Tinder or dating talk. Just old-married-couple time.

Time together, which was all too easy to take for granted after nearly a decade of married life, took on a new significance and vibrancy. Being intentional about togetherness became so much more important. We couldn't just fall back on parenting as a default, or treat the never-ending tasks involved in running a household as quality time. Neither could we simply occupy the same space while scrolling mindlessly on our phones or watching TV. What truly revived us was focusing our full attention on each other, sharing small pleasures that we enjoyed as a unit, like cooking or having a glass of wine, to replenish the emotional reserves that dating eroded.

*

I was working one afternoon when Daddy Dom texted me. *Where are you?*

Working at a café.

Where can I lick your ass in public today? Just like that, no preamble. The urgency in his desire for my body was an immediate turn-on, together with the thrill of conducting our secret rendezvous in a public place, the risk of possibly getting caught, and the dopamine rush of reward if we could successfully pull it off. Thinking fast, I named a nearby co-working space.

'How are the bathrooms?'

'Big enough.'

Within ten minutes, another message: *I'm here, and I'm hungry.*

This was the kind of demand Daddy Dom loved to make. A week later, he called me to an event at another venue where he was working. This time the risk was even greater: people knew him here. Taking my hand, he led me into the elevator, punched in a random floor number, pacing through the hallways at speed, trying doors until he found a room that was unlocked. Inside, he settled into a chair with a naughty grin.

'On your knees, my little slut.'

Eager to please, I obeyed and went to work.

I saw Daddy Dom about three or four times in as many months, including a few rendezvous at his apartment. My anticipation for our meetings was tremendous, but looking back, the sex wasn't particularly kinky. More than half the excitement was from the newness of it all. In retrospect, I believe he was taking it slow, biding his time until I was as malleable as he wanted me to be.

In a way, I was already familiar with this dynamic of online dominance. I thought I was getting to know him, but his endgame was opaque to me. In between dates, we chatted for hours on WhatsApp. What I didn't realize at the time was that our WhatsApp chats were the space in which he wanted to test my boundaries, try out fantasies to see how I reacted, make me comfortable with him and his ideas, and gain my trust. He was working on me with his words, nudging me ever closer to what he wanted.

Daddy Dom enjoyed recounting his sexual exploits to me, his captive audience. He was seeing and dominating several other women but had been on the receiving end of female domination as well. His experience appealed to me, as did the praise he heaped upon me for being what he called a cock-hungry slut.

He was full of questions: *Are you being a slut for other men? Does your husband get turned on knowing you were with me last night? Does he treat you like a bad girl or a good one?* He drilled into my sexual preferences and fantasies, my soft limits and hard ones, and my sexual dynamic with Marcus.

His probing felt flattering. His intensity made him hard to resist. And his finely honed instincts made it easy for him to zero in on my buttons from the get-go. But it also made it easy for him to steer me into the grey areas where the lines were blurred and limits had yet to be explicitly drawn, where he found it most exciting to play.

Daddy Dom filled our chats with elaborate fantasies that revolved around him ravaging me while Marcus watched helplessly from the sidelines. Thinking, *Oh, this is just fantasy talk*, I played along anyway.

He understood that permission to be bad excited me after a lifetime of trying to be good. He picked up on my craving for sexual validation long before I learned that the kink world had a name for it: a *praise kink*. Gradually he started to turn up the element of possessiveness in his sexts, drawing me into a virtual world where I was *his* cock-hungry slut, *his* good little girl.

My little slut. My little whore, he called me. *You're my good girl, aren't you?*

Yes, I would reply, *of course I am*.

Daddy Dom never verbally humiliated me or made me feel deficient. He only affirmed what I already secretly knew, that the world had told me was bad and wrong: that I was a slut, that I loved sex and had an appetite for it. I was turning out to be intuitively good at it and invested in becoming better. In Daddy Dom's world, these qualities were pleasing and to be encouraged. It was, in itself, a kind of recognition. Instead of being rejected, I was rewarded. Instead of the anger I had once faced from my own husband, I was showered with approval.

*

Something was up.

I came home late one night from Daddy Dom's apartment to find a plate of food on the dining table, and Marcus waiting up for me long after he'd put our daughter to bed. Without a word, he sat across from me as I ate my dinner alone, watching. For a change, he seemed not to be avoiding me, but I couldn't tell why.

He spoke, a whip slashing through the silence.

'Have you been a dirty girl today?'

Was this a trick question? Damn the rules.

'Um . . .' I squeaked, swallowing hard. 'Yes?'

'Finish your dinner. When you're done, I'm going to show you how a naughty girl like you deserves to be treated.'

WELL.

'Yes, Sir,' I said, pushing my fork and knife aside on the plate.

Like all women who've read *Cosmopolitan* and watched *Sex and the City*, I knew couples were *supposed* to dabble in this kind of thing to keep the fires burning. Unlike our earlier, somewhat dutiful attempts at role play, this was raw, real, and charged with an electric tension – a sense that *anything* could happen, instead of what was *supposed* to.

Marcus closed the door that led to the hallway and bedrooms and stood in the middle of our living room and kitchen. 'Stand in front of me.'

I did as he commanded.

Without a shred of gentleness, he undressed me, stripping away every single article of clothing from my body until I was naked under the gaze of the lights, every last one of them ablaze.

'I'm leaving the lights on so that all the neighbours can see what a naughty girl you are,' he said. As he leaned in close, I spotted a wicked gleam in his eye I'd never seen before. I was on high alert, trembling with anticipation, but I couldn't help stifling a smile.

'Get on your knees. He's had you tonight. Now it's my turn.'

His belt, pulled tight around my wrists.

The table, shaking with the force of his punishment.

My bottom, red and stinging from his slaps.

My face, flushed and gleaming with my sweat and his cum, at the very end.

Marcus had always been careful not to truly dominate me, ever the upright husband held back by respect for his wife. This time each slap stung as though he meant it.

It was the first and only time he would ever ask for explicit details. *Did you suck his cock? Did you lick his balls? Where did he put his cum? Has he fucked you in the ass?* Every answer only fuelled his 'punishment' with more ferocity.

It was new. It was intense. It was hot.

I loved it. So did he.

Hours later, we collapsed in bed, his frustrations released, my guilt assuaged, enveloped in a post-coital haze that brought us closer to each other than we had felt in weeks.

'This is a *much* better strategy for dealing with dates than trying to avoid you,' he murmured, pulling me into his arms and planting a kiss on my forehead.

'I agree,' I panted, snuggling into his sweaty embrace, cherishing the return of our affection.

After Marcus dozed off, I lay awake, still aglow with the exhilaration of being ravaged by not one, but *two* men in one evening. *Today is a prime example of why people are in open relationships. Achievement unlocked!* were my last thoughts before I finally fell asleep.

The discovery that intimacy was a far more satisfying response to the aftermath of dates than the silent treatment reshaped our post-date-night dynamic. It reinvigorated us with a sense of playfulness, the erotic spark that our sex life needed to come roaring back after the rift of the affair and all the weeks of tension and uncertainty that followed.

The angry daddy and naughty brat became roles we would inhabit with greater confidence and ease over the years. We would explore this more in-depth together and with other lovers – Marcus took particularly well to it – but that night was a glimpse of possibility.

If the sex was going to be anything like that from now on, maybe there was something to this after all.

*

Daddy Dom and I were deep into a sexting marathon one night when he suddenly asked: *Do you have any idea how much I want to cum inside you from behind?*

Tell me, I said.

Look back at me while I'm fucking you. You'll do as I say, won't you, my little slut?

Yes, I will.

Then beg me to cum inside you.

I sat up and reread the text. This was just fantasy talk . . . wasn't it? Was I supposed to continue the game? Or should I shut it down now?

It was minutes before I replied: *I can't. I've told you before. Rules are rules.*

Yes, he replied. *But we all know who's the boss here, right?*

Feeling queasy, I stared at my phone as his messages pinged, one after the other.

I know your husband's wishes. But I also know you don't want our little adventure to end.

Only I choose where I cum.
And you will lie to your husband every time.
Because you want my cum inside you more than anything.
Why aren't you begging for my cum, little slut? Do you know you're robbing me of a special feeling?
Do you?

I seized my phone. *I fantasize about it sometimes. Isn't that enough for you?* I wrote, a sudden fear roiling, rising in my throat, threatening to overwhelm me.

I don't want anyone limiting us. Neither should you, came the reply.

It's a hard boundary. I thought you understood that.

And I thought you understood that I love pushing boundaries.

This no longer sounded like fantasy talk. I swallowed hard. *I can't go on with this conversation,* I wrote. Then I hit the mute button on the chat, shoved the phone under my pillow, and left the bedroom, feeling shaken.

In one WhatsApp chat, my fling with Daddy Dom had taken a distressing turn, leaving me feeling unsafe around him. Could I trust him to respect my limits after this? Or was he simply out to get what he wanted?

Safe sex is non-negotiable. However, the real punch to my gut was the suggestion of lying to Marcus. I could never go anywhere near that again, not even in fantasyland. The thought of lying made me feel physically ill, like retching. The radical new honesty between us, as raw and shaky as it was, felt infinitely better than the secrecy I had once learned to live with. There was no way I was ever going back there.

When Daddy Dom left for a work trip, I was relieved I wouldn't have to deal with him. I should have ended it then and there. Instead I dithered, made excuses and avoided responding to his messages. While he was away, Daddy Dom kept his messages light and casual, but I could tell he knew something was up.

How's my little slut? he said after several weeks.
We need to talk, I replied.
What's going on, Deepa?
Message me when you get back.

The atmosphere couldn't have been more different between our first date at the taco bar and our last one at a brunch place at the south end of the Vondelpark. I sat dazed in front of Daddy Dom as he chattered on about work. The charismatic man who'd had me in the palm of his hand was almost a blur before my eyes, as though I could finally see through the smoke and mirrors. With my trust in him shattered, so was the illusion of charm and mystery. Suddenly I couldn't stomach the thought of having sex with him ever again.

It was close to an hour before he addressed our last conversation. 'Listen, I know I said some things to you –' he began.

I cut him off. 'I can't. I'm sorry. I can't continue seeing you.'
He nodded, expecting it. 'I understand.'
'Do you really?' I replied.

He tried to explain: he had been in a much more dominant headspace than usual; he needed the mind games to get turned on, otherwise it was just fucking. But he knew he had pushed at boundaries I had clearly stated as hard limits, and none of his justifications could make things right.

'I understand you need what you need, you want what you want,' I said, 'but I can't give it to you.'

As soon as Daddy Dom realized there was no luring me

back, I could see him trying to get out with his ego intact. He launched into stories about various other women he was fucking and attempted to console me, saying, 'You'll find someone.'

My mind flashed to the list of unexplored matches in my Tinder account. *Maybe I already have your replacement lined up*, said a voice in my head – a voice that sounded like me, but different.

Perhaps it was Daddy Dom's good girl, but a little sharper, a bit wiser.

Rules can make the new and unknown feel safe as we venture out into uncharted territory. But no matter how many rules we lay down, or how specific we try to make them, they only provide an illusion of safety and control. It is virtually impossible to anticipate every situation we might face, or the people we might encounter.

In the undefined and unknown, it would be my own boundaries – my own internal compass for what I believed was right or wrong – that would show me what to do. I had to learn how to listen to them and how to enforce them. My encounter with Daddy Dom was only the first step.

By honouring our rules, Marcus and I would learn to trust each other; by honouring my boundaries, I would learn to trust myself.

In the meantime, my curiosity pulled me onward to seek what else was out there.

7

Are you ever jealous?

With shaking hands wiped clean of lubricant and various human secretions, I typed the following words into Google on my phone browser:

what to do when a butt plug gets stuck in your ass

butt plug stuck in anus

lost butt plug

Salvation appeared in the form of a magazine headline.

HERE'S EXACTLY WHAT TO DO IF YOU GET A SEX TOY STUCK IN YOUR BUTT.

Before I could scroll down to the rest of the article, an alert leapt out at me in bold, black letters.

WARNING! DO NOT ATTEMPT TO POOP OUT THE PLUG!

Going to the toilet may create a vacuum that sucks the plug further up the anal canal instead of dislodging it, pulling it into the intestinal tract.

I scrambled to the toilet and banged on the door.

'Theo! Theo, stop! Stop pooping!'

'What?' replied a muffled voice.

'Google says don't poop! You might make it worse!'

'I already took a dump!'

'Stop! Just come out right now!'

The toilet flushed, the door creaked open, and a two-metre-tall tower of strapping muscle emerged, looking worried and sheepish. 'I don't know if I got it out,' Theo said, running his meaty hands through his long blonde hair. 'But I definitely did a number two.'

'Why did you flush?' I shrieked. 'How will we know it's gone?'

We stared at each other.

'Fine. On the bed. Face down, ass in the air,' I commanded, rolling up my sleeves and reaching for the lube. 'I'll check.'

Never had I been so grateful that having a baby had eliminated any qualms I might have had about poop. Crooning soothing words to calm Theo, I plunged in and squished around with my fingers, feeling for the sly little feet of the silicone plug that had disappeared into Theo with shocking ease.

'That's it. We're going to the emergency room,' I pronounced, withdrawing my fingers and heading to the bathroom to scrub them clean.

'Are you fucking kidding me?' he yelled. 'I can't go to the hospital! What if someone recognizes me?'

'I can't find it. We have to make sure it's not lodged in your intestinal tract.'

'My *what*?'

I took a deep breath. 'Theo, I'm sorry. I can't let you go without getting a doctor to check you out – and get that thing out properly if they have to. If you start coughing up blood at two in the morning, or worse, I'll never forgive myself.'

'Fuck. You're right.' With a groan, Theo rolled off the bed and began clearing the hotel room of debris – sex toys, ropes, handcuffs, condoms, half a dozen kinky costumes – and stuffing them into his duffel bag.

'Um, Theo? I'm going to need my clothes back,' I said.

He glanced down at the silk scarf I'd knotted around his neck as a collar and leash, the frilly white blouse straining across his broad chest, and the black miniskirt that circled his narrow waist – ending, obscenely, just above his penis.

'Oh, right,' he said.

He unbuttoned my blouse and thrust it at me with one hand, wiping red lipstick from his mouth with the other. 'Here you go.'

The doctors at the local *Eerste Hulp* stifled their chuckles through the ultrasound, but to my overwhelming relief, they pronounced Theo's digestive system clear of sex toys. He would live to play and be dominated another day, but probably not by a first-rate amateur like me.

'Thanks for not leaving me there,' Theo said as he drove me back to the train station where I would catch the Sprinter home to Amsterdam. 'I really appreciate how you tried to keep me from panicking.'

'Of course I couldn't leave. I'm not evil!'

'I was right about you. You really are quite caring,' he said. 'Must be 'cause you're a mom.'

'Caring makes me a great mom. Not a great Dominatrix,' I said.

'Everyone has to start somewhere,' he replied, pulling up at the train station. 'Preferably not at the emergency room.'

'No, preferably not,' I said, stepping out of his car with my bag. 'Thanks for being so cool about it. I'm sorry again.'

'No problem. It was fun . . . before all of that,' Theo said. Then he winked. 'We'll just have to leave the butt plug at home next time.'

'Next time?' There was going to be a *next time*? I thought there was no way this man would ever let me touch him again.

'We're just getting started,' he said. 'Don't you agree?'

Indeed, I was just getting started.

After kissing Daddy Dom goodbye, I flung myself back into Tinder with appetite and abandon. The renegotiated terms of my marriage freed me to pursue the variety and adventure I'd glimpsed from my online life, which now seemed like a lifetime ago, though it had only been six months between the end of my affair with Thomas to my emergency-room escapade with Theo.

Neither variety nor adventure were hard to find. After sex with the same man for most of my adult life, everyone was variety, and everything was an adventure.

At first, I was shocked by the Tinder matches and male attention flooding into my phone. Back home, I had never been anyone's type. Filipino men displayed an overwhelming preference for what we called *the simple girl*. When asked what kind of girl they are attracted to, Filipino men will almost always say, *'yung* simple *lang'* (just the simple kind).

The simple girl was the Filipino cultural ideal of feminine beauty. We all went to school with someone like her: fair-skinned and petite, with a tiny waist and stick-straight hair pulled back into a prim ponytail. She had neat handwriting and a preppy wardrobe, wore ballet flats and pearl earrings, always smelled fresh and never laughed too loudly. She was agreeable and docile, unassuming and self-effacing, unthreatening and uncomplicated. Impervious to the ageing forces of marriage and motherhood, her arrested development made her forever desirable and worthy of admiration, her girlhood (along with her gamine figure) a trophy she clung to for life.

Half-Indian and wild-haired, ample-bottomed and opinionated, possessed of a healthy appetite and complex longings, I was none of those things. My non-existent dating history, coupled with the insecurity of a former fat kid, had convinced me no one would ever be attracted to me. Even Marcus, when I first met him, belonged to the cult of the simple girl. I considered myself lucky that he had noticed me at all.

In the Netherlands, where the dominant feminine type was blonde, blue-eyed and tall, I was suddenly, strikingly different. And being different changed everything.

I had been brought up to believe that my body, like all fat bodies, was ugly and better hidden. But now, my curves were sexy, my mixed Filipina-Indian features exotic. My butt, which I could never squeeze into simple girl jeans that strained to contain it, was now my most sellable feature. Being just over 1.5 metres, a full head shorter than the average Dutch woman, prevented me from reaching the tops of supermarket shelves or fixing my make-up in the mirror in public toilets; it also made me adorable, appealing, and easy for tall Dutch men to pick up and throw around in bed. I wasn't short, I was fun-sized.

Being in an open relationship was now the most intriguing thing about me. It made me seem liberated. Sexual. Cool. Shedding the invisibility cloak of marriage and motherhood, I became a magnet for men I thought would never give me a second look in real life. They professed 'mad respect' for me, my husband and the road we'd chosen, showering me with high-five and fist-bump emojis on Tinder and, later, on dating apps like Happn and Bumble. Men sought my advice on how to bring this up with their girlfriends; wanted to meet me more out of curiosity about my marriage than actual attraction to me; claimed they would never 'allow' 'their women' to do such a thing, but were more than happy to bone me nonetheless.

Men rushed at me like an avalanche, leaping at the promise of no-strings-attached sex from an uninhibited woman who made unconventional decisions, whose emotional needs were taken care of at home, would never become clingy or demand more than a casual encounter, and claimed freedom from entanglement and responsibility as well as guaranteed it.

Years ago, Thomas's hands on my belly had shown me that it was a part of me that deserved attention and brought me fully into my body. What might other hands, and other lovers, teach me about myself? What might I learn if other parts of me that had been hidden and excluded were allowed to come to the table – or invited to bed? What else might be possible?

Now I was free to find out.

Dating apps brought Craigslist, my old cornucopia of curiosities, to life, and I embraced it in the flesh. Flirting on apps helped me overcome the shyness around men that my upbringing had drilled into me. Trained to be the prey, never the pursuer, a decent Filipina woman never made the first move. As single women, we were praised for our ability to keep men at arm's length, not reel them in; we were judged on our elusiveness and patience, never our wit or flair. When we aged into mothers and wives, we were valued for our selflessness and suffering, not our sex appeal or style.

As a result, I'd reached the age of thirty-six without ever having acquired any of the skills required to ensnare men in the wild: how to make eye contact, read a man's signals, or chat up a handsome stranger at a bar. I had zero game.

The written word had always been my secret weapon. Words came easily to me on dating apps, where I had time to think about what to say and the risk of face-to-face rejection was low. The Tinder chat box became my playground as I found my inner flirt. Now seen as exotic and attractive, with wit flowing from my fingertips, I entered an arena that I'd believed was closed off to me, where only beautiful, skinny, perfect women reigned.

The gates were open, the game was on, and I was killing it.

An extrovert liberated from the isolation of new motherhood, I emerged with a voracious curiosity about people, which dating both whetted and satisfied. I met people I never would have encountered in my child-sized cocoon: a social worker who cleaned homes for the elderly; an artist who travelled around the world painting murals; the CEO of a posh rehab facility; a mob sidekick on the run from Beirut; and those rarest unicorns of all in a city of over a hundred nationalities, born-and-bred Amsterdammers.

By this time, our daughter was in daycare twice a week to prepare for her entry into preschool. On days when writing was easy or slow, I met up with freelance creatives who were down to do it in the daytime: art directors and account executives; film-makers and artists; too many photographers to count. Coffee turned into quickies, and lunch breaks into afternoon delights.

I had a weakness for chefs and bartenders, whose late shifts ultimately made them unviable as a source of potential dates. *Where are you, gorgeous?* the bartenders would text at 3 a.m. after closing time. *In bed beside my husband*, I would quip, which cracked them up. *Try me in the morning.* I had no physical type, but was drawn to mental agility, a sense of adventure, humour and entertainment. I came for the sex and stayed for the stories. Tall tales were my pillow talk.

I was fascinated by them all, and free to leave when the novelty faded. I could breeze through men's lives and bedrooms without the obligation to stay, take care of them or cater to their needs. All I had to do was be good company:

sparkling, delightful and sexual. I didn't even have to be that good in bed. Sometimes all I had to do was show up.

I rediscovered Amsterdam, overwriting my mental map of playgrounds and diaper-changing facilities with lovers' addresses, day-use hotel rooms and temporary trysting grounds. With my bike, I could be anywhere and everywhere in no time: at the hip brunch spot where a sexy cook dished out eggs Benedict in the morning and bent me over the tables at night, after wiping down the kitchen and locking the door; the shop where a bearded barber offered me a private shave in his vintage chrome-and-leather chair; the five-star hotel where a mischievous concierge and his magic keycard gave me my pick of designer suites; the rockabilly boudoir in an abandoned office building, squatted by a tattooed accountant with a taste for bondage and bourbon; the secret music studio tucked under a bridge in the ancient heart of the city, where thick brick walls and heavy iron doors muffled the sounds of drums, rap, and sex.

My city was unfolding, and so was I.

An 'Erotic Blueprint' quiz I took at the time christened me a Shapeshifter, whose sexual make-up changed ever so slightly to please every new lover. I found pleasure in meeting men, but I relished getting to know all the women inside me even more. I was beginning to discover that I had as many sides to myself as I did lovers. What men saw in me, desired in me and projected on to me was fascinating and instructive.

I was something different to everyone. To a 23-year-old advertising wunderkind, I was the married professor he had secretly lusted after, but could never make a pass at. To Caribbean-born Ibrahim, I represented the broad-hipped women of his native island, whose tropical warmth and caramel curves he missed after emigrating to Amsterdam. And to

Theo of the lost butt plug and small-town emergency room, I was the first-time Dominatrix who 'forced' him into wearing women's clothes, indulged his most secret desire, then teased and taunted him for it.

From his days as star coach to his role as one of the corporate godfathers of Dutch sport, Theo occupied a position of authority and respectability in a hyper-masculine world. His fiancée knew about his fetish but refused to facilitate it. It was easier to turn a blind eye to casual encounters where, due to his social stature and powerful build, he was expected to be dominant. But beneath his sharp suit and TV-worthy smile, Theo hid the desire to shed all responsibility and relinquish all his power to a woman who would force him into feminine costumes as the ultimate mark of his subservience.

For a brief, bizarre, yet altogether not unpleasant moment in time, that woman was me.

Why me? I wondered after I matched with Theo on Tinder, and he confessed to his kink and the role he wanted me to play. What did he see in me? Could I pull this off? But Theo was so *hot*, so into me, and seemed so confident in my yet-to-be discovered powers of dominance, that I decided to try it at least once. Going the complete opposite of my experience with Daddy Dom appealed to me: exciting and novel, but also safe. If I controlled the power, no one could trample on my boundaries.

I spent days poring over blog posts, forum threads and articles on the fetish of feminization: the process of training a submissive male to be feminine. In theory, I was the boss. In reality, Theo exerted power over having me cater to his kink – and he was *demanding*.

On his days off from corporate life, he would beg me on

WhatsApp to choose his outfit for the day. I replied with pictures ripped from cosplay websites. Lace made him lusty, and frills were his freedom: the pinker, puffier, and more ludicrously feminine, the better. He would race to dig into the stash of women's clothes he had amassed in secret, put together a look, then send me pictures of himself modelling for me. 'Does this please you, Miss?'

'What a pretty sissy you are!' I would croon, delighting and arousing him with my approval. I started out by lifting direct quotes from articles with titles like 'FemDom 101' or 'How to Train Your Sissy', but quickly learned to improvise.

'What would your team say if they saw you like this? I bet they'd love to take turns fucking your tight little sissy asshole!' I worried that I'd gone too far, but Theo ate it all up.

Watching hardcore femdom videos on Pornhub made me realize I didn't have the stomach for complete and total degradation. I could never be a mean Mistress; instead I found it easier to be a playful one. I commanded Theo to turn over his entire collection of women's clothing – including a size 52 pair of white patent high heels, the biggest I'd ever seen – and teased him to delirium with snaps of myself masturbating in his favourite outfits.

To win back each item, he had to complete tasks I devised, such as delaying orgasms for hours or even days, until I pronounced my satisfaction. He never succeeded in taking them all back; I still have a delicate pair of lace-cuffed white socks and a marvellous Oktoberfest dirndl with puffy sleeves and a flouncy, royal-blue satin skirt.

All this teasing culminated in a hotel rendezvous, where I painted Theo's face to complete his transformation into the woman he so desperately wanted to be. The sheer novelty of the experience was thrilling, the push–pull of shame and desire on his face and body fascinating to watch. When his make-up was done, I clapped my hands with delight as he adjusted his blonde braided wig and batted his false eyelashes like a bear cosplaying as Barbie.

Then I flung a French maid costume at him and ordered him to dust the furniture, make a cup of tea and paint my nails. It was the strangest foreplay I had ever experienced, more amusing than arousing, but it worked – at least for one of us. Feminized to a frenzy, Theo begged to wear my clothes while we had sex. As I clambered up on to his massive frame and lowered myself on to his stiff cock, I had to wonder if he wanted to *do* me or *be* me.

Unlike the woman in Theo's life, I could tolerate his kink, cater to it, even get a kick out of it. But when I realized that it ultimately did nothing for me in bed, the endless messages and dress-up games began to feel like time I'd never get back. He'd bossed me into bossing him, but I wanted to return to what mattered most: my own sexual satisfaction. Instead of learning what gave *me* pleasure, I'd been sidetracked by the force of Theo's will into catering for his.

'I'm sorry, Theo,' I said to him after our third date. 'I've had fun, but I think you're better off finding someone who really enjoys doing this.' He took it like a gentleman and a champ, and we parted ways warmly. I glowed with the pride of having tried something so different from every sexual experience I'd had so far and discovering that I could stretch myself in directions I'd never considered.

Back on Tinder, I was happy to enjoy the modest excitements of novelty and the subtle shifts of behaviour each new lover prompted in me. After so many dates, I could hear something in the first-date small talk, the tall tales, the compliments murmured in bars and groaned in bed. They were all saying one thing: not that I was sexy or hot or interesting. They were all telling me: there was nothing wrong in wanting or enjoying any of this.

Hearing it so often, I began to believe it.

It felt like the beginning of something. Of thriving.

But if I was thriving, Marcus was not.

*

In the aftermath of the affair, the nights when Marcus and I cuddled on the couch and giggled over Tinder profiles together brought affection and buoyancy back into our marriage. Laughter was our medicine, a sense of shared discovery our soothing balm.

Feeling like two crazy kids with a naughty secret, Marcus and I goggled at the sheer variety and mind-boggling specificity of the kinks we stumbled upon on FetLife, one of the largest kink-oriented online communities in the world. We rolled our eyes at the early-1990s aesthetic and clunky user interface of Swingers' Date Club, where we posted a profile as a couple and scrolled through invitations to swingers' clubs and couples-only sex parties. Those moments felt like the promise of adventure, the first ticklish sip of bubbles before a wild night out on the town.

Reality set in when I began racking up dates and Marcus began striking out. Before long, I was the only one with any dubious Tinder matches to show or cringeworthy opening lines to chuckle at. The fantasy of fetish parties and swingers' nights fizzled into the ether when we realized that they all started too late for us, the parents of a three-year-old, to attend. Living half a world away from family meant that we couldn't drop our child off at the grandparents' for a night off or a weekend away, a luxury the Dutch parents we knew took for granted.

As kinky and involved as it was, my little experiment with Theo was the least of Marcus's concerns. It was easy for him to roll his eyes and brush off the sight of me posing for selfies in Theo's billowy blue dirndl. Feminization was nothing he'd ever been curious about or wanted to experience for himself. 'No thanks,' he quipped, shaking his head. 'Knock yourself out.'

But when my dating life took off without him, he struggled. 'This was supposed to be fun for both of us!' he complained.

Tension would fill the house as I dressed up for dates, as though Marcus was steeling himself. I would head out after bedtime, leaving him home alone to discover what new motherhood had taught me: that it was entirely possible to be lonely in a marriage.

Loneliness had been my constant companion in the wakeful nights I spent breastfeeding while Marcus slept; during the sleepless hours I spent in the dark with a teething baby while he jetted off on business trips to London and New York, watching Broadway shows after his meetings and workshops, wining and dining on the company dime; throughout the months I spent at home in the mind-deadening cycle of playtime, feeds and naps, while he enjoyed an uninterrupted career trajectory; every time I was called to pick our daughter up early from daycare when she felt clingy or fell ill, expected to surrender whatever freelance writing gig I had scored to lie down beside her and stare at the ceiling as she burned with fever.

Now Marcus chafed at loneliness as it intertwined with envy, a combination that had become familiar to me over the years. In retaliation, he took to Tinder with a grim obstinacy. A type-A overachiever and inherently competitive, he became bent on racking up his own score to bolster his ego. Was I having fun? He would out-fun me. Did I have multiple dates lined up? He would rack up more. Was I having a wild and exciting time? He would revel in so much wildness and excitement, I wouldn't be able to *stand* it. I would regret having asked for this and renege on the whole experiment, grovelling at his feet. His determination was a neon sign over his head, flashing in red: *I'll show you. Just you wait.*

A determined Marcus usually gets what he guns for, but the odds were stacked against him on dating apps. Women matched with him without reading his Tinder bio, then accused him of wasting their time. 'Why do you still want McDonald's when you already have fine dining at home?' one of them scolded.

This made us both explode into giggles. 'Oh girl,' I said, 'I'm so sorry you think of yourself as McDonald's!'

Besides, I reasoned, doesn't everyone have the craving for a big juicy Whopper or a gooey slice of pizza every now and then? Can anyone honestly say they want a Michelin-star experience for every single meal, every day until death claims them?

I couldn't. I love pizza too much.

Marcus railed at his perceived position in the unspoken pecking order of digital dating in the modern age. 'I'm a fluffy, married Asian man,' he complained. 'Black guys on top, white guys second. And you? A curvy, short, Asian MILF? You're queen of the world!'

'That's not true!' I tried to reassure him, without conviction. The reality was that it was far easier for me, a married woman offering no-strings sex to men, to find casual partners on dating apps than it was for him, a married man looking for no-strings sex from women.

I was having all the fun. Marcus was having none of it.

Sometimes our arguments felt less about making Marcus feel safe or protecting our closeness, than about controlling my behaviour. He brought up additions to the rules constantly, leading to quarrels about the frequency with which I saw particular people. Seeing any one person too often ran the risk of intimacy, forming an emotional bond. But how much was too much? Once a month? Two, three, five times? The idea of assigning a number felt pointless and arbitrary.

Marcus had problems with all the men I dated. They were too hot, too cool, too attractive, too interesting. 'You must think I'm so boring,' he complained. 'What's to stop you from running off with any one of these guys?'

'How do you even want us to resolve this?' I said, incredulous. 'Do you want me to date only boring, ugly people that I have zero connection with? Are we seriously going to make that a rule? What if I demanded the same of you? Ugly girls only? Are we going to screen each other's dates for attractiveness now?'

He protested, he sulked, but eventually he got the point. And I began to see that loneliness and envy were smokescreens for the ugly, green-eyed, and very real monster: jealousy.

The anxiety of being compared and coming up short, the fear that perhaps the *real* reason I sought sexual adventure elsewhere was because he wasn't enough for me, was visceral and deeply rooted. The threat of losing me to someone new was not only present, but palpable to Marcus, a complete reversal of where we had been just six months ago, when it was *his* empty suitcase on the bed, and *he* was ready to walk out on *me*.

At the heart of jealousy is a fear too great to be named: a fear of not being enough, of *never* being enough. Of being abandoned, left unwanted, unloved and alone. All it wants is to feel safe and to know – to *believe* – that it is enough.

Naming this fear is the beginning of its undoing, but it would take Marcus at least another year to admit this. He didn't need to; his actions said it all.

Jealousy reveals the face of that which you wish never to confront – about the relationship, but most of all, about yourself. Like anything that puts a relationship through discomfort and stress – becoming parents, life upheavals – it reveals the foundations of the relationship, testing its strength, but also magnifying its cracks.

In those early days, I wanted it all, and all at once. I struggled to be patient and kind, to steady my frustration at Marcus's pace, to keep finding new ways to help him process his jealousy. I wanted to be an inexhaustible fount of reassurance, a tireless champion of our love, but our conversations ground me down until I felt like a broken record shouting into a void. No matter how many times I told Marcus I loved him and could never replace him, it never seemed to be enough. No matter how I tried to make him understand that these dates were not auditions for his eventual replacement, he didn't seem to believe me. I often felt as though he was searching for the lie behind my words.

I wondered whether, if I hadn't shattered his trust, things might have been different. But I had done what I had done. Now we had to build something new and audacious, for which neither of us had a master plan.

All I could do was keep reminding him how much I loved him: that he was still my favourite person in the whole world, that there was no other life partner for me, that I wanted to grow old with him, just as we had envisioned when we set out to make a life together. In the distant future I dreamed of, the two of us would look back someday and laugh about all the crazy things we had done in our wild youth.

But at the end it would still be the two of us: grey hair, wrinkles, and all.

The tide began to turn when Marcus went on his first Tinder date, a Dutch redhead who lived in the neighbourhood. I was relieved: *at last!* Maybe this would take the heat off me, and he would start enjoying the perks of our agreement.

'She's cute,' I said, inspecting her profile when he held out his phone to me for a look. I couldn't tell if he was excited and wanted me to be supportive, or smug that he'd scored a date of his own and wanted me to be jealous.

My eyes fell on her age, beside her name: twenty-two. I felt a stab of something prickly and irrational in my chest. 'A bit young, isn't she?'

'Oh, I didn't notice,' he said with a shrug.

'Do you set your age limit so low? Is this your type?' I regretted the words as soon as they escaped my mouth. I sounded so . . . *petty*.

Am I jealous? I asked myself as Marcus's monumental first date drew closer. I wanted him to start having some fun of his own. I sensed how nervous he was and found it encouraging that he wanted to talk to me about this date. I did my best to respond with a light banter that I hoped would soothe and reassure him; recommended where to take her for a drink; helped him decide on an outfit.

Dating had boosted my confidence, so I no longer felt insecure about things that used to bother me: my extra kilos, post-baby belly, stretch marks and C-section scar. At this point in my life, I felt secure in how I looked and who I was, hard-won battles that took me the greater part of my adulthood.

Then her age would flash in my mind, and that twinge of irritation would strike again. I imagined all the things a younger woman might have that I didn't: a trim figure, perky boobs, perfect skin, boundless energy. Age was the one thing a younger woman would always have over me. No matter what I did, I could never turn back the clock. I would only get older, my skin would only wrinkle and lose elasticity, my breasts (and God knows what else) would only deflate and sag. If young was indeed Marcus's type, I would only ever be its opposite.

I would never win. But only if I saw it as a competition.

I had to trust that it was not.

Watching Marcus prepare for his first Tinder date, slicking back his hair and spritzing on the cologne he so rarely used, I wondered if there was something wrong with me. Surely if I truly loved him, I would feel even the slightest hint of jealousy?

The lie we're told about jealousy – the lie that comes all wrapped up in the romance novels and Hollywood movies, the diamond rings and white dresses, the myth of The One and the promise of forever – is that it's a sign of love. Being crazed with jealousy means being madly in love. The more agonizing the jealousy, the greater the love.

Jealousy is a difficult teacher, but she has much wisdom to impart if you calm down enough to listen. Staring her in the face, I saw that she looked nothing like love.

By the time Marcus had slipped his keys off the hook in our hallway and shrugged into his winter coat, I had come to the conclusion that I wasn't jealous. I was insecure. Whatever I felt had nothing to do with how much I loved Marcus, and everything to do with how I saw myself and our relationship.

But because I knew Marcus better than anyone, I knew that he'd grown up surrounded by shame around his body, and around sex and pleasure. Whatever insecurity I felt faded into the background, overridden by my excitement to see him enjoy himself free of guilt, shame and self-doubt. By the time I kissed him goodbye and closed our front door behind him, insecurity felt like a momentary blip, small and petty, something I could overlook in the face of what I wanted him to have.

What I felt was desire for Marcus to have experiences that led to discovery and growth, and curiosity to see how they unfolded for him. What I *didn't* feel was the need to own those experiences. I could enjoy how they affected him without having to cause, control or embed myself in every single one of them.

Isn't that love, too?

Marcus returned just before midnight. I lay awake in bed, listening to the familiar muted sounds of his homecoming: hanging up his coat in the hallway closet, kicking off his shoes, turning the shower on full blast.

He walked into our bedroom, his expression both dazed and thoughtful, as though he wanted to talk and had something to say.

Taking a deep breath to prepare myself, I asked: 'How'd it go?'

'I get it now,' was the first thing he said. His slow, deliberate cadence hinted at a mind still processing input, choosing words, making sense and meaning. 'I get it now,' he repeated.

I pulled aside the duvet and patted his side of the bed. He slid in beside me and lay back against the pillows, crossing his hands behind his head.

'I thought I would feel terrible about myself,' he said. 'In the beginning, something kept telling me, *This is wrong*. I'm a bad husband, and I'm doing something bad, even if I know it's okay between the two of us.'

'For you to even put yourself out there is a huge step,' I said. 'We agreed on this. I want you to feel good about it. You shouldn't feel guilty.'

'That's just it. In the end, I don't feel guilty,' he admitted. 'I'm surprised at how easy it is. Does that make me a horrible husband?'

'No,' I said. 'No, it doesn't.'

'I had fun. Really, I did,' he said. 'But when it was over, it didn't change how I feel about you. I was still excited to come home to you. And I still love being your man.'

There was something in his voice I hadn't heard before: tenderness, a mild curiosity, even a kind of wonder. Gone was the sharp tang of judgement, the stony indifference of numbness, the explosive fire of anger. These had given way to something else.

It was empathy: the softening of a lifetime of shame.

The softness felt like an opening. If I spoke reassurance to him now, he would be ready to receive it.

'You do get it,' I said. 'Nothing I do with anyone else

changes how I feel about you. It doesn't make me want you, need you or love you any less. And nothing *you* do with anyone else changes how I see you. It doesn't make you any less of a good man. That's what you are to me: a good man and a good husband. The best there is.'

The following night our sex would take on a new intensity. In the heat of the moment, with his arms around me, as I took him deep inside me, I would be possessed by the uncontrollable urge to know everything.

What did you do?
And then what did she do?
Did you like that?

Perhaps it was the thrill of novelty, the excitement of teasing out new and undiscovered things about him, just as he was finding them out himself. I have always loved words, and to hear my husband describe himself to me as a completely different lover rewrote the character of him in my mind, in a story that had just begun to pick up speed. Taking control of when and how I heard the words, turning his tryst into stimuli to serve *my* pleasure, on *my* terms, meant that my little experiment with Theo wasn't a complete failure.

Perhaps there was something to being in command after all.

Marcus would hesitate at first, years of shame stopping him. Then, when he realized how much it turned me on, he would pour out the details like gasoline on fire.

But that was later. On the night of my husband's first date after nearly a decade of marriage, I fell asleep in his arms feeling I was understood, and he fell asleep in mine knowing he was loved.

More dates would soon trickle in for Marcus – still fewer and less frequent than mine, but he found his groove. He began to notice what attracted his attention while browsing kink communities like FetLife, or a sex-positive dating app called Feeld, where we could also post a profile as a couple. I was always interested to hear about the kinks that sparked his curiosity – which aren't mine to disclose – but appreciated the freedom we gave each other from the obligation to facilitate those kinks.

The more often Marcus dated, the more confident he became. The more often we *both* dated, the more normal it felt. He began to see a pattern – *I'll feel sucky for a while, then I won't want to be around her, then I'll really miss her, then I'll be over it.* The sucky bits grew shorter, and the distant moods passed more swiftly, until he was almost impatient for us to feel close and connected again. This time, there was no stand-offishness, no toughing it out, no weakness in being vulnerable.

Ultimately, jealousy is a feeling, and feelings always pass. To ride it out, not to dwell in it, hold on to it or make decisions while in its throes, prevented us from doing more damage to our relationship than any date could. Looking past jealous feelings grew easier, knowing that what waited after was so much better. The sooner jealousy passed, the sooner we could get back to what mattered – each other, and the intimacy and joy of our life together.

On the couple of nights a month that I was out, Marcus began to rediscover things he loved to do, that had somehow gotten lost in the fog of early parenthood. Things that made him feel good about himself – working out, painting, inviting friends over and cooking for them – filled his nights.

The dead air that had preceded my nights out began to buzz with the hum of activity – music, the flop of his sketch pad, the clatter of pencils and paintbrushes on our dining table. When I heard those sounds I knew he would be fine, and so would we.

It sounded like normalcy. It felt like progress.

Marcus says it helped that I constantly reminded him of all the things he was to me, and that I wasn't looking to replace him – words he grew to trust over time. But in the end, jealousy is a personal confrontation. What made the greatest difference, and what only he was in control of, was how he felt about himself – and that's nothing I could have fixed for him.

Was I jealous? The truth is, I found it harder to deal with Marcus's jealousy than my own.

In the beginning it almost felt like a betrayal to enjoy myself so much while the person I loved struggled with the very thing that was helping me thrive. Then should I make myself smaller and deny my own expansion to cater to a partner's feelings, just as I set aside my own pleasure to facilitate Theo's kink? Where do I cross the line from care and consideration for his feelings, to shrinking myself to fit into his expectations of me? How can I help him grow to keep pace with me instead? I'm still trying to find that line, because it's fine, delicate and never static. I'm still trying to figure it out.

Confronting jealousy together taught me that waves of feeling can be intense and overwhelming at first; but, with practice, they calm and settle. I had learned that it is possible to overcome the discomfort by attending to what is exposed and giving it what it needs to be resolved. Easier said than done, when it takes courage, a willingness to look within, an ability to articulate and self-regulate emotions, and a commitment to a shared cause.

Jealousy is a visceral reaction to a perceived threat, an emotional response to the idea that someone has something over me that will make me come out the loser in a zero-sum game. It boils down to a fear of not being enough, and that this insufficiency will ultimately lead to pain and loss.

When all I see is richness in our entwined life – our lifelong growth project of parenthood, which we only share with each other; how we care for each other and enjoy being with each other; how we support each other's work, dreams, friendships and plans – I see everything that keeps us together.

I see everything I bring to the table as his life partner. If we made each other fundamentally miserable and I saw that he was only happy, excited or enjoying himself elsewhere, then I'd have a reason to be worried. Instead I see that I, and we, are more than enough, and are worth more to each other than anything else that might be out there.

We've had a look around, so we can say this with at least some authority.

And that is why I am unafraid to lose.

8

Do you have adventures together?

Springtime in Paris beckoned with the promise of adventure.

Choir mates from Manila were coming to sing at the Notre-Dame Cathedral, giving me a good excuse to save for the Thalys high-speed train and stay with a friend for the weekend. Arriving at Gare du Nord with my backpack on my shoulders and time on my hands, I wanted to explore the city with my camera before meeting my friends.

Heady with freedom, I craved something new and different, something I hadn't seen or done before. I turned to Instagram for inspiration, scrolling through the profiles of the Paris-based photographers I followed. On a whim, I decided to send messages to several of them, introducing myself and asking if anyone might be up for a cup of coffee and a stroll that afternoon.

The sole reply came from a Brazilian photographer named Rui. I knew him only from his photographs – he had an eye for colourful murals and black-and-white street scenes – and the few comments we had exchanged in the past.

Welcome to Paris! wrote Rui. *Yes! Let's meet!*

We agreed to rendezvous along the Canal Saint-Martin. Rui pulled up on a Vélib', one of the grey shared bicycles that I'd seen all over Paris. He was lean and pale, not particularly tall, with piercing hazel eyes, a thick shock of black hair, and a full, bushy black beard. Dressed all in black – T-shirt, skinny jeans, army boots, camera bag slung over his shoulder – he was a lightning bolt rendered in charcoal strokes, with a magnetic energy and effusive warmth that leapt off him and pulled me right in.

Quickly realizing that Rui didn't speak much English, I struggled to understand him at first. But he had bought a 50mm prime lens for his Nikon just before coming to meet me, and his excitement about his new toy was infectious. Soon we were stringing together bits of English, Portuguese, Spanish and French into an animated chat, our facial expressions and hand signals filling the gaps in our conversation.

As we strolled along the canal, Rui pointed out a building where the firefighters of Paris studied and threw a massive party in the summer. Rui seemed to be a party animal and had learned French entirely by going to parties.

Indifferent to partying, I responded with a polite smile-and-nod, until he added: 'The *pompiers* of Paris, they are beautiful men. They take off the shirt, they party all night.'

I stopped in my tracks. 'Did you say firemen? Shirtless firemen?'

He laughed. '*Oui!*'

I booked a cheap hotel and train ticket for a return trip to Paris three months later. It became a funny story to tell people we knew, and soon even Marcus's colleagues at work were rooting for me to go and see the hot French firemen.

By this time, our daughter had started preschool, a milestone that felt both like the end of an era and the beginning of liberation.

After navigating the application process and lottery system in Dutch, attending open days and coffee hours with administrators and parents, and introducing my child to her new school one hour at a time – then two and three, until she could stay for a half day – I brought her to her classroom one morning, commending her into the firm, capable hands of her teacher, a formidable lady who spoke Dutch with a heavy Portuguese accent, and waved goodbye from the outside.

My daughter ran to me and pressed her sweet face against the window, smudging it with her nose and cheeks. I breathed on the glass and drew my love into the steam with a fingertip: hearts, stars, smiley faces, and Miffy, the white bunny beloved by Dutch children everywhere. For a moment I thought she might cry, or was that me?

Then she was swept up in a circle of blonde heads and rosy cheeks, of clapping hands and cheerful songs. By some miracle, there were no tears: only tiny fingertips waggled in a wave, a rosebud mouth puckered wetly on to the glass, and the tentative flash of a smile as she took her first steps away from me into her colourful new world.

'I love you,' I mouthed, waving, but she was already gone.

With my child out of the house five days a week, I suddenly had time. Time to focus on my freelance career and finding new work; time to breeze into Marcus's office for a late Tuesday lunch; to invest in acquaintances that I wanted to turn into friends; to meet people for coffee and exercise and write and sit in the sunshine on the balcony, free of the guilt that time building my life and my self was time wasted.

Regaining more of myself, I had more to give. Marcus, who never took time off for himself, splurged on a week-long camper-van trip along the coast of Portugal. It was a trip I supported with enthusiasm; parenting solo for a week was so much easier now. Before he left, I bestowed a blanket blessing upon him to 'go ahead and have fun', which became our private code for: *You don't have to ask me first, just tell me after.*

Relaxing our rule about advance notice breathed a new ease

and spontaneity into our marriage. Having benefited from a wild night with a surfer chick in Portugal, Marcus reciprocated in kind with my return trip to Paris for the firemen's party.

The night before I was due to leave, Rui sent me a message on WhatsApp. He'd gotten the dates wrong.

The pompiers make the party last week, he said, apologizing. *But! Tomorrow, have another party called Possession. Is a good party. Very strong party.*

Clicking on the Facebook link he sent me, I was greeted by a profile photo of an open-mouthed nun clutching a black cross, eyes bleeding black and rolling up white in her head. Nothing could have been further from the shirtless Parisian firemen of my dreams.

'Looks like I'm going to a techno party called Possession,' I told Marcus. 'I hate techno.'

'Are you sure about this?' he asked.

'I can't chicken out now. I've already paid for my train and hotel room,' I said. 'So . . . yeah, I guess so.'

'Send me Rui's last name, address and phone number, please,' he said. 'Have fun, but please, stay safe. I'll see you on Monday.'

*

It was almost midnight. I hurried down the worn stone steps of the Quai de la Rapée towards a barge moored in the inky waters of the Seine, which rumbled with what sounded less like music and more like a battle between pieces of heavy machinery. A pale throng of students swathed in black and chattering in French swirled around me, cloaking the barge in its own mysterious climate of rhythm and shadows.

Was this what I had returned to Paris for? Suddenly I wasn't so sure. Before I could change my mind and turn around, a figure emerged from the darkness and reached for me.

'Rui!' I said, relief coursing through me as his grin lit the night.

'Deepa!'

He enveloped me in a warm hug, as though we'd known each other for years, and together we snaked with the queue into the barge, which turned out to be an underground club called Concrete.

For the next few hours, I was a lamb trailing in the wake of my nomadic shepherd. We paced in endless loops on the wooden dance floor on the top deck, and traced halting paths through the womblike basement in the vessel's steel belly.

Rui had been magnetic in the spring sunshine, on the day we first met. But in the darkness, in his element, he was irresistible. People were drawn to him, reaching out to stroke his beard or pull him closer for a chat. He seemed to know everyone, and everyone wanted to know him.

That day along the Canal Saint-Martin, it was Rui who had first brought up MDMA, the crystalline form of the key ingredient in Ecstasy pills. It must have been nearly 2 a.m. when he turned to me and said: 'MD. We talk about this before?'

I'd never done drugs in my life; I didn't even know how to smoke a cigarette. My only experience with mind-altering substances had been when I first moved to Amsterdam and lit up a pre-rolled joint in a red-light-district coffeeshop with Marcus out of a mild curiosity. Amsterdam might have built its reputation on weed, but after the sputtering, coughing let-down that was my first joint, I decided that I wasn't missing much.

I had asked Rui what MD was like. 'Everybody beautiful,' he said, closing his eyes, spreading his arms and lifting his face to the sky, like Moses welcoming manna from heaven. 'Have no problems. Love everybody.'

It sounded hokey. But something about the rapture in Rui's expression, the openness of his posture in that moment, had stayed with me.

Now I thought: *Okay, I'm in.*

Rui slipped something tiny, solid and vaguely conical into my hand. A swig of water, a hard swallow, then we were on the move again. As we wove through the mass of bodies in motion, I began to lose faith. I felt old, out of place, and uncool. What was I supposed to feel? What was I even doing here?

Rui and I peeled away from the wooden dance floor to lean on the railing that overlooked the Seine. 'How are you?' he asked.

'Rui, I don't think this will work,' I said. 'I think I might just go back to my hotel.'

The moment the words left my lips, everything went soft.

Whoosh, like the world breathing out a sigh.

The city lights reflected on the Seine coalesced into enormous four-pointed stars that blazed more brightly than anything I had ever seen, blotting out the darkness with their brilliance. Fierce and dazzling, the stars on the river were so huge, they were almost cartoon-like.

The Seine was on fire, and so was I.

'You feel something!' he said.

Aeons later, I dared to answer. 'The lights – the lights,' I whispered. 'They're so beautiful.'

When Rui embraced me, it felt as though he was welcoming me to a place he already knew, where he had been waiting for me to find him. Embracing him back, I arrived.

His hands on my shoulders urged me forward. 'Go, go, go!'

I lost myself in the crowd, where the music revealed itself to me. The bass became a command, and I could do nothing but obey. It began as a beating of a thousand hearts under the soles of my feet, gaining momentum as it pounded through me, coursing up my legs, spine, hips, shoulders, bursting through the tips of my fingers as I threw my hands up in the air. I'd never danced this way before, but I'd never felt music this way before.

I piled my sweat-matted hair on top of my head with one hand. Behind me, Rui leaned in close and blew cool air across my nape. His palms radiated heat into my shoulders, pulling me into a warm soup of sights, sounds and sensations. Thoughts fled, making space for the enormous rush of new stimuli. The roar of interference in my head – doubt, anxiety, awkwardness – disappeared, leaving only silence. I had found the off switch to a lifetime of noise.

Later, I would discover that I could flip the switch any time, or at least dial down the chatter of self-consciousness at will. But in that moment, there was only bliss.

I craved everything and feared nothing. Rejection slid off my back like sweat. If I wanted to tell someone they were beautiful, I could. Every touch was reciprocated, every compliment warmly received, every smile I beamed reflected back with charm and generosity. I had never seen any of these people in my life, but I felt that I knew them all and that they knew me.

I could have stayed rooted in one spot all night, taking it all in, but Rui was too restless.

'Walk with me,' he said. 'Talk to every people. Look all in the eyes.'

So I did. I became acutely aware of how I never usually made eye contact with strangers. In the streets of Manila, to lock eyes with a stranger was to become a target: to invite unwanted attention, even danger. I had learned to put on a mask and armour, to hide in plain sight.

But in this world, I was safe. I was ready. My eyes were open, and I wanted to see everything.

I wanted to remember it all. How colours flowed like paint on wet paper, sliding into new hues. How sound penetrated every available texture, every hidden corner, until shadows seemed to pulsate with life. How light captivated me: the glint of the strobe on a silver earring, the slick sheen of sweat on exposed skin.

I grew mesmerized by a rainbow prism glancing off a pair of clear eyeglasses, dancing in a transparent arc. 'Hey, nice glasses,' I said dreamily.

They belonged to a fresh-faced boy with luminous blue eyes and blonde hair, who I guessed couldn't have been more than twenty-two.

'Thank you!' he said in English with a marked French accent, moving towards me with a beer in hand. 'Where are you from?'

His name was Lucien, and he was in fact twenty-three years old. Within minutes of our first conversation, of which not a single word can I recall aside from the fact that he'd come to Possession with a friend and was a train driver for the Paris Métro, Lucien and I were kissing on the dance floor.

My head spun as this beautiful boy ran his fingers through my hair, flicking his tongue in my ear while whispering how hot I was. That was it? *Nice glasses?* If picking up a man was that easy, why hadn't I done it before?

Dawn painted the dark waters of the Seine a rosy gold when I decided that Lucien would come home with me. 'Find your friend and say goodbye. Let's go,' I said.

'To your hotel?' he said, leaping to obey. 'Okay, yes, yes!' Almost instantly, he caught the arm of a stocky, dark-haired boy who I presumed was his friend. They muttered to one another in French, eyeing me all the while. One word in English leapt out at me: 'MILF'. Was that what I was now? In this pulsating, upside-down world, the identity that had rendered me invisible now made me desirable. I decided I would be crazy not to embrace it.

With Lucien wrapped around my arm and an Uber on the way, I found Rui entangled in a knot of Brazilians. 'Rui, it's been wonderful,' I said, 'but I'm leaving now.'

His eyes lit up in surprise. 'He go with you?'

I nodded.

'*Bon, c'est bon*,' Rui said, chuckling. He gave me a tight hug, then took my face in both hands and kissed me on the lips. In that moment, I was incapable of guessing what the kiss might mean. I simply accepted it as a definitive end to a night unlike any other, not realizing that it was only the beginning of more nights to come.

Picking up a man for the first time was far more remarkable than the sex I ended up having that night. Ecstasy turned out to be excellent for my libido, but dismal for poor Lucien's equipment.

I returned to Amsterdam a newly anointed MILF – at

least in the eyes of one 23-year-old French Métro driver – in the throes of the longest, most lingering high of my life. I've since been told that your first twenty times on Ecstasy are magical, before the law of diminishing returns kicks in. But everyone says there's nothing like your first time – and I agree.

Back home, I spilled the events of my revelatory evening to Marcus. He seemed relieved that my gut-feel gamble on Rui and this strange party had worked out, but he also seemed envious. He'd only just begun to experience the fun that came to me so easily in our open marriage; now here I was, disappearing down a new rabbit hole.

Yet when I booked another train to Paris for Possession in November, Marcus didn't stop me. When I accepted Rui's offer to put me up in his minuscule apartment, I expected Marcus to put his foot down. Instead of feeling threatened by the unknown, he seemed content to hang back and see how things would unfold.

'So, what's the deal with this Rui guy?' he asked. 'Is it sexual, or . . . ?'

'I don't think so,' I said, thinking back to Rui's good-natured laughter when I'd left with Lucien, of his stories of sex and parties, of the French girls coiled around him all night long. 'If it was, it would have gone there already.'

My word seemed good enough for Marcus. Enough for me to hop on the Friday train to Paris and boomerang into a back-to-back weekender. In between daybreak and midnight, Rui and I hurtled home in the Métro with hands entwined, scarfed down breakfast in his tiny kitchenette, then slept the day away in his narrow bed like vampires curled into a coffin.

Despite the heat of our bodies and the serotonin in our blood, we never once turned to each other for sex. It was the beginning of something more lasting than pleasure. I was learning restraint: to allow a connection to unfold, recognize it for what it was, and respect its boundaries. I could find sex anywhere, but the nascent friendship I had with Rui was something far more rare.

My conservative, gender-segregated upbringing in the Philippines had taught me that friendships between boys and girls were not only impossible, but dangerous. The warning followed me into adulthood: girls were never to trust boys who wanted to be *just friends*, and wives were exhorted to shun close friendships with men. Instead of developing the skills we needed to navigate platonic intimacy and uphold the boundaries of friendship, we avoided it altogether out of fear.

It's too dangerous, we were told. *Temptation is everywhere. Protect your virtue. Protect your marriage.*

Rui's friendship showed me what was possible outside the iron-clad circles of high-school girlfriends and schoolyard mums. I felt that he understood me, or the wild in me that was capable of hopping on a last-minute train to Paris or surrendering to my senses on a crowded dance floor. Having left his buttoned-up life as an architect in Brazil to become a free-spirited bohemian in Paris, he had liberated himself in a way that I admired, with a bold optimism I wanted for myself.

Around Rui, I could be a different me, a Deepa who wasn't a caregiver, sex object or fantasy dispenser, catering to no one's pleasures other than my own. When I was with him, I was as free as he was. But I couldn't keep shuttling back and forth to Paris to be this alternate self – my bank account was feeling the pinch of one too many impulsive train tickets, and

I had a marriage and family to show up for on the daily. I needed to integrate my newfound pleasure – and this new aspect of myself – into my real life.

I wonder if there's something like this in Amsterdam, I thought to myself. Later I would realize how naive I was. Because of course there was – I just hadn't discovered it yet.

*

In the same way that it had gifted me with Rui, Instagram delivered my passport to Amsterdam's club scene in the form of a buzz-cut, bespectacled gay Filipino millennial named Joey. Like many of my queer friends from back home in Manila, Joey had a curious mind and witty tongue laced with Filipino gayspeak, which endeared him to me instantly.

When we first met for coffee at the Scheltema bookstore, Joey enquired into my musical preferences right away. 'Have you been to any parties in Amsterdam? *Anong klaseng* techno *ang* type *mo*?' he asked.

'I don't know,' I confessed. 'I just go for the people.'

'And the drugs. *Aminin!*' he cackled. *Admit it!*

This was, to a sonic geek like Joey, unacceptable. He took my musical education upon himself, taking me to my first party at his regular haunt in the basement of the shiny new A'dam Toren in Amsterdam Noord. He knew the door staff and security, put me on the guest list, introduced me to his vast network of party friends, and coached me on my outfits. Under his wing, I learned how to sense the vibe at a club, how to spot and avoid trouble, how to listen to the layers in the music. It was Joey who taught me that even an A-list DJ can't rescue a party from a bad crowd.

In time, clubbing would become more about line-ups and less about hook-ups. The nights when I craved to be touched would give way to nights when I wanted nothing more than to dance and be left alone with the music. But in the first flush of my entry into the scene, the club was the practice ground for skills I'd never learned before: making eye contact, reading signals, striking up conversations. Clubbing was how I developed game.

On a typical night, I would drift back and forth between the dance floor and smoking lounge, a narrow tunnel where overheated dancers went to cool off and light up. The irony was, I didn't even smoke. I only wanted to be where stories mingled with cigarette smoke and possibility pulsed in the atmosphere: where a casual hand rested on a shoulder could melt into a soul-searching kiss, a nod and a smile could morph into a mid-morning cuddle puddle in a student flat, and a blurry shadow could – all too easily – become a new lover.

In that hyper-sensitive cloud of chemical-induced euphoria, the lightest touches carried more weight, and the most fleeting of glances were loaded with meaning. In that dreamy underworld, my fascination with people found a new home, my social network exploded, and my boldness blossomed. Perhaps I could have been more discriminating, and half the men I made out with were gay, but it was all part of the fun.

Each time I returned home at dawn, wild-eyed with exertion, glowing with sweat and bursting with stories, I could sense Marcus fighting to keep an open mind. He vacillated between curiosity and disapproval and couldn't seem to decide whether he was more comfortable with me finding lovers on Tinder or picking them up in the wild at the club.

Sometimes I would get a whiff of envy rolling off him, and I would think to myself: *We need to do this together. Then he'll understand.*

He drew the line when I came home at noon from my first after-party with Joey. 'I don't like the idea of our daughter seeing you walking into the house like this,' he said. 'If you're going to be out all night, can you make sure you're home, showered and in bed before she wakes up?' More of Marcus's requests were becoming like this: reasonable, calm and clearly stated. I was happy to oblige, leaving the after-parties to the childless millennials who didn't have to parent the next day.

During the week, we were a textbook nuclear family: Daddy at the office, Mommy at home, child at school. We came together at dinner, took turns with storybooks and lullabies. But on Friday nights, as my parents did, we diverged from the script: Daddy and child would go to bed, and Mommy would put on her gold shorts and dancing shoes, sail into the club on Joey's guest-list privileges, and tear it up on the dance floor.

The morning after, I would take our daughter to her weekly lesson with Fräulein L., a strict and sprightly violinist with the National Opera Ballet, where she learned her strings on a tiny violin – A for Alligator, E for Eagle, G for Grasshopper, D for Donkey. Then, while I caught up on my sleep, Marcus would take her to the Saturday farmers' market on Lindengracht, where we'd shopped nearly every week since she was born. While he did the groceries, she would snack on free cheese, nuts, and other handouts from the vendors who doted on her.

Those walks through the Lindenmarkt became their father–daughter date, a counterbalance to the time Marcus spent at work and I spent mothering. I thanked my lucky stars that he had never been interested in cars or motorcycles, or basketball or football. On Saturdays, while other dads always seemed to disappear to watch football with the lads, few things excited Marcus more than coming home with a market find to turn into a special meal. And how he cherished his father–daughter time.

Shopping bags and stomachs full, Marcus holding aloft an inspirational ingredient – a live lobster as long as his torso, fresh oysters from Zeeland – our child munching on a shred of sausage in her chubby fist, father and daughter would return to a mother renewed. Those few hours of sleep would power me through whatever we had planned for the afternoon – the zoo, a playground, rainy-day finger painting – until the final crash at bedtime. A solid eight hours of sleep, together with Sunday morning cuddles and breakfast in bed, would restore me, and our family, to our full equilibrium.

One of my friends said to me: 'I don't know how you do it, woman. We're out together until 5 a.m. I'm twenty-nine, I don't even have a kid, and I'm shattered! But you're out there on the playground with Bebe while I'm a slug at home. I'm like . . . how? *How?*'

'You just love them,' I told her. 'Then you just get up and do it.'

By opening up a wider world beyond the responsibilities of family and motherhood, my nights out gave more energy than they took from me. I saw new facets of myself reflected in the faces of the characters I met; the more diverse the cast and the crazier the conversations, the more of myself I discovered. I found freedom, joy and release on the dance floor – and I wanted Marcus to experience it, too.

For Marcus's birthday, I bought tickets to a party where I knew the music would be chill and melodic, the crowd open and gregarious – a perfect first time, I thought, to ease him in. I arranged for our daughter to sleep over at her best friend's so we could enjoy a precious night off together, not as Mama and Papa, but as Marcus and Deepa. It would be good for him and bring us closer together.

Descending into the darkness of the basement, my heart beat with excitement along to the now-familiar pounding of the bass. After we'd secured lockers and put away our coats, I led Marcus on to the dance floor brimming with optimism. I would be his guide, just as Rui had been mine.

Over FaceTime, Rui had shown me how to fashion a bomb like the one he'd pressed into my hand that first night at Concrete, wrapping up all my hopes and dreams for this evening into a tiny package of rolling paper and crushed magic.

I was in line for the toilet when the bomb hit, peeling apart my senses and loosening my tongue. The unmistakable sound of French uncurled itself from the muted layers of music and drifted towards me. I turned towards its source.

'You speak French!' I said to a tall, dark-haired man standing behind me.

'Yes, I do,' he said. '*Parlez-vous français?*'

'No, but my shirt does,' I said, gesturing to the words '*Bon appétit*' in pink script on my chest.

'Aha,' he said, leaning closer. 'In France, we say *bon appétit* before eating something delicious.'

I felt Marcus tense up. Before I could respond, a toilet-stall door opened. 'My turn!' I sang out. 'Have a nice night, see you around!'

On the dance floor, I melted into Marcus, whose face was inscrutable. I held him tighter, swaying with him to the music, willing him to be where I was. At last, I felt him relax. His breathing quickened and his body grew warm in my arms; as if seeking sensation of their own accord, his fingertips drifted to my head and began to stroke my hair.

'There you are,' I murmured, tipping my face up to his. 'Welcome.'

Marcus's lips on mine felt softer, wetter and fuller than I'd ever tasted. When our kiss deepened, mouths slanting open and bodies pressing together, I knew he felt it too.

This is it, I thought in an upswell of euphoria. Things would be different from now on. This night would change everything.

We might have been wrapped up in each other for an instant or an eternity, when a hand grazed my waist and a voice whispered in my ear: '*Bonne soirée.*'

For the second time that night, I turned towards the voice. Still wrapped around Marcus, I reached for the dark-haired stranger with my free arm and drew him closer, sliding between the two of them.

I looked up at Marcus as if to ask, *Is this okay?*

In reply, he kissed me, making no move to stand between me and the other.

Behind me, unfamiliar hands drifted down from my waist and up my skirt, settling on the curve of my ass; unfamiliar lips grazed my nape and nibbled at my ear. When one kiss ended, a new kiss began; first one, then the other. For a few slow, infinitely delicious heartbeats, I was a woman whose desire was so powerful that my husband couldn't help but be carried away by it. After taking turns with dating all this time, each of us exploring on our own, we were both on the same wavelength of pleasure at last.

'Fuck this shit,' Marcus said suddenly, pushing me away. 'I've had enough. Enjoy yourself. I'm leaving.' He stalked off into the crowd, heading towards the exit.

'Marcus, wait!'

I caught up with him as he was removing his coat from the locker. 'Marcus, wait. Don't leave!'

'This is not about my birthday. This is not about me at all. This is about you and what you want. It always is!' he snapped.

'I'm sorry,' I started. 'I thought that was okay with you. I thought you were into it.'

'I thought so, too. But, well, I'm not!' He threw up his hands, dropping the locker key, and I scrambled to fish it off the wet, sticky concrete floor. 'None of this is about dancing or music or having fun. You just come here to find guys to fuck. You didn't waste a minute. You started with that French guy the moment we got here!'

'I talked to everyone, guys *and* girls!' I protested.

'Why do you even want me here? This fucking sucks!'

'Marcus, please give me another chance.' I tugged on his arm. 'I just want us both to have fun. I want you to feel what I feel when I'm here – ow!' I banged my forehead against the sharp steel corner of the open locker door.

'How? How is any of this supposed to be fun for me?' He slammed the locker door shut. 'If you want me to be here, fucking be *with me*. This was supposed to be our night – just us!'

'It is!' I said, my eyes stinging with tears of regret. 'It *is* our night. I'm sorry.'

He sagged against the wall of lockers just then, as if the fight had gone out of him. 'Take care of me, Deepa,' he said. 'I'm not used to this. I'm not like you.'

I pulled him closer until our foreheads touched. 'I'm so sorry,' I said. 'I got too caught up in my own fun. I forgot that this is all new to you.'

He was silent, breathing hard.

'I want to take care of you. I *will* take care of you. From now on, tonight will be about us.'

'Promise?' he asked in a small voice.

'Promise.'

Marcus let out a deep sigh, then patted his pockets. 'Do you have another two-euro coin for the locker?'

Pulling our night from the edge of disaster jolted me out of my euphoria. This moment had been necessary, because I needed to be reminded that Marcus and I were different, moved at different paces, and had different needs. My enthusiasm required boundaries, and it was important that Marcus felt he could set those boundaries. Caught just in time, course-corrected in the moment, disconnection would not fester into resentment.

Back on the dance floor, I tried to hold us together with sweaty embraces, deep kisses and the sheer force of my will, but I could no longer fully let go. I saw myself as responsible for Marcus's mood. It was my job, for the rest of the night, to protect our fragile bubble.

Burning through a pack of cigarettes faster than I'd ever seen, Marcus seemed to warm to the smoking lounge, where he drifted from one group to the next. I watched through smoke-stung eyes as he shot me a wink from across the room, where he was deep in conversation. He was fine; we were going to be fine. Relieved, I slumped against the wall, hoping my butt would land on a bench, but there was none.

Across the narrow tunnel from me, the brim of a brown felt hat lifted to reveal a pair of dark eyes, followed by a dark, neatly trimmed goatee and beard below it. We locked gazes for a few beats. Then, without a word, he scooted over and patted the bench next to him.

'Thanks,' I said, squeezing into the gap he'd opened up. 'My feet are killing me.'

'Welcome,' he replied with an easy smile, tipping his hat. 'How's your night going?'

'It was almost a disaster,' I said, 'but I think I managed to save it.'

'A disaster! What happened?' His name was Khalil, and he wanted to hear the whole story. 'No way! You're here with your husband? Where is he?'

I waved across the smoky room at Marcus, who waved back.

'Seems like a nice guy,' Khalil remarked. 'So you're in an open marriage. What does that mean, exactly?'

'It means that we see other people,' I answered. 'You know . . .' I shot him a side-eye glance. 'Casually. Just for fun.'

'I see,' he replied, holding my gaze. 'You look like a lot of fun.'

'I am.'

'So you mean,' he said, 'if we wanted to, you know, you and I could . . .'

'Yeah?'

'Have some fun?'

'Not tonight, no. But in general, yes, we could.'

The space between us was closing fast. 'I'm so high right now,' he said.

'That's okay,' I said. 'Everyone here is. So am I.'

'I really want to kiss you.'

'I'm sorry,' I said. 'I'd like that too, but I can't. It's been a rough night for my husband, and I need to stay close to him. It wouldn't be a good decision right now.' I pulled away.

Khalil drew a deep breath, his body language mirroring my retreat. 'I totally understand,' he said. 'It's good that you want to take care of your man.'

'I do,' I said. 'Maybe we'll see each other again sometime.'

'I hope so,' Khalil said. Then he gently took my hand by the wrist and laid it on his lap, right on top of a significant – and impressive – erection. 'I really hope so.'

Out of the corner of my eye, I could see Marcus coming towards me. Snatching away my hand, I fumbled at the tiny purse slung over my shoulder.

'Who knows what the future will bring,' I said, handing him my phone. 'Why don't you give me your number?'

*

Later in the week, after we had both recovered, I phoned Rui about our failed night. When I wondered why Marcus hadn't experienced the same luminous revelation as I had, Rui replied: 'Marcus. I think he need more.'

'More what?'

'More you. More love. More,' was his enigmatic, but also uncannily astute answer.

I'd managed to turn the night around just enough to leave Marcus receptive to the idea of a do-over. I wasn't about to give up. I knew better now. I would do better by him. I would bide my time and wait for a different night, party, and vibe.

Something special. Something big.

*

Spanning 7,000 square metres of concrete and steel, with over 300 towering drums squatting atop a 20-metre-deep concrete basement, the Maassilo — a century-old complex of former grain silos along the banks of the Maas in Rotterdam — was nothing if not big.

Six months after my first disastrous night out with Marcus, the Maassilo announced a massive rave called the Wall of Sound, named for the monolithic wall of speakers built to dominate the space and render everyone within earshot into sonic oblivion. It was the brainchild of DVS1, a Minnesota-born DJ and producer who wanted to pay homage to the 1990s rave culture of the American Midwest, where the sound system, not the DJs, took centre stage. Beyond achieving volume, the size and scale of the Wall of Sound was designed to explore what music could do to the physical body.

I felt it in my bones: this would be the perfect do-over.

In just under a year, my appreciation for electronic music had developed under Joey's tutelage. I understood the shades of variation between subgenres, which kind of partygoers they tended to attract, and which ones I liked the most. I knew Chicago house made me festive and buoyant, minimal turned me sensuous and dreamy, and hard techno plunged me into sweat-drenched catharsis. I knew I could show up at VBX in a colourful riot of print, but that skin and leather were de rigueur for Vault Sessions. Tonight, I knew that I should expect to be pummelled by a wall of sound. But nothing could have prepared me for the force of its impact.

Emanating from the speakers taking up the entire front wall of the Maassilo, the hot energy of pure sound reshaped the very air before me into ripples and waves. It was the sheer power of music, imbued with such heft that it both flattened and animated me. Sound pressure formed a physical field that I could feel as I walked through it, and I could almost trace a visible bassline through the main hall. My body moved as though of its own volition.

There would be no hesitating, thinking, or resisting. The speakers and the artists who controlled them demanded nothing less than total submission.

It was only a matter of time until the masses forced us apart and Marcus and I lost each other in the madness. Remembering how vulnerable Marcus had been on our first night out together, I searched the cavernous halls for him. The last of my clarity was slipping away, replaced by the now-familiar slide into oblivion; I had to find him soon.

The throng parted to reveal Marcus, all waving arms and writhing bulk and flying drops of sweat, flinging himself into the music as though his life depended on it, dancing as I'd never seen him before. 'Marcus!' I shouted, stunned. His eyes were screwed shut and the bass drowned me out. 'MARCUS? ARE YOU OKAY?'

He opened his eyes so wide, I almost fell into his pupils. 'My wife! My beautiful, beautiful wife!' he cried, his voice peaking in unadulterated glee. He smothered me in his sweat-soaked embrace with such ardour that I staggered backward into the force field of air in front of the subwoofers, squished between a literal wall of sound and a wall of flesh.

'Marcus, what have you had?' I shouted. 'How *much* have you had?'

'Enough!' he cried with a goofy grin.

'How much is enough?' I yelled, panicking.

'Enough to see!' he yelled back.

'See what?'

'Enough to see why you do this!' he cried, taking my face between his hot, damp hands. 'I understand you now. I know why you dance. When you dance, you're free. I know because it's happened to me, too. For the first time in my life, I can finally shed all my burdens. I've been carrying around so many. And they're so heavy. So, so heavy.'

Marcus burrowed his face into my neck. 'So many anxieties, insecurities, judgements. I've been judging you. I've been making you wrong for everything you've been doing, when all you want is to be free. I'm so afraid of losing you. But all you want is to be you. And all I want is you. Because I love you. You have no idea how much I love you.'

'Excuse me, is this guy bothering you? Should I call security?' From the depths of Marcus's arms, a thumbs-up wobbled into my peripheral vision.

'It's okay, he's my husband!' I called out, forming a heart with two cupped hands. 'Thanks!' The thumbs-up wobbled away, but Marcus didn't seem to notice.

'All my burdens. All my doubts. All my fears,' he breathed into my ear. 'I can throw them away like this' – he waved his arms again like an octopus possessed – 'and I get lighter. Lighter and lighter. And now they're gone!'

He paused, stroking my face. 'And it's all because of you! Because you brought me here. And now I'm free! Free to love you the way you want to be loved. Free to just be me.'

Forget pretty lights and sensuous kisses: this was a sledgehammer to the impenetrable walls of Marcus's emotional fortress, unleashing all his pent-up feelings in a tidal wave. I'd never hoped for nor asked to hear any of this, but sensed I could trust the fierce, raw emotion behind his words. I knew it was safe to let go, and we held on to each other amidst thousands of dancing bodies, sealed off in our own reality.

'I'm so afraid of losing you,' he said, touching his forehead against mine.

Through the bass, in the cocoon of his embrace, I heard his fear and spoke to it. 'You could never lose me. I love you more than I could ever love anyone else. And I always will.'

Time lost all meaning in the vortex of heat and sound, a place beyond listening, where we could only feel. At last, Marcus had come to meet me there.

'What now?' I asked, wiping away a tear when we broke apart.

'Don't find me, I'll find you,' he said.

'What?'

Eyes gaping like portals in the dark, he whispered: 'Fly free, little bird!' Then he flung himself into the crowd, octopus arms undulating to liberation.

'Marcus!'

But he was already gone.

The sun was high, its harsh rays glinting off the Rotterdam skyline and the waters of the Maashaven, when we stumbled out from the belly of the beast. I don't know how we made it through the city on foot, towards the hotel room we'd rented for the day. I only know that we tumbled into bed and possessed each other with a desire that had been building up inside both of us, a hunger that had tasted faceless mouths and embraced nameless bodies throughout the night, only to find relief in each other. I know that after waking, we sped home on the train, collected our child from her sleepover, and fulfilled the basic duties of parenting in a daze until it was time for bed.

I know only that things were different after that night. Two years later, when the pandemic forced the closure of clubs in the Netherlands, we would hear about a protest against the loss of our beloved nightlife culture. Marcus would joke: 'I ought to show up with a sign that says "Techno saved our marriage".'

It's an oversimplification, of course. Just as jealousy can't be resolved in the bedroom, trust can't be rebuilt overnight in a club. We'd had a vague notion that our shared adventures might be found in threesomes, swingers' clubs or sex parties. Perhaps unlike many who have explored the non-monogamous lifestyle, we have yet to do any of those things. But we found something else on the dance floor.

Through some inexplicable alchemy of rhythm and feeling, the Wall of Sound had shifted us forward. We had broken through to a new ground of understanding and discovered a new landscape of pleasure we could explore together.

It was the first of many shared nights that chipped away at Marcus's restrictions and inhibitions, starting with my 7 a.m. curfew. 'It's so hard to leave at seven!' I remember Marcus exclaiming after we'd torn ourselves away from the furious peak of a weekender at another club we came to love, housed in the sprawling halls and garden of a former technical college.

'I know!' I said. 'But I did it anyway, because you asked me to.'

Over time, our nights out and the magic we shared on the dance floor gradually shut off what I call Marcus's critical brain, and I began to notice him becoming more open-minded and malleable, less judgemental.

I've seen Marcus grow in many ways, both subtle and seismic. I was by his side for his first *and* second kiss with a man, which both happened in clubs. 'Bristly,' he said later when I asked him how he found it. I was delighted to see him temper his curiosity with respect, and consider it a privilege to have witnessed the layers of toxic masculinity and homophobia of his all-boys Catholic school upbringing fall away, bit by bit, to reveal a new man.

I've seen Marcus grow in creativity. It was in the smoking room that he started sketching quick portraits of random people he met, rendering them in glowing, vibrant lines on his phone. The drawings became his way of making new friends and staying in touch with them. The artist in him comes alive on those nights, finding inspiration in the colourful souls we meet.

I've seen Marcus grow in confidence. When we meet people who tell him how great he is, I can see it sinking in, reshaping his insecurities about his body and rewriting his image of himself as dull and unappealing. In time, he began to see himself the way I and others do: attractive, interesting, warm and radiant.

Marcus and I often take turns going out dancing, so one of us can stay home parenting. But on the rare nights we can be together on the dance floor, people gravitate towards us for the energy we generate. Marcus as a single male might come across as more threatening to a woman at a club, but as a couple we are magnetic in our joy. My presence changes the dynamic, making me the perfect wingman.

Instead of threesomes and foursomes, we found a whole

community as familiar faces became friends. We met musicians, artists, creatives – some of the most interesting and knowledgeable people I know – but also professionals, parents, even the occasional grandparent, who simply need a space to be free from roles and responsibilities, just as we do.

This community affirmed our choice to be non-monogamous, expressing admiration for a beautiful, difficult endeavour. Among kindred spirits, our open marriage wasn't strange or sinful or crazy. We met students from all genders and sexual preferences who told us they want this for themselves too, and couples who want to know how we manage it. We appear as a kind of possibility for long-term relationships: parents of a young child, a married couple of seventeen years, still partying together, still in love, who haven't given up.

You have a daughter? the younger ones squeal when we reveal that we're parents, cooing over the pictures that we inevitably flash them from our phones. *Couple goals!* they sigh.

When Rui finally came to visit me in Amsterdam, he and Marcus greeted each other like brothers. Rui dropped his bag on the floor of our living room and enfolded Marcus in a warm hug that bore the full force of his charisma.

'He's so good-looking!' Marcus hissed when Rui went to unpack and shower. 'Are you sure there's nothing between you two? I mean, look at that!' I had to laugh, shaking my head.

We all went out dancing together, of course, and it was one of the most unforgettable club nights of my life. It felt like coming full circle: the man I loved now knew the joy and freedom I had found that first time with Rui, on a barge moored in the Seine.

*

Every night out must come to an end. The DJ plays the final track, the crowd winds down and throws its arms in the air, whistling and shouting gratitude. House lights come on, limbs are disentangled, numbers exchanged, coats retrieved from lockers, eyes shielded from the first light, bicycles mounted and ridden into the morning.

For some, the party never ends but changes venue, resurfacing at a stranger's flat or a cuddle puddle on a friend's couch. If we're lucky, we'll get home in time to squeeze in a blowjob in the shower, maybe even a full round in bed.

But inevitably, the urgency slows, heat cools, pleasure fades. Promising connections are forgotten, potential lovers disappear into the past, never to text again. Permissions granted and passions indulged fall on to a heap of dirty laundry along with last night's sweaty black tank top, booty shorts and ripped thigh-highs.

All that remains is the life we've chosen. Those of us with responsibilities must face them. So we slip back into lives designed for security, stability and routine, not novelty, variety and exploration, where the point so often seems to be maintaining equilibrium rather than pushing boundaries. When you're married for seventeen years and raising a young child, that's what you have to do, in order for that life – and that child – to thrive.

I learned to accept my appetite for new, intense experiences as part of me. Understanding it would always be there in some shape or form helped me tend to it – and treat myself – with kindness. But I also knew that there would always be options upon options available to me. It would be all too easy to slip away from my own life, become a novelty junkie, seeking highs everywhere but my own home, in the arms of everyone else but my husband.

Nights in the club would have to end, but I wanted the transcendent pleasure and sense of adventure they gave us to last. Could Marcus and I take what we'd found and bring it into our marriage, where it would make us stronger rather than pull us apart? Or would we – would *I* – become used to chasing thrills elsewhere?

I wasn't ready to let that happen.

9

Do you still have sex with your husband?

For the first year of our non-monogamous experiment, I was only ever quizzed on its inner workings by strangers on dating apps. The casual curiosity of men who wanted to sleep with me was easy to navigate. I could be an open book to someone I might never see again after I slithered home at 2 a.m.; the risk was low and the pay-off relatively high. My openness about my – well, openness seemed to boost my appeal and made me more interesting.

The rules? Sure. Jealousy? No problem. When their questions were straightforward, uncomplicated, almost predictable, the answers rolled off my tongue with a knowing wink and a toss of my hair.

All of this was practice. For all my breezy confidence, I was wary of opening up to the people in my real life who were closest to me. When I finally did, I found that the mildly curious ask different questions than those who truly care.

'What does this mean? Are you just co-parenting now? Are you still in love or are you only staying together for your daughter's sake?' asked my sister, alarmed and disbelieving, when I told her about us on our annual trip back to the Philippines for Christmas. Five years older, unmarried and living in Manila, she couldn't comprehend why I would risk the Holy Grail of marriage and family for the fleeting satisfaction of casual encounters.

'Partying *and* dating? How do you have the energy for this?' asked my friend Elise, incredulous and ever practical. A tall, blonde Canadian with a sunny, capable disposition, Elise had started out as an acquaintance on the fringes of my loose circle of moms. Her daughter was the same age as mine, so we took them to the same playgrounds, signed up for the same toddler classes, and arranged playdates at each other's houses.

Elise was the most like me of all the moms I knew. She had an adventurous streak; having lived in Asia, Africa and the Middle East, she understood what life was in a non-Western society. Like me, she returned to work within a year of the birth of our children. She understood that work brought a different fulfilment than family, and was too sensible to conflate the two. She was chattier and more animated about global politics than domestic projects, and both of us were just about the same level of crafty, which was to say: not at all.

One rainy afternoon at her tiny Jordaan apartment, after the girls had disappeared into a corner of her daughter's bedroom and were absorbed in play, Elise turned to me with her usual bright-eyed smile. 'So,' she said, leaning back and tucking her legs under her, 'how have you been?'

She probably wasn't expecting a long answer, but I was ready to give it.

'Well,' I began, 'Marcus and I have been going through something recently. We're trying out an open marriage.' Elise's eyes widened and her smile froze. But she listened. One by one, her questions came. I answered them all, laying out everything from the schism of the affair to my newfound clubbing career.

By daring to breach the barrier of polite conversation beyond the pleasantries of holiday plans and the minutiae of motherhood, I had taken the risk of being vulnerable with Elise. Vulnerability gave depth to our friendship of convenience, transforming it into one that was real, present and immediate – not online like Thomas, or distant like Rui. I was most afraid of being judged by other moms, but Elise was the first to accept me and listen to me without criticism. Our conversation that day gave me hope that she wouldn't be the last.

Opening myself up to the questions of those who truly cared was one of the first crucial steps along the road of having nothing to hide. My sister, Elise – and later my closest friends from Manila – enquired into the intimate details of my marriage not to satisfy idle curiosity or bestow judgement, but out of a genuine desire to understand how we were. They wanted to know if we were happy; they were rooting for us to make it.

Are you staying safe? Are you still in love with each other? I opened up to one friend at a time, observing, gauging, sometimes waiting months for the right moment. As I did, one concern came up with increasing frequency.

What about your sex life? Do you two still have sex?

*

After being married for seventeen years, Marcus and I know every inch of each other's bodies as intimately as every nook and cranny of our home. Familiarity leaves no unexplored corners and few untested surfaces. Sex on the kitchen counter, dining table, even the bathroom floor, which all felt so naughty the first time, loses its spark after so many years.

Sex almost always begins the same handful of ways, at the same times, in the same places. Sometimes it begins on the couch, with the curling smoke of a joint and the throbbing pulse of our favourite tracks from the club. Like most windows in Amsterdam, ours are bare, open to the twinkling of the street lamps, the flashes of a football game from across the canal, curious eyes of neighbours known but unseen. The thought that anyone could see us – if they look into the right window at the right moment – makes him nervous, but it turns me on.

Most of the time, it starts in bed, right before we go to sleep. He'll turn to me and touch me where he knows I like it, because he knows I like it, and he knows we don't have a lot of time. He won't have to keep going for too long, until I turn to him and part my lips and sigh out loud and kiss his neck and bite his ears, because I know that's what he likes.

I spread my legs and wriggle out of my sweatpants, wishing he'd started earlier and not left it to the last minute. We need to wake our child up to pee before we go to bed because she still can't sleep through the night without peeing and I don't want to wake up to a pee-soaked bedsheet for the third time this week because I have so much to do in the morning and it's already so late and I don't know how we're ever going to have a second baby because I'm the one who can't function on less than six hours of sleep because I just need more and he just needs less because he's always fine after the first four cups of coffee.

He reaches between my legs and I freeze. I think I hear her footsteps, a warning for which I'm always on high alert. Sometimes she climbs into our bed because she's had a bad dream; sometimes we find her already beneath the covers, right between us, before the alarm goes off for school. He jokes about waking me for sex at 5 a.m. before she comes, then he sees my face and gets that it's a terrible idea. Morning sex was my favourite, and I miss it. But then I think: *How many years of this tender sleeping face between us do we still have left?*

I'm ashamed that in my own bed I choose sleep over sex,

because in other arms, in other beds, sleep is the last thing on my mind. Why is that?

When I reach for a toy in the dark or fumble in the closet for lingerie, it isn't for him. He doesn't need it. A kiss on the neck or the tip of my tongue in his ear or a whisper to go to bed early can make him hard for me in an instant. No, the lingerie is for me. I'm the one who always takes so long to get turned on. He might need more coffee to get going in the morning, but I need more stimulants to get me going at night. High sensation, high intensity: that's me.

So I grasp for something I've never worn or felt or seen before: whatever's newest before it becomes too familiar. Every new shred of fabric, every delicious new texture, every smooth new curve is a gamble on sensation, and my pleasure is what's at stake.

Sometimes it's the way my nipples look against red lace, or the way the glass dildo sounds hungry and wet as he pushes it into me, one fat round bulb at a time – some visual, aural, sensual spark ignites the engine of my desire, a steam train that keeps going even after slamming on the brakes.

Sometimes it's enough to make me forget my child in the next room, to pull me out of my head, to stop me from being a mother in my own bed. And for a moment, the thrill of something new transforms me into what I'm supposed to be, what he wants me to be: the slut I'd rather be instead.

Sometimes all I want is to not have to come up with it myself, then to be allowed to want it. Demand it. Beg for it. Then surrender to some new and unknown pleasure I didn't even know I craved until moments ago.

Familiarity cements the life Marcus and I have chosen to build together, but it can also dull our senses to pleasures we've experienced a hundred times before. Sometimes it could feel as though all the years we had spent as a couple, moulding ourselves into each other's contours, worked for us in every area of our life except sex. Sometimes it felt as though our years together were stacked against us where passion was concerned.

Dating other people introduced new ideas and influences into our sexual dynamic. I discovered that the crackling electricity of a novel experience, once savoured, could be channelled into our bedroom in some shape or form, even if it was only feeling sexy after a date, or high on the energy and confidence of having tried something new and bossed it.

At his own pace, in his own time, Marcus was discovering the same. An impassioned bite on my shoulder one night was a direct result of a hook-up with a Finnish blonde who turned out to be a biter. A Filipina dancer who'd shown him photos of herself tied up in intricate knots and suspended from the ceiling in *shibari*, the Japanese art of rope bondage, awakened his imagination to new possibilities for our once-forgotten ropes.

From golden showers to foot fetishes, I was delighted by unusual requests from new lovers, although I drew the line at an invitation to fart into a man's mouth. I figured if I tried something at least once, it would become part of my repertoire. So my bag of tricks grew bigger, but I always brought it home. Influences from outside the marriage started to feel less threatening as we discovered new pleasures elsewhere and shared them with each other.

Dating gave us both the space to follow our curiosity into areas of sex we wanted to explore without obligating each other to do so, or risking the resentment that might have arisen from resistance or refusal. We've felt free to say, 'I'm not really into the idea. But I see how that could be exciting for you, so you go ahead and try that out with someone else if you want to.'

By far the biggest transformation that opening up our marriage brought into our sex life was the way we talked about sex.

I don't just mean discussing likes and dislikes, positions and preferences, new toys or things to try. I mean allowing each other – without judgement or resentment – to become curious about who we were as sexual beings, what made us that way, and deciding how we fit together. We went over histories and conversations, sifting through memories and opinions, to find the things that shaped our sexual selves as individuals and as a unit, and to understand how society had shaped our views of ourselves, our bodies, and sex.

My Filipino Catholic background – an upbringing I shared with Marcus – had deemed curiosity about sex sinful and wrong, shrouding it with shame and secrecy from childhood into our adult years. Now, in a culture that encouraged it and a marriage that allowed it, we could ask each other anything and talk about everything. Now, talking about sex meant asking myself questions like: *Why did I like that? Why am I avoiding this? Where did I learn to think that? Why does this excite me? Why does this scare me?*

It meant asking Marcus questions like: *Hey, so, I tried this thing with someone. Why have we never tried this before? Would you like to? Why do you think this is dirty? Why do you think that's embarrassing? What if I really liked it? What if you did, too?*

For Marcus, it meant being honest with his discomfort, and being brave enough to admit his vulnerability. It meant asking me questions like: *Why don't you feel you can try that with me? How have I made you feel like you can't ask me this?*

And one night, it meant asking the question: 'Sometimes

I get the feeling that you're always so much more excited about sex with other guys, and not as excited about sex with me. Why is that?'

*

I paused, lips parted in a pouty O, red lipstick in hand and halfway to my mouth. It was not a great time for this question, but I understood why it had come up. I was getting dressed for a date I was excited about, and Marcus was picking up on that excitement.

Capping the tube of lipstick, I turned from the mirror to face Marcus, who sat on our bed watching me get ready. 'Well,' I began, thinking it through, 'when we're at home, it's super-hard for me to switch off being Mom.'

'I think we've talked about this before,' he said, nodding. 'You can't feel sexy and be Mommy at the same time.'

'Exactly,' I said, pleased that he remembered. 'The moment I step out the door for a date – automatic off switch, Mom hat comes off. Then I'm somewhere else, physically and mentally, where I don't have to be Mom. It makes it that much easier to slip into sexy-time mode.'

'You need time to switch hats,' he said.

'Right. Here at home, reminders are everywhere. Laundry hamper. Toys. Clutter. I mean, she's right *there*,' I said, jabbing the lipstick at the wall between the two bedrooms, 'when we have sex! It has more to do with that, than anything about you.'

'Is that it?'

'Well, then there's anticipation.'

He considered this. 'Say more.'

'When I match with someone, we're messaging each other on WhatsApp for however long it takes until we meet,' I said. 'Could be days, weeks, months. All of that, if they're any good at it, is build-up for the date, or the sex, or whatever. Take this dude I'm seeing tonight.'

'The one from the club. What was his name?'

'Khalil. We met, what, over a month ago?' I said, shimmying into my tights and zipping up my miniskirt. Weeks had passed since that near-disastrous night with Marcus, when Khalil had placed my hand on his erection and saved his number in my phone. We'd both been busy since, but tonight, the stars – and our calendars – had finally aligned for a drink to test the potential of our connection.

'Well, sometimes these things take a while. Or they go nowhere.'

'Sure. Point is, we've been messaging each other this whole time,' I said, pulling my sweater over my head. 'All of that builds anticipation.'

'So what you're saying is, you're really excited about this guy?'

'What I'm saying is, anticipation builds desire,' I replied, coming over to stand in front of him, wrapping my arms around his neck and leaning in for a kiss.

'Hmm,' he said after we broke apart. 'Noted. It's not easy, though.'

'I know,' I agreed. 'Your work takes up so much more energy than mine. After bedtime, there's always so much household stuff to take care of. Like, the fucking laundry! It's never-ending.'

'I know, but I want you to get excited about me, too.'

We kissed again, longer this time. 'Hmm, noted. And

now, thanks to you, I'm going to have to redo my lipstick, *and* I'm going to be late.'

'He's been waiting long enough,' Marcus pointed out, running his hands under my miniskirt, up the curve of my ass, pulling me close. 'What's fifteen minutes more?'

*

I'm so not done with you.

Khalil's message, sent the night we first met in the smoking lounge, had kindled a months-long simmer of anticipation that bubbled over in the warm glow of his bedroom. Exertion and pleasure flooded our bodies, confirming the chemistry both of us had intuited from the get-go.

Khalil was the only lover I've had who never came, not even once. He simply couldn't, no matter what I did. 'Most women get stressed out about it,' he confessed. 'They think it means something's wrong with them, or they're not doing something right. Don't take it personal.'

'Okay, I won't,' I replied. 'As long as you're sure you're having a good time.'

'Oh, I am,' he said, turning me over. 'I'm having a very good time.'

It was freeing. Without orgasm as a goal, our meetings were a languid unfolding, instead of an urgent pursuit of an abrupt end. In the heat of the moment, Khalil was a generous and relentless lover; in the cooldown, he was easy and chill. As sweat evaporated off our bodies and our breath slowed, he would dial his Philips Hue lamp down to a shade of pink I might have found kitschy elsewhere, but seemed to suit his trippy tenderness and the warmth of the hours we shared.

Curled up in a damp cuddle, we explored each other's histories: my Catholic schoolgirl years and his upbringing as a Turkish-Moroccan in Amsterdam; my married life and his experiments with psychedelics; my dating adventures and his experiences with group sex. He seemed to be a frequent guest at three-, four- and moresomes with friends.

'I'd like to have friends like that,' I remarked. 'How do I find them?'

'I have a theory,' he said. 'Wanna hear it?'

'Sure,' I said, stroking his bearded face with both hands.

'There are two kinds of people: robots and aliens,' he began. 'Robots do what they are programmed to do. The whole nine-to-five, marriage, kids, car, house, everything. They don't know anything else. They never question. Aliens look like robots, but – well, aliens know they are different. They're just not from here. They don't fit in, or maybe they never did. They don't follow the script. They're open, searching, curious.'

'So, what are you?' I teased, as if I didn't know.

'Alien, for sure!' he answered. 'Aliens recognize each other. They know other aliens when they see them. That's how I know you're an alien, too.'

'You sure? I mean, I did the whole marriage thing. I have a kid.'

'I think you're an alien who grew up among robots, so she thought she was one of them,' he said. 'But now you're discovering who you really are. And now the other aliens will start finding you. You'll see.'

I laughed. But secretly, I thought he might be on to something.

*

The tricky thing about anticipation is that it never guarantees a pay-off. It is a fickle ingredient in attraction: easy to spark, yet hard to sustain, with as much chance of fizzling out as of building into a satisfying crescendo.

Some men were experts at creating anticipation. Like Aron.

With his tight black curls, deep olive skin and long, muscular legs, Aron was as handsome and charismatic as a movie star, sleek and statuesque as a Greek god, and smooth and charming as James Bond. Matching with Aron on Bumble was like striking gold. He turned up for morning coffee in a dark red velvet blazer that would have been theatre on any other body, but was poetry on his. Was this guy for real?

I felt giddy as he gazed into my eyes, laughed at my jokes, and grazed my wrist with his large, elegant fingers. His matinee-idol looks and refined flirtatiousness seemed at odds with his professed sexual inexperience. With a touch of shyness that made him almost gentlemanly, he expressed eagerness to explore new territory with me. The way he spoke about me made me sound like sexual liberation on legs. I was so *different*, he enthused, so open, so unapologetically sensual.

I was convinced I was batting way out of my league. But the steady stream of sexts Aron sent blitzing into my phone for two solid weeks, not to mention the sex toys that arrived in discreet plain cardboard boxes at my door, whipped me into a frenzy of erotic expectation. 'I can't wait to see you fuck yourself with that big glass dildo that's coming in the mail,' he wrote, 'and those plugs in your gorgeous ass while I fuck you. It'll be my first time seeing that. It's going to be *so* hot.'

'You always remember your first,' I wrote back.

Because Aron worked in a high-profile tech company, pinging back and forth between Amsterdam and London every two weeks, our rendezvous was booked in a luxury hotel suite with a freestanding bath and a view over the city. I arrived two hours early, delicious anticipation and nervous energy barely contained in a black lace bodysuit, tight neoprene miniskirt, and thigh-high nylon stay-ups.

Aron greeted me with a peck on the cheek. Then he placed his huge hands on my shoulders, spun me around, dug into my bra and squeezed hard. 'Why don't you get naked and start fingering yourself. I'll get the toys,' he murmured.

Great start.

When I turned around, there he was, naked as David, the bag of brand-new sex toys spilled out on to the bed. Weeks of drawn-out digital seduction had driven me delirious with desire. This was the moment! I couldn't believe this supernaturally beautiful specimen of manhood was finally about to fuck me.

And he did.

Except – it was like ticking boxes.

Glass dildo. Check.

Butt plug. Check.

Ass trainer. Check.

Bigger butt plug. Check.

There was something cold and dispassionate about the way Aron watched me, just *watched*, as though I was a hired performer. Within minutes he had me flat on my back while he stood by the side of the bed, ordering me to continue playing with myself the whole time.

He came in my mouth and on my face, silent, impassive and inscrutable.

No touching. No kissing. No words.

It was the same in the shower and when we returned to bed. This time Aron plunged into me while the plug was inside my ass – just as he had wished, just as he had promised. Yet he seemed to derive no satisfaction from it. He pulled out, stood beside me again, and came on my face once more, with a slow half-smile that was more amusement than pleasure.

Then he crawled into bed, pulled the duvet over his glorious, sweatless body, and fell fast asleep.

I lay awake for two solid hours, trying to wrap my head around what had just happened – or not happened. Was it him? Was it me? Did we just have zero chemistry? Had I been expecting too much? Hadn't we been stirring this pot for weeks? How could such a meticulously stoked frenzy of anticipation turn out to be an underwhelming disappointment?

The longer he slept, the angrier I grew. Was the dead log snoring beside me the same magnetic charmer who'd begged me to stay all night so he could pleasure me to oblivion? How could someone so perfect, so charming in his flirting, so passionate in his messages, be so distant and aloof? So – dare I say it – boring?

Finally my mind turned in on itself, questioning why I was here with this man, in this bed, with nothing to show for my time but doubt and dissatisfaction. What did I really want from these encounters? Was it too much to expect fireworks and earthquakes the first time – or every time, for that matter? Why couldn't I have taken the bull by the horns and turned this night around, into the kind of sex that satisfied *me*?

But what kind of sex was that? Did I even know, or was I too busy pleasing and being a good girl, as I had my whole life?

It wasn't even midnight when I tiptoed out of the hotel room with my bag of lingerie and sex toys, closing the door softly. Judging by the muffled snoring from under the duvet, he didn't even realize I was gone.

I arrived home to find a half-empty bucket of KFC on the dining table and Marcus glued to an MMA match on TV. *Well, that's a lot more groaning and sweating than I had tonight*, I thought. *At least one of us had some excitement this evening.*

'You're home early,' Marcus said. I must have still looked bewildered; he glanced away from the screen and stopped short at the sight of my expression. 'Hey, are you okay? Is something wrong?'

I hesitated, not knowing what to make of my night, or how much he was willing to hear.

'What is it? What's the matter?' he asked, switching off the TV. 'You can tell me.'

For the first time, I poured out the details of an entire date to Marcus – and for the first time, he listened. Fully, openly, without tension or hostility. As I came to the conclusion of my story with Aron, Marcus leaned forward and set his hands on his knees in the resolute manner of a man about to deliver a come-to-Jesus speech.

'Look. Reality didn't meet your expectations. That's all it is,' he said. 'But you're trying so hard to rationalize an unsatisfactory experience. Why?'

'Well, I . . .' I didn't know either.

'It was disappointing,' he stated. 'You're allowed to be disappointed. Why is that so hard to say?'

'Because he's so perfect on paper!'

'But why does that matter?' he asked. 'You're trying to convince yourself you *should* be satisfied because he was so attractive, or smart, or respectful, or provided decent conversation. Okay, it was nice that he was all these other things, but none of that changes the fact that the sex was bad and left you unsatisfied.'

'I feel like I ought to be satisfied with what I got because — because . . .' I started, faltering. 'Because he's just so far out of my league and I should feel lucky I even got to fuck this guy.'

'Honey . . . please. No. Just no,' Marcus said. '*He* should feel fucking lucky to get into bed with you, because look at you. It sounds to me like he's been in basic bitchland for so long that he doesn't even know what a satisfying sexual experience is, let alone a boundary-pushing one.'

'He did say that his wildest sexual experience was with a woman who had K-cup boobs,' I said.

'Wow,' Marcus said, rolling his eyes. 'Big tits. So wild.'

I giggled.

'It sounds like you have way more experience than him,' he continued. 'It's okay to admit you weren't satisfied and want more.'

'I'm not used to being the experienced one,' I admitted.

'Well, you've come far since we started this two years ago,' he said.

'So have you,' I said.

We looked at each other over the grease-stained bucket of leftover fried chicken and smiled.

*

Karma.

The scent, delicious and familiar, wafting from the Lush store in the IJ-passage, caught me in mid-rush from train platform to bicycle parking at Central Station, plunging me into a warm froth of memory and longing.

I stopped, remembering what it felt like to be in my twenties, plugging through the Manila rush-hour carnage, racing to the mall to pick up a bubble bar on the way to Marcus's hotel room, flying to him on wings fuelled by anticipation. Lush's Karma bar, with its heady tang of sweet orange, patchouli and pine oil, had been our favourite scent in those early long-distance years.

I remembered how it felt to be apart from him, all those weeks of separation stirring up my need, sliding into the sensuous pleasure of a bath, then emerging into a cocoon of bliss, the comfort and safety of our closeness wrapped around us like the fluffy white hotel bathrobes we wore. Bubble baths in hotel bathrooms had been our ritual of reunion and release. Now that we had a bathtub in our own home, we didn't use it as often as we should.

It turned out Lush still stocked Karma bubble bars. They still smelled the same, even a child, a continent and a lifetime later.

'I've been thinking about what you asked me,' I began late one night, when Marcus and I were in the bath together. 'About getting excited about sex, and anticipation, and all that.'

'And?'

This had been on my mind since Marcus had first brought it up. I'd been able to answer his questions off the top of my head, but something else had come to me since then — something I'd never said out loud. Now felt like a good time to talk about it, lying damp and relaxed against each other, brought closer by the memories of bubble baths past. But it wasn't going to be easy.

'Have you ever . . . have you ever noticed that I'm the one who always buys new lingerie and sex toys?'

'I buy you lingerie,' he replied.

'When was the last time?'

He fell silent. I felt my feet grow cold, even in the warm, patchouli-scented water.

'Okay, so what are you trying to say?'

The words tumbled out in a rush. 'I mean – I just wonder – sometimes – why am I the one who always finds new things for us to try?'

He didn't like that. 'That's not true. I initiate new things, too!'

'When was the last time? Do you even remember?'

'You're bored with me, is that what you're saying?' he asked.

'Answer the question. *Do you even remember?*'

'So I'm boring in bed. And that's why you have to get your thrills elsewhere.'

'Answer the question, Marcus!'

He stared at me, thinking. 'That time I tied you up,' he said at last. 'Remember? You loved it.'

A flashback: slippery white nylon ropes around my wrists and ankles, face buried in a pillow. Knots tied in haste, bindings I could have slid out of if I'd wriggled hard enough. But I'd been far too eager to stay bound, to believe myself the wild animal and my husband the tamer, willing the fantasy to hold.

Marcus had picked up the ropes at the corner hardware shop, used them on me once, then never again. Afterwards, he had stuffed them deep into the shelves that lined the sides of our headboard, where they lay gathering dust until our daughter found them one afternoon after school.

She had galloped into the kitchen, adorable and gleeful, with the rope tied around her waist, and announced: 'Mama, Papa! Look, I have a tail!'

We had laughed – *awww, so cute!* – but also exchanged looks – *Uh-oh. You should have hidden those better.*

So the white nylon ropes were hidden better. Then they were forgotten.

'Yeah, I loved it!' I said. 'But how long ago was that? You did it once, and then what? Just forgot all about it. Like all your other great ideas.'

I regretted the words as soon as I said them. Oh, we were heading into character flaws now, threading familiar complaints into fresh ones. But old hurts have a way of doing that.

'It feels like . . . it feels like I'm the one who always brings something new into our sex life,' I said, softening my tone, trying again.

'Well, you're the one who likes new things all the time.'

'I know, but knowing that about me . . . wouldn't you want to do that for me too? If you know that that gets me excited about sex?' I took a deep breath.

'What I'm trying to say is sometimes I feel like I'm doing all the thinking for our sex life. Like I'm the only one who puts effort into how to keep things fresh and exciting and . . . surprising for us. Like you can just tap me on the shoulder whenever you're horny and expect to get it, without putting any effort or energy in.'

'I put a *lot* of effort and energy into us!'

'Into our *family*. But our family life and our sex life are separate things,' I said.

Pulling my dripping hands out of the water, I held them apart and drew a column in the air. 'Our family life is awesome, and we get so much out of it, because we put so much into it. But sex –' here I sketched a second column '– sex is another category altogether, and requires its own effort. At least that's how I see it. A lot of times, I feel like I'm the only one who's putting anything into it. Anything new at least.'

'But I don't need much to get turned on!'

'But I do.'

In the silence, I noticed Marcus was gripping the sides of the tub. Beneath the surface of the water, I reached across to him with soapy hands, willing him to listen.

Honesty was the thing that made all this work. Throughout the mistakes I'd made and the difficult confrontations we'd had, honesty was the one thing I could rely on to make everything better. It was the only way that whatever needed to be fixed would get fixed; the only way both of us could get whatever we wanted or needed.

If what was on the other side of a hard conversation was worth it, I was willing to brave that conversation. And my pleasure – and our intimacy – was worth it.

'It's not easy for me to say any of this out loud,' I said quietly. 'But it came up because you asked me, and I think it's important enough that I shouldn't ignore it. I don't want to hide any more. And if anyone should know this about me, it's you.'

His hands slid off the sides of the tub and down into the dissipating foam to find mine.

'What this makes me sound like is a man who expects sex as a reward for being a good father and a good husband. A reward for working hard, for taking care of this family,' he said. 'What makes me angry about your dates is that they're not putting in the work, but they're getting the reward.' He puffed up his cheeks with air and let it out in a long whoosh. 'It's not a pretty thing to see about myself.'

'It feels like that sometimes,' I admitted. I hadn't expected him to make this connection, but now that he had seen it on his own, I felt relieved and grateful.

Now that he had seen something, Marcus began to make more connections. That was how it worked sometimes – one glimpse led to another, one insight sparked the next, until we found something that gave way.

'I don't want our sex to feel like an obligation. Like a duty,' he said with sudden feeling, looking down at our wrinkled hands among the suds. 'I don't want it to be like that for us.'

'It doesn't have to be,' I said. 'I mean, you don't jump my bones because I'm a fantastic mom or a great cook, do you?'

'Definitely not. You're a terrible cook,' he said, screwing up his face, and we both chuckled. 'I jump you because you're hot and you make me horny for you. And I want you to jump me because you're horny for me. That's all it ought to be. Not because you owe it to me. Because you don't.'

The swell of warmth in my chest as I heard his words told me: *So this is what it feels like to stand up for my own pleasure.*

I had been taught that my desire was a dangerous animal which, left to run rampant, would destroy me and tear my marriage apart. But now I knew that wasn't true. Desire wanted to be heard and known, seen and felt. Given room to do so, desire could help us grow.

'So make me horny for you,' I said.

His fingers left mine and slid deeper beneath the surface of the water, searching until he found me.

*

'I really liked our conversation last night,' Marcus said.

It was a Sunday afternoon at our neighbourhood café. He

and I had the unexpected luxury of time: two whole hours to ourselves while our daughter played at a friend's house.

'What did you like about it?' I said, looking up from my book.

'The way we listen to each other is different.'

'How so?'

'In the beginning, I didn't trust you.'

'Understandable. I broke your trust.'

He squeezed my hand across the table. 'I thought you just wanted to do this for your own pleasure, your own freedom, without caring for my feelings at all.'

'Well, I *am* doing this for me,' I reminded him gently, squeezing back.

'I know,' he said, 'but there's a diffcrence between doing this for yourself, and not caring about anyone *but* yourself. Over time I saw that you do care. About our family, about my feelings, and about me.'

My heart leapt. In my mind, I heard a distant echo from our first session with Amanda, years ago. Marcus's voice, cold with hurt. *You put your own needs above my feelings. You only cared about what you wanted. You disregarded my feelings to get your way.* It had taken time, but Marcus had just acknowledged that the work I had done – that *we* had done – was finally paying off.

Instead of saying all of this, I simply said, 'Of course I do. You're my husband. So when you say the way we listen to each other is different, what you're really saying is that the way you listen to me is different.'

'Hmm, yeah, true. My listening has changed,' he agreed. 'You've always said the same things from the start, but now I hear you. Now I believe you.'

'I'm really happy to hear that,' I said. 'We've been doing this now – what? About two years?'

He shook his head. 'I didn't think we'd make it this far.'

'Believe me, neither did I!'

'Is it weird that I didn't feel jealous when you were telling me about your date?' he asked suddenly. 'Not even when you were talking about how hot that guy was. Not even when I was hearing about the sex toys. I didn't even feel relieved that you're obviously not going to see him again.'

'It's not weird,' I said, 'just new.'

'It *was* a new feeling for me, yeah,' he said. 'I wondered for a minute if that means I've just become numb. Maybe I've gotten to a point when I don't care any more. Does it mean I care about you less? Do I love you less?'

In the pause, I could hear the low hum of conversation, the clink of cups and saucers punctuating a jazzy playlist. 'And?' I asked softly.

'Funny, but I'm just annoyed with him for spoiling your evening. I just want you to have what you want. You deserved more than that.'

Marcus reached for my hand.

'I still love you,' he said. 'I still want you. I still want your attention and affection. I still feel close to you, and want to be even closer. The big difference is that I feel better about myself now. Plus, I feel like I *can* tell you what I want and need, and get those needs met. It makes me feel considered and cared for.'

'That's huge! That's exactly how I want you to feel.'

'Thanks for sticking with it,' he said.

'You can't shake me off that easily,' I said.

*

One night, Marcus waits for our daughter to fall deep into sleep. Then he decides it's time. He takes my hand and leads me into the darkened bedroom, which flickers with the glow of candlelight and throbs with the rumble of bass. 'Black Russian' by DVS1, the architect of our incandescent night at the Wall of Sound, plays on the Bluetooth speaker. He remembers this detail and gives it a place; I love him for it.

On the bed, coiled into neat figure eights, lie four lengths of jute rope, each the matte red of wine-stained lips. When I see them, anticipation wets the corners of my mouth, a river rising under my tongue and behind my teeth. My breath swells from deep in my belly high into my chest. As I stand before the bed, a silken blackness descends over my eyes.

The first knot is tied behind my head.

I swallow hard but say nothing. Instead, I slide into blissful silence like a warm bath. Now I understand: the ropes are not for my body. They are for my mind. They pull my mind into my body and bind it there, where I so desperately need to be. I only want to feel, and now the one thing that stops me from doing so has been silenced and tamed.

He doesn't need to tell me what he wants. The ropes do it for him.

Framing my breasts, tied in a knot that presses against my clit, threaded down between my lips and up between my cheeks, the ropes become burning paths of friction. The tiny hot tongues of their fibres lick me open: teasing, priming, sensitizing. In his hands, they do the work of spreading me, turning me over, preparing me like a delicacy to be savoured; our bed is the table, and the feast is laid.

The ropes are his messengers: guiding my wrists behind me, laying the backs of my hands against the skin of my tailbone, pressing my arms to my sides, binding my ankles and feet. They whisper: *You need not do anything. Pleasure is coming. Wait for it.*

There will be more experienced lovers, more deft hands and devious minds. But no one knows me, cares for me or loves me as he does. This is why I trust him as I trust no one else. This is why my surrender is instant, effortless and complete.

His knots are far from expert, his movements far from sure. He must pause and consider, retrace and redo, many times. But these are no longer the loose, hasty knots of his first, clumsy attempts. Between this moment and our last conversation, he has taken the time to study, practise, and learn.

And this is what I need. Time.

This is what I want. Adoration.

This is what I deserve. Pleasure.

Every length of rope, stretched over every centimetre of skin, is a measure of time. Each second that he spends to consider where the next rope will fall, where the next knot will be tied, is a gift. Each pause whets my appetite and fuels my need. When he lavishes my body with this much time and attention, I feel as though I truly deserve it.

So that everything he wants from me, I yield to him. When he finally pushes me face down on to the bed, I am hungry, wet and willing. And when he finally takes me, I am grateful.

The ropes allow him to take what he wants from me as hard and as often as he pleases. But it is my desires that have been granted. It is I who have been given everything I long for.

Hours after he unties me, I feel close to him, as though still bound. We fall asleep cocooned in each other, wrapped in a deep, satisfying intimacy.

Later, when we replay the moments he filmed on his phone, he will berate himself for the messy tangle of ropes at the back. We will take a private course together under a teacher with a blonde ponytail and swift hands. In time, the ropes will become other things: a costume, a reward, a stopper that corks the sounds of my pleasure, and so much more.

When he looks at the pictures from that night, he sees all the things he could do better. But when I look at them, I see knots like rubies adorning my throat, heart, solar plexus and navel, ropes around my wrists and feet like bracelets and anklets, criss-crossing in diamonds on my skin from one jewel to the next. And I will remember what it feels like to be precious. Worshipped. Adored.

I see a constellation of red on my body, knots like stars in the deepest crevices of my sex. And I will remember what it feels like to be a galaxy: vast, limitless, and yearning to be explored.

10

How much do you tell each other?

Content Warning: Sexual Assault

Whenever people ask me, *Do you really tell each other everything?* I always hear two questions.

The first, asked out loud, is about surface-level transparency around the graphic details of sex. *How much detail do you share with each other? How much can you handle? How much is healthy or harmful?*

The question that's left unspoken is about honesty at a deeper level. *How honest do you need to be to make all this work? Is 100 per cent honesty even possible? Because that would hurt.*

When Marcus and I first opened our marriage, I felt liberated from my previous double life. I became a zealous convert to the cult of honesty. If we had promised to be 100 per cent honest with each other, I would tell Marcus *everything*. Even if we had mutually agreed to spare each other the intimate details of our sexual encounters, there was still plenty I could share.

So I did. Whenever I felt like it. Because it was my *duty*. Because it made me feel *good*. After all, there's nothing like the blind zeal of the newly converted. I was washed clean! I had nothing to hide!

It hit me that this was unnecessary self-gratification while I was telling Marcus about a single dad I'd hooked up with.

'– and you'll never guess what his son's name is? Marcus! Isn't that funny? Just like you!' – when I looked at his face and stopped mid-chatter.

He didn't look the least bit charmed, amused, or grateful for my noble honesty. Far from it. Instead, his expression read: *Why on earth does she think I want to know this?*

This taught me what honesty isn't. Honesty doesn't mean dumping information on someone because it makes *me* feel good, without first pausing to consider how it might land on them.

When I felt unsure whether I should share more or less, I asked Marcus to draw up his own boundaries around what he was comfortable hearing. I wanted him to know that his feelings mattered to me – more than my desire for his approval or acceptance, more than my need to share or feel close to him.

It was the first warm day of spring. We'd cycled to the Vondelpark and wheeled our bikes to a sunny spot on the grass. Our daughter flitted about, showering us with the first daisies of the season from her tiny cupped hands, then running off to pick more.

I asked Marcus how he felt about the men I'd been seeing, and what he thought of everything I'd been sharing about them. Maybe it was the spring sunshine, or the pleasure of being sprawled out on the grass beside each other, heads and hands touching, but bringing this up felt light and natural. Lately, we'd begun to feel more ease, less tension in our conversations.

'They all feel like a faceless wall of strangers to me,' he said.

'Well, you won't let any of them be more than that,' I pointed out. 'Sometimes I try to tell you more, to humanize them. You withdraw, shut me out. I get the feeling you find it threatening. I don't know what's okay to say, and what's not okay.'

He paused to consider this. 'All I want to know is who the guy is, how you feel about him, and what you're getting out of it,' he said.

This became the general principle that defined our approach to honesty: go for the broad strokes, instead of the graphic blow-by-blow (pun unintended). 'We had a strong physical connection' is no less truthful than 'he fucked me all night in positions I never even dreamed existed', but is easier to hear. 'I think it'll be fun to explore new things with this person' tells me what I need to know and respects everyone involved, while 'she wants to be tied up and hung from a hook in the ceiling, and I'm into it, so we're going to do that' doesn't.

The rules we sketched out when we first opened our Tinder accounts shifted over time. Those boundaries became less controlling, less prescriptive of each other's behaviour, and more descriptive of our own comfort zones and ability to deal with new information.

Two years in, we found that we could say to each other: *Please don't spring something on me when I'm in the middle of work. Let's wait until we're more relaxed. Let's wait until she goes to bed. I've had a long day, I'm fried and I don't have the bandwidth for details. Can you just give me the high-level download? I need time to process what happened. Can I share it with you tomorrow?* The morning after a new date, we could ask each other over coffee: *How was it? How did it go?* If I started seeing someone more frequently, Marcus could ask: *Do I need to worry? Where is this heading?*

Inviting each other to define our own limits around what we need and don't need to hear, and respecting those limits, enabled us to create a kind of casual honesty – one with low stakes and low risk. But even casual honesty demands an awareness of my own mental and emotional state pretty much all the time, so I'm always prepared to give simple, truthful answers to these questions. What Marcus wants to know isn't what the other guy was like, or what we did in bed. What he's asking is how I am, and how we are.

Honesty demands emotional housekeeping: tidying up my own inner space so the person I love can feel comfortable in it. It's my space and I'm responsible for it, but he can drop in any time. This means posing questions to myself like: *How did this new date make me feel? How much do I want to see them again? Is there anything I'm considering doing with this person that I would feel uncomfortable sharing with Marcus if he asked?*

All of this helps us make honesty considerate and kind. There need not be anything brutal about it. Sometimes the truth itself is brutal enough.

Then honesty takes on a different dimension. It means not backing down from the tough stuff. Asking each other the important questions, even if you're afraid of the answers. Telling each other high-stakes, high-risk things. The things that shake you to your core to admit out loud – especially to the person who means the most to you, the one you're most afraid of losing, whose rejection will hurt the most.

Because life – like people, feelings and relationships – is unpredictable and messy, there will never be a shortage of hard things. Mistakes will be made. Feelings will be hurt. And rules – even the most sacred ones – will be broken.

*

It happened on the eve of King's Day, the biggest, most raucous holiday in the Netherlands. On the night before

King Willem-Alexander's birthday, Amsterdam swells up with booze and bodies: tourists flood into the city in the tens of thousands, every club and bar is packed to bursting, and house parties spill out on to street corners besieged with drunken revellers dressed in orange, the colour of the Dutch royal family.

I was out by myself at my favourite club, which was holding a King's Night edition of a minimal techno party with a colourful, chill local crowd – the same party I'd taken Marcus to on that disastrous birthday outing. By this time I was a regular: being granted free entry by the door staff made it easy to pop in alone for a few hours, confident I would run into familiar faces or make new friends. With so much going on that night, because of the number of parties all over town, the usual crowd had given way to an influx of strangers – tourists, first-timers, people for whom King's Night was their one night out a year, an annual dispensation to go wild.

Ferro, one of my favourite DJs was on the decks, stretching his tracks like toffee, as though the morning would never come. I danced on my own, flitting from group to group in the smoking lounge, floating wherever interesting people and stories could be found.

I made an instant new connection in Gal, a 59-year-old mother who'd been inducted into the party scene by her adult children and now went clubbing with them on the regular. 'My mother had a tough life,' her son Pieter told me as I watched Gal dance beside him. 'Her first pill was like cracking an egg. She couldn't stop crying in my arms. And now she comes with me to every one of these parties.'

With the sparkly dregs of half a pill still percolating in my system, I felt like I could keep going for hours. It seemed like

I wasn't the only one. After the house lights came on at 7 a.m., clubgoers were reluctant to leave, coalescing into stubborn clusters at the couches by the exit or upstairs outside the door, sniffing around for an after-party.

Exhilarated and sweaty, I plopped down on a couch. 'Wooh, what a night!' I said to no one in particular.

'*Ja*, heh?' said a voice beside me.

I registered the presence of a pale, gangly Dutch guy, I guessed in his mid- to late twenties, all elbows and knees topped with a mousy brown mop. Dressed in a nondescript T-shirt and jeans, he struck me as quiet and nerdy, like the harmless wallflower in a sitcom.

'Too good, gotta keep it going.'

'Oh, for sure!' I said. 'What's your name?'

'Pim,' he said, holding out a thin hand.

'Deepa,' I said, shaking it. 'So, Pim, do you know where there's an after-party?'

It took him a few beats to reply. 'Yeah,' he said slowly. 'Yeah, actually. I met these Spanish guys earlier, and we were talking about an *aftertje* at my place' – the Dutch diminutive making it sound small and casual. 'They had to go home to get some stuff, but they have my address and they said they're going to follow. Do you wanna come?'

'Okay, cool,' I said. 'Where do you live?'

'Close to het Spui. We can walk there and pick them up on the way.'

'Sounds good,' I said. I'd been to enough after-parties to be familiar with how they came together just like this – spontaneously, with not a lot of fuss or details. 'Let's go.'

I followed Pim into the city centre on the morning of King's Day, as gay and chirpy as a princess in a Disney cartoon. The sun shone, birds twittered, and bright bursts of orange filled the narrow streets with a festive air.

Pim was silent as we walked, except for a call he made on his phone. 'The Spanish guys aren't answering,' he said. 'I'll try them again later.'

Almost at random, a few minutes later, he stopped at a door somewhere along the Spuistraat. 'Let's just stop by and pick them up,' he said, ringing the buzzer on the stoep.

'Is this where they live?' I asked as we waited. 'Did they give you their address or –'

'I guess nobody's home,' he said, cutting me off. 'Maybe they already left for mine. Come on.'

Pim's apartment was a cramped one-bedroom flat with low wooden ceilings, bare except for a black ergonomic office chair and a rickety computer table next to a wall of tiny square leaded-glass windows overlooking the Singel.

After hanging up my coat and kicking off my shoes, I drifted to the window, leaned my forehead against the cold panes, and stared out on to the tram tracks below. 'Hey, can you try the Spanish guys again?' I asked.

It was only when Pim came up behind me and said, 'I think we should forget about them,' that it dawned on me.

There was no after-party. There were no Spanish guys. There had never been.

'You mean it's just us,' I said.

Pim placed his hands on my waist. 'It's just us.'

I turned around and looked up at him. With absolute indifference, I thought: *Oh, why not. I'm already here.*

His lips on mine felt hollow and dry; I had tasted cigarette filters with more softness and moisture. The final wisps of chemical euphoria were stretched thin now, creating the illusion of a vibe where none was there, filling in for a chemistry that didn't exist.

But he seemed excited by my body and my presence in his sorry, empty flat. As we kissed, he pulled me closer, ran his hands up my short skirt and over my butt, and led me to the bedroom. If that was where it was going, I thought, I had to lay down the law, and quick.

'I'm married, but it's okay, it's an open marriage,' I told him as he laid me down on the bed. It's ironic to me now how *honest* I was compelled to be, that even in my dreamy stupor, I thought no one deserved to be duped into a situation they hadn't bargained for.

'You have to use a condom,' I said, reaching for my party purse, which was still slung around my body. I had learned to keep at least a couple of condoms on me in various sizes, especially for men who believed they were too well endowed and might be tempted to wield their unsheathable girth as a reason to squirm out of using protection. I'd heard it all before.

'Here,' I said, pressing the foil packet into his palm. Without a word he took it, ripped it open, and turned me so I faced the wall.

I blinked, and it was over. He groaned and shuddered and came quickly, too quickly for me to register any pleasure. I swivelled my head to see his face in the frozen mask of orgasm. Then I caught sight of the limp, shrivelled condom in his hand.

My first reaction was confusion. Why was he already holding the condom? How had he taken it off so soon after ejaculating?

'Why —'

'Shhh,' he said.

'Did you catch the stuff?' I blinked hard, trying to clear away the fog, until the condom came into focus.

It was empty. It wasn't even wet.

'Where is it?' I said, my voice rising, panic rearing in my chest, instincts awakening from their slumber in the bottom of my gut. 'Where's the stuff? Did you catch any of it? Where is it?'

He lifted his weightless frame off the bed, stepping away from me, still holding the empty condom. 'Shhh,' he said again.

'Where is it? Is it inside me? Did you come inside me?' My voice was shrill as I reached down between my legs and touched a slimy unfamiliar wetness that was not my own.

'I took it off, okay, sorry –'

'You fucking asshole!' Anger propelled me up off the bed, into his face. Then he was careening away from me into the front room, and I was charging at him in a rage, crying, 'How could you fucking do this to me! I told you to use a condom! I told you! You fucker, you asshole, you lying fuck!' until I had him backed up against the windows.

He collapsed in the black office chair. Then, to my horror and disbelief, he produced a key and a white plastic baggie from his pocket and snorted a bump of cocaine right in front of my face.

'What the fuck?'

'Calm the fuck down,' he said, the cocaine instantly granting him some measure of a spine. 'It's not a big deal.'

'Don't fucking tell me to calm down!'

'There's a pill for that,' he said, wiping at his nose.

'Get me the fucking pill, then! Where's the nearest pharmacy? Take me there, let's go. Now!'

'No.'

'What do you mean, no?' I couldn't believe what I was hearing. Where was the nice guy, the harmless wallflower? Where was the apology, the mortification?

'No, I'm not going with you. You can get it yourself,' he said, digging into his baggie and sucking up another bump of cocaine with a loud, wet snort.

'What the fuck?'

'You sleep around, you should know. Haven't you taken it before?'

His attempt to shame me enraged me even more. 'Never, because no one has ever done this to me before!'

'I don't know why you're making it such a big deal,' he said, snivelling. 'Other girls have been fine with it.'

'Other girls? So you've done this to other girls?' All I could do was parrot his pathetic words in shock, a shrill and broken record. 'I'm not leaving until you get up and go get it with me.' I wanted to drag him from his chair, down the stairs and out the door to the pharmacy. It was the only thing that made sense in the moment. I wanted him to acknowledge he'd done something wrong and try to make it right. There had to be a shred of decency in him somewhere.

'Then I guess you're not leaving,' he said, every word from his thin lips a waking nightmare. 'I guess we're just going to stay right here, and you won't get your pill, and we're going to have a baby together. I've always wanted to be a father,' he finished with a sneer that I could only describe as evil.

That was when I broke down in deep, wracking, humiliating sobs. *Please please please*, I heard myself beg, willing my knees to hold so I wouldn't crumple in front of him, hanging my head so I wouldn't have to look at his face, so he wouldn't see me cry.

Finally he must have realized it was the only way to get me out of his apartment. 'Okay, stop it, come on, let's go,' he said.

He refused to enter the pharmacy or give me cash. I found the pill, paid for it, walked out and told him how much it cost.

'I don't have any cash on me,' he said.

'Find an ATM!'

'Send me a Tikkie,' he said.

I thrust my phone at him, he keyed in a number, and I sent him a payment request that he never paid. I never called the number or found out if it was really his. I only wanted to forget, and to disappear.

Because after he slunk off, leaving me outside the pharmacy clutching the morning-after pill in a sealed cardboard box, I had to go home to my husband. And I had to tell him what had happened.

Several times, I stopped on the street and tried to call friends. No one answered. King's Day was already in full swing, with boat parades, street parties, and shitty speakers cranked up to top volume. The city was too frenzied, too boisterous, too happy to hear me.

With blurry eyes I managed to find the most recent contact on my Facebook Messenger: Gal, the 59-year-old mother I'd met that night and added as a friend a few hours ago.

Gal, I typed, hands shaking.

I'm walking home from an after

A guy took off the condom and came inside without telling me

I'm so angry

I'm crying on the street

What do I tell my husband
I got the pill
He was such an asshole

She responded immediately. *That's terrible! I wish I was there with you, but I'm at an after in Purmerend. Do you have a close friend you can go to now?*

I'm going home to my husband, I wrote.
We have no secrets
He's my best friend
Sorry to mess with your vibe

Don't worry about me, she wrote back. *Honesty is the basis of love. I hope you can work it out. I'm worried about your health, Deepa. We can keep talking until you get home, if you like.*

A pause, three dots flashing as she typed.

Then: *It's rape if he did it against your will.*

Rape.

I stared at the screen, pixels forming the words that described my reality.

I shoved my phone into my purse and kept walking.

Tram services in the city centre were suspended on King's Day. I trudged home, dread weighing down my every step, fear a leaden shroud thrown over the wild animal of panic inside me. I braced myself for Marcus's anger. I knew he would blame me, for in that moment I blamed myself. Why wouldn't he?

In the twenty-five minutes that it took me to walk home, telling Marcus became the most important thing. It was the one thing that was clear to me, the one thing I held on to as I stumbled along in a daze, feeling numb and invisible amidst the bustle of a city caught up in its biggest celebration of the year. The one thing that would save me was the one thing that made all this work. There was no other choice but honesty.

I knew from my old life that there were ways to hide. I could take the morning-after pill, do the STI and HIV tests in secret, make up a lie for each act of medical damage control. I could conceal my devastation as a comedown, sleeping away the worst of it as though it was any other party weekend. I could escape into the impenetrable lair of my shame and lick my wounds in the dark. I could heal on my own, even if it took forever.

I didn't want to. I had lied and hidden before, and I never wanted to again; it would only tear me and my marriage apart. Marcus was my partner; I couldn't survive this without him. We had promised to be honest with each other. It was that simple.

Honesty demanded that I refuse to let myself be silenced by fear or shame; instead, it meant letting the person I loved the most see the worst of me. The utter vulnerability of exposure was almost unbearable, but I had to put my faith in the relationship we had worked so hard to rebuild together. I had to trust that Marcus would still love and accept me, as we had once promised each other.

Most of all, I had to believe that I was worthy of his love and acceptance.

It would take a long time until I did.

*

I wish I could remember exactly how I told Marcus and how he responded. But just as panic and adrenaline engraved every detail of my assault into my memory, shock and exhaustion erased the words. My brain had reached its limit; all it wanted was to fall into darkness and forget.

All I can remember is pulling him into the bedroom with me, whispering, *I need to talk to you.* I remember closing the door to muffle the jarring cheerfulness of our daughter's favourite cartoons from the living room, and being grateful for this small mercy that distracted her from registering the state I was in. I remember that I tried to tell him as slowly and evenly as I could manage, as if this would help, and that it felt like a superhuman effort to keep from shattering as I spoke.

I can't remember if I said *I'm sorry.* I'm sure I did.

Marcus demanded the address. I refused to give it to him. I didn't want retribution; I longed for comfort and care, to be held and reassured it wasn't my fault. But Marcus was consumed by anger and hurt. And I knew that although he wanted to take his rage out on the man who had done this, part of it was also directed at me.

The only words I remember tumbled out a few days later.

'This wouldn't have happened if we hadn't been in an open marriage,' he said.

If I hadn't felt free to go out partying by myself. If I hadn't thought it was okay to go home with another man. If I hadn't fought for the conditions that somehow, directly or indirectly, led to my own violation. If I hadn't wanted any of this. If I hadn't been so naive.

His words stayed with me for weeks, months.

He would take them back, of course. After the string of people I'd tried to reach in my panic began returning my calls. After a gay friend told me I needed to get PEP, a last-ditch emergency treatment for HIV, which ideally should be taken within twenty-four hours of unprotected sex. After the emergency-room doctor refused to give me PEP because I was a straight woman and my assailant was a straight white male, and the odds of either of us contracting HIV were statistically insignificant, making the treatment unnecessary in their eyes. After I broke down weeping, *I didn't want this, he deceived me*, the doctor's silence invalidating me, making me feel invisible. After I swallowed the morning-after pill and disappeared into a hormonal black hole for the next forty-eight hours.

Only after all of that, Marcus would see me suffering and take back what he'd said. He would gather me into his arms and let me cry. He would tell me all the things I needed to hear: that it wasn't my fault, that he would take care of me, that it would be okay.

But it took time. It took weeks for him to absorb his own shock and deal with his own anger, wrestle down the instincts of his baser self, and find the strength to give me the love and support I needed. It took him months to ask my forgiveness for how he reacted, for blaming me. It took me even longer to stop blaming myself.

Looking back now, I see that fixating on Marcus's reaction allowed me to delay confronting my own responsibility. It was easier to expect his blame, to prepare myself for his anger, and to strategize how to soothe and diffuse it, rather than face the truth of what had happened and accept my own role in it.

For hadn't I put myself at risk: going to a party alone, taking a pill, opening myself up to intimacy with a total stranger?

Deep down inside me, I knew I had.

I just wasn't ready to deal with it yet.

In the weeks that followed, all the emotional resources I could marshal went into taking care of myself, my family and my marriage.

Our marriage closed up naturally, and so did I. Marcus didn't even have to ask. I deleted my dating apps, devoid of the enthusiasm, curiosity or passion I once felt for dating or sex – or any kind of pleasure, for that matter. I was numb: tastes dulled, sensations muted. All the life had gone out of everything. I couldn't enjoy anything because I felt I didn't deserve any enjoyment. I didn't know how to get any of it back, which scared me.

I felt something inside me turtle up, guarding me. The tension of holding myself so tightly was exhausting. I slept all the time, then became paranoid that fatigue meant the morning-after pill hadn't worked and I was pregnant. When my period came gushing out of me, so did sobs of relief.

Whatever energy I had, I channelled into caretaking. I functioned well enough to tend to my child's daily needs. I felt alone and hurt, but because I blamed myself for what had happened, I believed it was my duty to set aside my own feelings to support Marcus as he dealt with his. What happened to me also hurt him. By focusing on my family, I dissociated from my own difficult emotions.

I couldn't ask for support or sympathy without blowing up at Marcus or disintegrating into a sobbing mess; I found it hard to balance what I needed with what Marcus felt. I didn't have the fire to take action against the man who had assaulted me. The wordless indifference of the emergency-room doctor had chilled me to the core. Perhaps if they had met me with compassion instead of silence, I might have felt differently. I saw only an uphill battle that would drain me, one for which I didn't have the strength or support.

The path of least resistance was to turn inward, forget, and move on. It was a bitter lesson: now I understood why so many victims of sexual assault did the same.

*

About a month after the assault, Marcus received distressing news from his family in Manila. His mother, who had been living with a non-malignant brain tumour for years, had agreed to surgery to excise the growth. The procedure had caused her brain to swell, leaving her bedridden; now, the diagnosis was late-stage brain cancer.

He flew home to the Philippines to see her. It would be the last time.

I devoted myself to childcare in the two weeks that Marcus was gone. During my daughter's waking hours, I threw myself into school runs, playdates, ice cream in the park after school, crafting, collages, outdoor play, violin practice, violin lessons. I found a sense of accomplishment in hitting solid, predictable marks. I treated it like parenting bootcamp – it didn't have to be, but I preferred it that way. The more relentless the routine, the less room for anxiety or self-doubt.

After putting her to bed, without the distractions of dating and socializing, with no caretaking left to do, I finally had the time and space to sit still and think.

From the night I had first seen stars on the Seine with Rui, the vast majority of my experiences with club culture had been positive, if not overwhelmingly so. Like fluffy, rose-coloured clouds around a mountain peak, those experiences had obscured the risks, lulling me into a sense of security. Reality had pulled back the clouds, revealing the dangerous crevices where I could slip and fall.

Some clubs claimed to be safe spaces for self-expression and intimacy, but there would always be dangerous people lurking in the shadows, disguised as sexy strangers, carefree dancers, even harmless wallflowers from sitcoms.

My safety relied on my own ability to assess risk, register threats, and make judgement calls in the moment. MDMA created a sense of trust where there was none, flooding my body with pleasure to the exclusion of all other feelings. By numbing my instincts, I had cut off my own risk-assessment system, thrown out my personal safety gear.

There were things I could have done to mitigate the risks. I could have arranged to meet up with friends, made sure there would be someone to look out for me. Knowing I was alone, I could have cut my dose in half, or gone out dancing sober. I'd certainly done that before. I could have let Marcus know where I was going, as I would have on a date. I could have waited until I had sobered up, or at least taken a cold hard look at my own mental state before deciding to leave with someone I had just met.

These were not difficult things to put in place. I would when I was ready. There was too much joy and pleasure in my nights on the dance floor to give them up for good, even after this. I would return, and I would be wiser. Yet after retracing my steps to find out where I'd gone wrong and what I could do better, I realized that it went back much further than the moment I'd decided to step out of the club with a total stranger.

The uncomfortable truth was that I didn't value myself

enough. I tended to settle for what I *could* get instead of holding out for what I really wanted or what truly excited me. Being careless with my time and body had cost me dearly. I knew now what it felt like in my head when I was seeking validation – a restless, frenzied energy; a low roar of noise in the background of my thoughts – and that it could cloud my judgement.

By numbing my feelings with drugs, I had been jamming the signal, amplifying pleasure to the exclusion of all else. By limiting myself to transactional sex, I was preventing myself from feeling things for and about people. By seeing hook-ups as discardable, I had also opened myself up to being used and discarded. I had to see and treat people differently if I wanted to be seen and treated differently. And I had to learn to use, trust and hone the built-in personal warning system I had inhibited myself from using until now. I had to feel.

What if I could put that ace into play, and also manage Marcus's discomfort around creating closer connections? There was only one way to find out. But I had to go slow and feel my way through.

Being honest with myself was a necessary reckoning, one that I had avoided long enough. Or had I just given myself time? The benefit of time was that, somehow, it seemed easier to separate blame and responsibility.

Taking responsibility for my actions was one thing, but it wasn't the entire picture. The assault had revealed a fundamental inequality neither Marcus nor I had ever experienced or foreseen. As a straight man, Marcus had more power than I did; he was less likely to be vulnerable, as I had been, to being violated by a man and forced into non-consensual, unprotected sex. If he'd gone home high as a kite with an unknown woman he'd just met, *he* would have been the danger to *her*. That woman would have had to drug him unconscious to climb over his brawny body and violate him the way I had been violated.

Safety wasn't just a matter of me learning to be smarter or 'clubbing responsibly', dosing less or taking extra precautions. As a woman, I would always be more vulnerable to assault and abuse than my husband. It was a hard reality to confront, but we couldn't do things exactly the same way in this open relationship; we had to acknowledge how I was, in this way, at a disadvantage, just as Marcus was at a disadvantage on dating apps. We had to acknowledge the inequality and find ways to address it.

Redrawing these parameters didn't happen overnight, or even in the two weeks that Marcus was away. Like feeling safe and ready to trust the world again, it happened in trickles, over time. But the desire to be wiser, the awareness of how I could do better, and the dawning recognition that I deserved more, began in those summer nights after I'd kissed and sung and loved my daughter to sleep, when I tended to myself in a cocoon of solitude.

On the morning Marcus returned from Manila, our daughter was curled up asleep in bed beside me. 'It's Papa!' I whispered.

She sprang to wakefulness, eyes wide open in a flash. Her whole face lit up. 'Hide!' she whispered back, pulling the duvet over our heads. She could barely contain her excitement, clamping her hands down over an imminent explosion of red-cheeked laughter.

I heard Marcus chuckle as he came into the bedroom to find a lumpy duvet masquerading as an empty bed. 'Where's my family?' he called. 'I missed them, but I guess they aren't here!'

She burst into giggles and yanked down the duvet with a shout. Then the three of us were together again, all laughter and cuddles and love, and it was so good.

After taking her to school, I came home to a suitcase full of familiar flavours and smells: ripe yellow mangoes; buttery, sugary pillows of *ensaymada*; and salted, smoked milkfish – all my favourite comfort foods from home. We left Marcus's unpacked belongings in the living room and crawled into bed together. For the first time in weeks, I fully and deeply exhaled.

Marcus was, and still is, my safe place in the world. His presence made me feel I could relax, stop trying so hard, and just be myself. My own actions had undermined my sense of self-worth, and I'd been hard on myself to make up for it, to prove that I was good – even if what had happened and who I was as a woman, wife and mother were all separate things. I told Marcus as much.

'Sometimes I need to hear it from you, for you to say that it's okay,' I said.

His response was immediate and unhesitating. 'It's okay, Deepa. You don't have to prove anything. To me or to anyone.'

Marcus's time away had been bittersweet. He was grieving his mother's diagnosis and the loss that he knew was coming, but he'd also had time to reflect on what had happened to me and his reaction to it.

'I know in the past I've behaved in a way that's made you not want to share things with me,' he said. 'I've made you feel like withholding details to protect my feelings, but you shouldn't be afraid of telling me things.'

He was right, of course. He'd just never acknowledged it before, or never this clearly. My breath grew deeper, and I felt myself soften even more into his embrace. I had been holding myself so tightly while he was gone.

'I want you to be safe,' he said. 'Tell me where you're going, who you're with, how the person is, how he's treating you. It's not for me to control you, but to protect you. Next to your happiness, your safety is important to me too.'

Enveloped in the quiet strength of Marcus's love, I could feel safe again.

I could even begin to heal.

The question was: how?

11

Aren't you afraid of feelings?

On the day my mother revealed the truth about my father's death, she looked right at me and asked the question that stopped my world. 'Do you know how your daddy died?'

My mother told me many things in the eternity that followed: all the things she could not say to me all those years I had been her daughter. Sitting face to face as mother to mother, wife to wife, woman to woman, a lifetime of secrets found their release.

It is hard to recall her exact words, for after too many years of silence, too many things needed to be said. The one thing I will always remember was not something she said, but something she did.

She had received the call while she was at work. Shocked into autopilot, she couldn't remember how she had left the office, gotten into her car, and driven all the way to the hospital. It was in the car that the fury seized her.

Rising in her belly, spilling over in hot tears, until she was shaking and slapping the steering wheel in futile rage, crying out and cursing him in words she would never have dared utter to his face – *putang ina, punyeta, putang ina mo* – until she tore into the hospital in a blind frenzy, and saw his body lying cold before her.

Then, my mother said, she saw the peace of his expression, the smoothness of his brow. The lines etched by months of paranoia and pain, furrows carved by sleeplessness and suffering, were gone. In that peace, the face of the man she loved had never looked more beautiful.

Then she understood that she should have let him go sooner. For this peace was all he wanted, and she had been too selfish to give it to him. *I'm sorry, Daddy*, she said. *I'm sorry I wasn't strong enough to let you go.*

Then she said to me, '*Kinuha ko lahat ng galit, tapos –*'

('I took all the anger, and then I –')

She clenched her hand into a fist and held it just below her chin. She dragged her fist down the front of her body, slowly, painfully, as though pushing something down her throat, past her solar plexus, into her stomach, forcing her anger down into the bottom of her gut, and holding it there, she blinked back her tears and swallowed hard.

My mother banished her anger somewhere deep inside of her, where it lay powerless and forgotten, covered up by smiles and stories, weighed down by all the years like a sleeping dragon draped in iron chains.

Anger had no part in the life of a mother with a family to protect, provide and care for. Anger would only tear her apart, not move her forward; it could not turn back time or undo the past; it would not help her forgive or forget. Anger would not bring what she had lost back to life.

It took me a long time to realize that this, too, was what I learned to do with anger.

I never took legal action against the creep who violated me. I'm aware that you might be disappointed by this. I never went back to his apartment, rang his doorbell, or confronted him. I never gave my husband his address or the permission to avenge my honour and release his rage by beating him to a sorry pulp.

It's not worth it, I told myself. I imagine I'm not the first to think that.

Later I learned that the violation had a name: it was called stealthing. At the time, stealthing was considered a criminal offence in less than a handful of countries, such as Germany and Canada; the first conviction in the Netherlands would not come until 2023. It took me years to find the information I desperately needed then: how to contact the Centrum Seksueel Geweld, or Sexual Assault Centre, the national authority that would have helped me secure immediate treatment and tests and supported me if I'd chosen to pursue an investigation.

When I imagined myself lodging a formal complaint, I found myself staring down a draining, thankless road that would keep the asshole in my life longer than I wanted. I believed that the righteous anger required to fuel me through such a process would be a destructive force, rather than a cleansing, healing or empowering one. I was afraid that anger would consume me and turn me into someone I didn't want to be.

Anger is not an acceptable emotion for a woman to feel – this is what we're taught. A temper is expected, but rage is unbecoming. Good girls never get angry. If we did, how would we grow up into good wives who turn a blind eye? Women are not meant to hold on to anger; instead we are expected to give selflessly and forgive endlessly.

The culture that shaped me is not one that is adept at using anger to set boundaries, demand accountability or pursue justice. After all, Filipinos glorified our colonial oppressors for centuries after they ravaged us; we elected back into power the son and namesake of a dictator who amassed a chilling record of human-rights abuses and billions of dollars in looted public wealth.

We are notorious for our resilience, forgetfulness, and toxic positivity. As a people, we are too malleable to be containers for righteous anger, but we are excellent repositories of humour and happiness. We sing and smile through our wounds, laugh and pray away our pain.

Tumahimik na ka lang (Focus on the positive). *Hindi ka naman aasenso diyan* (Just keep quiet. That won't make you rich). *Be grateful for what you have. Stop being so negative. Pray for your enemies. This too shall pass. Time heals all wounds. Everything happens for a reason. You'll get over it. It could be worse.*

I did not know how deeply I had internalized these messages until I let the man who had sexually assaulted me disappear.

To remain angry was to let him win. I did not want this person and this moment to rob me of every opportunity that still lay before me to grow, explore and feel. I did not want to give him that power. My instincts told me that my path to healing lay elsewhere.

I did not become wiser or stronger overnight. I did not have a plan for feeling safe, reopening our marriage, or returning to my beloved dance floor. Life simply took over and, surrendering with relief, I let it carry me away from what had happened.

*

Summer had gotten off to a mild start in Amsterdam, but it was sweltering when I arrived in Berlin. I stepped off the U-Bahn, wheelie suitcase in tow and backpack on my shoulders, and headed upstairs to the entrance of the Warschauer Straße station.

He arrived at almost the exact spot where we first met a lifetime ago. This time, it was midday, not midnight. The baby sleeping in a hotel room on the opposite bank of the Spree was now safely ensconced at home with her papa. This time there were no more secrets, no more need to hide.

This time, Thomas called me by my real name.

If he was aware of the full-circle significance of this moment, at this meeting place, he didn't let on. Instead he strode towards me with a grin and took my suitcase from my hand. Together, in the blinding noontime sun, we crossed into Friedrichshain.

The idea of visiting Thomas in Berlin came to me out of nowhere and roused me from the depths of my languishing. After weeks of numbness and indifference, a trip to one of my favourite cities and most trusted friends gave me something to plan for and look forward to.

It wasn't long after Marcus and I agreed to open our marriage that I'd asked him if I could be friends with Thomas again. 'You're already sleeping with other men. It seems pointless to stop you from talking to this one,' he'd said at the time. 'If you can assure me that friendship is all you want from this, and promise me you'll be honest with me if that changes, then I guess I can accept that.'

I promised. Time would help me show that I was true to my word. I wrote an email to Thomas, blank except for the subject line: *Still wanna be friends?*

Where do I click? he replied within minutes.

Thomas became my trusted reader and critic for the essays I produced in my first writing classes; in the final stretch before turning in his dissertation, I called him at 7 a.m. so he would wake up and write. In between trading takes on pop culture, music, books and politics, we shared the ups and downs of dating and relationships: I as a beginner non-monogamist in

Amsterdam, and he as a single white male looking for love in New York, London and, now, back home in Berlin.

Being here was no longer a secret or a risk; it felt like a triumph. It spoke to how far Marcus and I had come in the years since the affair. I didn't know many husbands who would be fine with their wife becoming friends with a man she'd had an affair with, or trust her to stay in his apartment for four days, but here we were. 'I keep asking myself: Am I stupid? Am I actually letting this happen?' Marcus confessed before I left. 'Conventional wisdom tells me I'm not supposed to be okay with this. But I know you and I are far from conventional.'

It was too stifling to stay indoors, so Thomas took me out to a lake in central Wedding for an evening swim that promised relief from the oppressive heat. We passed freight trains working up the momentum for a laborious escape on scorching tracks, through the tree-shaded canals and islands of Westhafen, a massive port within the city, until we reached a renegade beach on the banks of the Plötzensee.

Thomas was the first to dive in. His body sliced into the lake precisely where the sunset glittered on the water, turning rich green ripples into deep rose gold.

I plunged in after him. For the first time in months, I *felt* something. It took me a few moments to understand the signals my body was sending me, to put a name to what I was feeling.

It was pleasure.

Pleasure in the icy shock, then electric bliss of the water against my overheated skin; pleasure in my own strength as I pulled myself forward with long, sure strokes; pleasure in realizing a resolution to my past with Thomas that I never could have foreseen. This pleasure came freely, without trepidation or guilt.

I was safe in the company of a trusted friend. Marcus knew everything there was to know. I had nothing to fear or hide. In the fading August heat, I felt another piece of shame's brittle armour break off and fall away.

I wanted to remember everything about this. How it felt to reawaken to a sense of trust in myself and in the world. How it felt to be myself again: joyful, curious, and open to wonder. How it felt to be in a relationship — platonic, committed, or otherwise — where trust and respect were paramount.

Being in Berlin with Thomas was proof that I wasn't doomed to suffer from my mistakes forever. I didn't have to be stuck in the same patterns, making poor choices again and again. I could learn from my careless actions, clean up my own mess and, with time, incremental effort and commitment, leave the past behind and create something new.

I had turned things around and remade a disastrous choice into a life I loved.

I had done it once. I could do it again.

I could choose differently.

I could be free.

For the first time since the assault — sitting on a concrete shore listening to laughter, music and yells echo across the water, watching tanned bodies cannonball into the darkening Plötzensee — I could *feel*.

In my recovery from a sense of violation, feelings were what told me that I was going to be okay. That I was operating normally. That it was safe to be myself once more: exploratory, curious and joyful. That I was alive, healing, and happy to be so.

So whenever people ask me if I'm afraid of feelings, my answer is a resounding *no*.

In the world of dating and casual sex, feelings are forbidden. Feelings can mess up everything. *As long as I'm vigilant and keep sex strictly feelings-free, I will be safe, and so will my marriage.*

The truth is, I *like* feeling things about people. I was never wary of 'catching feelings', as people say. In fact, I welcome them. Sex with feelings is great! What else is sex but embodied feeling? Without feelings, it's just body parts and friction.

Feelings are the secret sauce that makes sex juicier, more stimulating, more fascinating. Feelings are the fairy dust that makes connections more human, less transactional. Feelings are the whisperings of my body and the urgings of my gut, all of which are valuable information. If I don't feel anything, what is the point of it all?

I enjoy mulling over what I feel about a person and what made me feel that way about them. I enjoy figuring out which shades of feeling are evoked by particular lovers, moments or experiences.

I can like someone. I can be attracted to them. I can be stimulated, fascinated, intrigued by or even infatuated with them. To confuse any of these feelings for love is a mistake made by people who can't handle complexity, for whom feelings only come in a few dull hues, rather than a delicious, dazzling rainbow.

Those first flickers of feeling – anticipation for my visit to Berlin, exhilaration on the shores of the Plötzensee, fulfilment in having rebuilt a valuable friendship and thriving marriage from the wreckage of the affair – were a tenuous, glimmering lifeline. Holding on, I let my feelings pull me back to aliveness once again.

AREN'T YOU AFRAID OF FEELINGS?

I feared I would return to a resentful husband who'd regressed into the Marcus of years ago. But when I came home, Marcus only pulled me close, quite literally clinging to me. His mother had just passed away; he wasn't angry at all, but sad, alone, and grieving.

Weeks passed, and we went on with the motions of life as usual. But underneath the surface Marcus mourned the only way he knew how: walling up, denying his feelings, and powering through his grief.

We settled into our comfortable routine of family and home life until, nearly five months after the assault, I felt ready to return to dating. Wary of risking my re-emergence into pleasure with someone new, I chose one of my favourite lovers, someone I knew well and felt safe with.

Massimo was a blue-eyed, street-smart produce importer from Sicily. A beast in bed and a *nonno* in the kitchen, he was my go-to for bedroom-only dominance and farm-to-table aftercare. Though he was in his twenties, there was a bit of the old world about him. He loved classic rock, taught himself how to play the piano, and though he lived across the IJ in Amsterdam Noord, he always picked me up and drove me home. With Massimo, there were no mind games, no attempt to take control over any other area of my life, no kinks to facilitate. I only had to look sexy, get in the van, and prepare to be ravaged.

Massimo's recipe for pleasure was simple: rough me up, then feed me. He would tuck a blanket around me as I recovered from several hours of *carino brutal*, then root through the back of his cold-storage van for the pick of the season. 'I have a beautiful burrata,' he would call out to me, 'but not as beautiful as you.' I ate it up, as I did his homemade gnocchi and meaty *cuore di bue* tomatoes, washing them down with limoncello from his father's farm. Dessert was served in the form of outrageous tales from his teenage years as a runner for the Palermo mafia, with a naughty drizzle of nymphomaniacs and strippers for good measure.

When Massimo roared up in his vegetable-loaded van, Led Zeppelin blaring out the windows, Marcus blew up. At first I was dismayed — hadn't we already made so much progress, built confidence and trust, left the jealous rages behind? — but I began to see a pattern.

My dating was Marcus's pressure valve, the only acceptable excuse for him to lash out and unleash the feelings he bottled up to get through the day. I couldn't tell where his jealousy ended and his grief began, but I knew I didn't deserve to bear the brunt of emotions that had little to do with me.

Marcus was accustomed to me helping him process difficult feelings, but I was still on my own path to recovery. I wasn't equipped to handle his grief, and neither was he. Both emotionally maxed out and unable to support each other, we agreed to call in backup.

Our therapist, Noam, had a lifetime of experience in what he called 'alternative lifestyles', and was polyamorous and bisexual himself, with children of his own. In his office, our roles were clear: Marcus's was to talk, mine was to listen, and Noam's was to mediate. Whenever I became defensive, Noam would gently nudge me back into my role. At first I bristled, but soon his approach made sense.

Marcus needed to feel safe to express difficult, complex emotions. The more secure he felt, the stronger our marriage would be. As the partner who was getting far more sex and pleasure out of this, I was in a position of power. As the more vulnerable partner, Marcus needed my attention and support, especially now that his emotional bandwidth was completely taken up by grief.

Sometimes listening to Marcus made me feel selfish, made me want to cave in and say, *Let's not do this any more*. But I had been doing this long enough to know that despite recent events, I was thriving in the freedom of our open marriage. I had to make it clear to Marcus why I was intent on returning to dating: it made me feel more myself, fully alive. It satisfied my needs for sexual variety, adventure, exploration and discovery. None of that had changed.

When we stepped out of the therapist's room, Marcus was visibly shaken: I could see it in the set of his jaw, the tightness of his shoulders, the slight tremor in his hands. I offered him time to gather himself before we got on our bikes, so we found a park bench outside and sat down together.

'I'm still angry,' Marcus said, 'even though we already talked about it. Is that weird? Even though, logically, I know we've resolved it. I feel rubbed raw.'

'Welcome to the real world, Neo,' I deadpanned in a reference to *The Matrix*, playing the grave Laurence Fishburne to a newly awakened Keanu Reeves. Then I softened. 'That's what it's like when you allow yourself to actually feel the shitty stuff, like the rest of us do.'

Once a month or every six weeks, we combined a therapy appointment with a date night out. Both were good for us: time off from parenting to enjoy each other, and time to work on our relationship with therapy as a resource, rather than a cure.

'I feel more at ease with our open set-up these last few months,' Marcus told me one evening. We were at a tiny Japanese bar off the Albert Cuypmarkt after our appointment with Noam.

'I'm happy to hear that,' I said, setting down my yuzu sour and taking his hand across the table. 'What's clicked for you?'

'That I can ask for what I want and need, and not be ashamed of it, and trust that I can actually have that need fulfilled,' he said. 'I know, you've been telling me this the whole time. You never changed your tune. But now it's different. Now I really get it.'

With each expression of safety and trust, I gained a little more security and freedom. Before long, I was ready to spread my wings again.

*

Forever late, I sped through the frigid January air, hurtling towards De Wallen as fast as my bicycle could carry me. After double-locking my bike – gloves between my teeth, fingers bitten by freezing metal – I hurried towards Brouwerij de Prael, a craft brewery tucked into a quiet back alley in Amsterdam's infamous red-light district. Standing by the door, a figure edged by lamplight glimmering off half-frozen puddles on the cobblestoned ground was waiting for me.

It had been an entire year since I'd first matched with Charlie on Happn. Normally I would be annoyed that someone who lived two hours away by train was trawling for dates in Amsterdam, but Charlie looked too damn sexy in his profile picture to write off. Not only did he come across as warm and engaging over WhatsApp, but he was also openly polyamorous and had two girlfriends.

I was intrigued. Our on-again, off-again chat survived a lost phone, the death of a relative, several holidays, and too many reschedules and cancellations to count, until we were finally about to meet. I liked him on sight, but I already knew I would.

Charlie was tall and muscular, with close-cropped dark-blonde hair, warm brown eyes and a reddish goatee. He had the clean-cut, boyish appeal of a prep-school student and the ripped physique of a boxer – *Dead Poets Society* meets Ultimate Fighting Championship – a combination I would find irresistible. Something in the lift of his eyebrows and the brightness of his eyes gave him an open, interested expression, with a hint of mischief not too far beneath the surface. His cognac leather satchel, athletic socks and burgundy loafers underscored his schoolboy vibe; a tiny silver hoop glinted in one busted-up ear – cauliflower ears, he called them, from sparring in the ring.

Charlie and I talked for six hours that first evening. At first, he came across as cool and reserved, but it wasn't hard to draw him out. The way he spoke about his girlfriends – his long-term partner Eva, who also had a boyfriend, and Maya, who he'd broken up with since we matched – was both candid and thoughtful. When he reached for my hand across the table, it felt natural: less an escalation in a process designed to culminate in sex, and more an acknowledgement of the ease and connection we both felt with each other.

Charlie was an involved and responsive listener. I found it easy to open up to him about everything from the very beginning: my infidelity, Marcus's struggles, my dating escapades. 'What a dick! Fuck him!' he said in response to a story about a hook-up who'd ghosted me, making me feel like he was on my side. 'Give me a month. I will get to the bottom of this!' he said, making me laugh. His playful energy was infectious; I could tell we'd have a great night out at a club or party.

When Charlie told me, 'I feel I already know you,' it didn't feel like a line; his sincerity was palpable. But I'd dated enough to know that people can say all sorts of things in the moment because it feels good. What matters is what they do after the moment has passed.

'Well, we *have* been chatting for a year,' I pointed out.

'It feels absurd to refer back to my digital... *voorordelen?* –' here he paused to search for the English word, but I waved him on '– of you, even if it does match your IRL self. For one thing, I expected you to be taller, but I didn't think you'd be so cute. I like talking to you and how open you are.'

'I like you too,' I replied, 'and I think you're charming. I'm sure I want to see you again, but I'm wondering why we haven't kissed yet.'

'Oh, that can still happen!' he said. 'But not in this setting.'

He did kiss me, as I walked him back to Central Station to catch the last train to Nijmegen. There was a moment of hesitation right before he turned towards me, which felt almost as if the kiss was an expectation he felt pressured to deliver. Later I wondered, if I hadn't put him on the spot in the pub, whether he might have kissed me at all.

But his hesitation was too brief, and my anticipation too strong. So when he pushed me against the brick wall of Molly Malone's Irish Pub and kissed me full on the lips, warm hands scooting into my puffer jacket, reaching around my waist and down the back of my tights for a quick, juicy squeeze, I welcomed it.

'You're so hot,' he murmured when we broke apart. 'Why don't you stop by sometime?'

Infatuation.

That's what it was.

AREN'T YOU AFRAID OF FEELINGS?

Infatuation was what got me on the two-hour train ride to visit Charlie at home in Nijmegen several weeks later. Infatuation was what made my breath catch in my throat at the sight of his chiselled torso in the bedroom mirror as he took me from behind for the first time. Infatuation was the source of the giddy thrill that bubbled up like a hot spring inside me, as I watched him bring an oven-hot pizza into the bedroom wearing nothing but a tiny apron and a cheeky grin, looking adorable and sexy as hell. Infatuation made me sit back in his and Eva's bed, flushed with pleasure and aglow with self-satisfaction, as he scampered off to the kitchen for more red wine to refill my glass, his perky butt peeking out obscenely from behind his apron.

Marcus and I had spent the previous evening wrapped up in each other, enjoying an intense rope-play session. His interest in *shibari* had deepened since we'd done the workshop together with a private instructor. Now he was part of a WhatsApp group that exchanged tips and photos, where teacher and students critiqued each other's technique. The afterglow of our rope play had lasted until the next morning; having invested time and energy in our intimacy, the parting was easy, the send-off tender.

My wrists and ankles still bore rope marks from my own husband the night before. Not twenty-four hours later, here I was being ploughed and plied with pizza and wine by this beautiful man. *This is pretty fucking sweet*, I thought to myself. *I must be doing something right. Finally.*

The rope marks didn't escape Charlie's attention. 'Marcus seems like such a cool guy,' he said, after I told him about the night before. 'I'd love to have a beer with him sometime, ask what it was like from his perspective.'

I laughed out loud. 'That's never going to happen,' I said. Marcus would never agree to it. He preferred the boundaries between our dating life and home life to be iron-clad, never to meet any of the men I dated – to make it easier, I suspected, to pretend that they didn't exist.

'Why not?' Charlie asked. The way he said it was so guileless and open, almost childlike, that I stopped and thought: *Why not, indeed?*

I discovered that this was a particular talent of Charlie's: distilling the complexities of polyamory into simple questions that made me stop and think. The way he walked, talked, lived and breathed the *open* in open relationships made me pause and examine my own beliefs and assumptions about myself, my relationships, and the people involved in them. Talking to Charlie helped me articulate some new insight that was already simmering beneath the surface, and I liked that.

Charlie and his girlfriend, with their multiple partners, were doing polyamory at another level. He was a relationship geek who'd done his homework, read all the right books, used all the correct terms. Eva wasn't just his girlfriend, she was his *nesting partner*, the one he lived with and anchored his daily life to. Their partnership was *non-hierarchical*: whereas I had promised to prioritize my marriage to Marcus over all else, Charlie's relationship with Eva didn't necessarily take precedence over his romance with Maya, even though they lived together and had been together longer, and he strove to give equal weight to both women's feelings and desires. What he felt for Eva when she had expansive experiences with her boyfriend or other lovers was *compersion*, loosely defined as the opposite of jealousy. Discourse in polyamorous communities often points to compersion as a goal and measure of health in open relationships, a feeling that takes skill and practice to achieve. Compersion means being genuinely happy for a partner, even if that happiness has nothing to do with you.

Though Charlie was clearly a very sexual creature, his thoughtful approach to open relationships hinged on the belief that feelings were natural, always involved, and had to be considered. I began to see that there could be more to open relationships than casual sex. It might seem more complex, but it didn't have to be. It could simply be kinder and more genuine.

Too often in my escapades, I'd felt like a kink dispenser – as in the case of Theo, whose attraction to me seemed secondary to my ability to sissify him – or a box to tick. I had lost count of the number of times I'd heard a man say: 'I've always wanted to fuck an Asian woman/mom/somebody else's wife/⎯⎯⎯ [insert kink or physical attribute here].' I wanted to be treated like a human being, not an item on a bucket list. Surely other humans wanted that, too.

The thought of being more myself and bringing feelings into intimate encounters appealed to me. It might sound counterintuitive, after so recently having recovered from a violation of trust, but I had handicapped myself then by numbing what I sensed and felt. If I allowed myself to feel, express and consider feelings, I could choose better – and treat people better in return. If the way I was with Charlie, and he with me, was any indication, it felt easier and more natural.

On paper, Charlie was the perfect lover: an experienced non-monogamist, tender and tough, engaging and interested, charming but not cocky. We got along well and could talk and laugh for hours. The sex was good because we both brought considerable experience to the table. In the past, this would have been good enough for a casual hook-up, but a spark was missing, and I couldn't pinpoint why.

Infatuation made me like the *idea* of a sexual relationship with Charlie more than what was actually there. Infatuation made me ignore the little niggling doubts in our connection, the same pinpricks of hesitation as before our first kiss. Infatuation made me override my doubts – was this worth a two-hour train ride each way? Could I hold his interest? Was this really for me?

So I persisted in seeing him anyway.

At first, my willingness to date Charlie didn't sit well with Marcus. Was Charlie so special that I – who'd arranged the logistics of my daily life, from our child's school to her daycare to the desk I rented at a creative studio, so that nothing was further than a ten-minute bicycle ride from my front door – would literally go the distance just to see him?

'Did you just decide to sleep over at his house and not tell me?' Marcus snapped after I'd straggled in once at 3 a.m. My commute from Charlie's that night had been slow and arduous, plagued by a series of train delays in the bitter cold, but as far as dates went, it wasn't particularly late.

'Well – no. I'm here, aren't I?' I said, trying to keep a soothing tone. He must have been feeling particularly incensed – or threatened – to wait up for me. Conventional marital wisdom says never go to bed angry at each other, but this time I chose a hot shower and sleep over a fight. It was the far saner option.

In the morning, waking to each other, Marcus curled up in my arms and laid his head on my chest. 'It made me irrationally angry, thinking how you'd gone all the way to

Nijmegen for this guy,' he said. 'I'm sorry. I forgot about all the times you've gone the extra mile for me.'

Just like that, we were good again. Marcus's resilience and ability to take responsibility for his own feelings was growing; in turn, I no longer felt like the guilty party, compelled to placate him.

One evening, I stopped over in Nijmegen on the way home from visiting family in Brussels. Charlie and I were naked in bed, catching up over steaming mugs of cinnamon tea.

'Hey, darlin', guess wut? I'm gunna be on the tee-vee!' he drawled. Sometimes when he was feeling playful, Charlie loved to put on the character of the strong, silent type in an old country Western. It suited him, and when his accent skewed more towards Yosemite Sam than John Wayne, he would always get a laugh out of me.

'Well, gosh, darlin', that's excitin'!' I replied. 'How come?'

'Eva and I were in a panel interview about polyamory that's going to be on Dutch TV. I'm afraid they're going to make me come out looking like an asshole.'

'Why?' I asked.

'They wanted to know why we're polyamorous,' he said. 'At first, everyone was like . . . deeper connections, more community, more love. Okay, fine. I get that. But for a roomful of people who are supposed to be honest about everything, nobody wanted to talk about the elephant in the room. So I felt it was my duty to say it.'

'Which is . . . ?'

'Sex!' We both laughed. 'Isn't it true, though? If you want to be honest about it, sex *is* the primary motivation behind all of this. Sex is why we're here.'

'That's true,' I said, 'and I can see how it might be hard to admit, especially on national TV. But even if sex *is* the main reason I'm here, it's not just about sex any more. I find that the conditions that need to be met for me to enjoy sex are more complex now.'

'Like what?'

'Like, I need to find you interesting as a person. I need to like you.'

'So you like me?' he teased, a grin playing on his lips as he leaned in for a kiss.

'I like you a lot,' I said. 'Like, I need to get a sense of our dynamic, or at least what it could be. And – this has become really important to me recently – I need to feel good about myself. I don't *need* good sex to feel good about myself. It's the other way around. The sex can only be as good as I feel about myself. And that won't happen if I'm not treated well. At the very least, like a human. With consideration and respect.'

'Very mature,' he said, reaching over and squeezing my hand. 'By the way, I feel like I should apologize for my low libido tonight.'

'Oh no, don't,' I protested. We'd made out a little, but neither of us could seem to muster up the gusto for a full round.

'You have certain expectations coming here. I'm aware of that, especially now that we're talking about sex as the primary motivation for being here.'

'You shouldn't apologize, or feel you have to,' I said. 'I like that I can come here for a good conversation, as much as good sex.'

Previously, I would have considered a two-hour commute that didn't end in sex a bad evening, a waste of time. But here I was, content with cuddles, cinnamon tea, and a deep, easy intimacy that felt almost better than sex, if not at least as satisfying.

With Charlie, my definition of what felt good – and, more importantly, safe – began to shift. Sticking to random hook-ups and casual sex had been my way of making Marcus feel secure as we ventured beyond the confines of monogamy, by assuring him that no one would ever get too close to pose a real threat. But the territory that Charlie seemed to occupy so comfortably – a terrain of deeper connections, of feelings both involved and considered – began to appeal to me, a safe place just outside my comfort zone. It dawned on me that not only was our marriage worthy of safety and protection, but so was I.

Spring came and, with it, a clarifying moment in my relationship with Charlie. I was too infatuated to have initiated it; Charlie, with the thoughtfulness and honesty I admired, led me there.

We'd decided to go to a music festival in the woods on a rainy April Sunday. Charlie was a great date: he looked smashing in my outfit, a vintage red-and-gold floral jacket that had belonged to my mom and a pair of red cat-eye shades, and he loved to dance. We were waiting out a downpour inside a canvas tent before making a mad dash for the shuttle bus back to the city. The final beats of DJ sets about to end echoed through the festival grounds, fading into the night as Charlie cradled me on his lap, his strong arms around my waist.

'I've been thinking about us,' he began.

As soon as he said the words, I knew where he was headed: this was the end of our sexual relationship. I did not resist.

It was, as Charlie always seemed to make it, uncomplicated, clear and honest. Though we enjoyed each other's company and shared a deep connection, what we didn't have was the sexual or romantic urgency needed to fuel a cross-country affair. We were, quite simply, friends.

I thought: *Yes, that's exactly it.*

I expected my ego to be bruised, but instead I felt . . . free. Free from disappointment and expectations. Even relieved. It felt less like something ending than something clicking and falling into place with an *A-ha! So that's what this is!* It felt less like rejection and more like recognition.

Then I blurted out: 'But can we still have sex sometimes?'

He laughed and squeezed my waist. 'You're so cute! Sure, if the vibe is right.'

Charlie and I headed back to the city soon after, and back to our separate lives. Our friendship has since outlasted many casual lovers, our intimacy effortless and reliable even if we only see each other once or twice a year.

It was Charlie who found the right term for us in the polyamorous lexicon: comet partners. Comets are occasional lovers who exist at a comfortable distance from one another, but remain connected without the expectation of romance, commitment, or even sex.

When life brings us into each other's orbit, our connection comes alive, burning intense and bright in each other's presence, no matter how brief the moment. Then we shoot away into space until the next time we meet, whenever that might be.

My brief romance with Charlie taught me the quiet ease of recognition. To give a connection with someone time to reveal its nature instead of forcing it. To pause and reflect rather than chase and react. To learn to recognize something for what it is and acknowledge it for what it's not. That way, it feels easy and natural, like everything just makes sense.

Meeting Charlie made me ready for connections beyond casual adventures. I just didn't know it yet.

*

After being off dating apps for months, I reinstalled Tinder on my phone long enough to swipe through and wince at what a cesspool it had become. The app had reached mass ubiquity since Marcus and I had joined three years earlier, but a bigger user base didn't necessarily translate to better pickings. It seemed I had to swipe five times as much to reach even a moderately appealing profile. But in the 24-hour window before I deleted Tinder again, I found Rick.

Rick had grown up shuttling between a rough neighbourhood on the fringes of Amsterdam and a city on the banks of the Amazon. He had just moved back from Brazil, where his girlfriend was stuck sorting out her immigration paperwork. While waiting for her to move to Amsterdam, Rick lived between his separated parents' houses and had agreed to an open relationship.

Rick was Dutch on the outside – blonde and bearded, towering and rugged – but Brazilian on the inside: warm, charismatic and spontaneous. It was a potent combination. He sent long, frequent audio messages over WhatsApp, his booming voice the audio equivalent of a crushing bear hug, creating instant familiarity. Our first date ended on the floor of his mother's living room, where he had dragged down the mattress from his childhood bedroom in a burst of impulsive energy that I would come to recognize as typical Rick.

Moments before the first of many orgasms in this setting, I wondered if I was too old to be conducting my sex life within the proximity of anyone's parents. But Rick simply covered my mouth with a meaty hand and urged me to 'let 'er rip'.

If I was infatuated with Charlie, I was excited by Rick. Sex with him was rough, sensual and intense, because he was intense – full of big feelings, given to obsessive moods. But it was also erratic, and he tended to become self-critical when he couldn't 'perform', a word he used that made me uncomfortable.

Rick fantasized about sex non-stop. He loved to discuss his fantasies in detail, casting me as the star in all of them. The thought of watching me with other men in threesomes, moresomes and gangbangs sent him into overdrive. I was secretly thrilled by the idea of seeing how much I could handle; of revelling in an abundance of bodies and feeling my way through the dynamics of more than one partner; of being the focus of so much desire all at once.

By now, I had a shortlist of lovers I trusted and could call on to help me fulfil this fantasy. But each time I suggested pulling the trigger, Rick would retreat. I began to wonder if I would ever get around to any of the things we talked about exploring together.

Though he was a good-hearted man and a wild, giving lover, Rick had a generous tolerance for alcohol and cigarettes, and was a self-admitted chaser of dopamine highs. While he was up front about his own addictive tendencies, it was this side of him that made him want to get too close, too quickly. He asked if we might go away for a weekend together and invited me to bring my daughter for a tour of the fire department where he worked.

'I want more than this stolen time with you between

sunset and sunrise,' he wrote me after a long, intense night. 'But I know my place. I respect what you have with your husband and family.'

When he broke up with his long-distance girlfriend, then went on a first date that lasted three days before fast-forwarding into an exclusive relationship, I felt almost relieved. I was fond of Rick, with his big heart and uncontainable feelings, but his intensity could swallow up someone with weak or ill-defined boundaries. That wasn't going to be me; it was clear to me how far I could go, or how much I could give. I couldn't afford to meet Rick where he was – not even halfway.

By autumn, the fiery tempests of Rick were cooled by calm interludes with Marc, a silver-haired, globetrotting poker dealer.

I was impressed by Marc. First of all, he pampered me. Because he shared an apartment with other casino freelancers from abroad, we met at a different hotel every time. He was delighted when I introduced him to my favourite French bakeries in Amsterdam, preferring from then on to end every rendezvous with a civil, almost old-fashioned cake and coffee. His lingering goodbye kisses tasted of lemon, buttery pastry crust and meringue.

Marc invited me to watch him deal cards at one of the world's most prestigious poker tournaments, which was held at a big casino in the centre of Amsterdam. I turned up dressed to kill in a tight black miniskirt, red lips and high heels, expecting *Casino Royale* only to find *Family Guy* instead.

In his slim-cut suit, elegant waistcoat and crisp bow tie, Marc was James Bond in a sea of unwashed men in stained hoodies, dad jeans and trucker caps. Dealers were forbidden from socializing with guests, so I watched Marc from a distance, sipping a cocktail as he exerted his quiet dominance over the table, his elegant hands moving with deft precision on the green felt. Now and then he glanced up at me with an electricity that crackled across the room; the sly wink and unexpected kiss he blew my way before he disappeared for a break sealed our secret connection.

Marc treated sex the way he handled cards: with skill, smoothness and finesse. Most importantly, Marc was reliable. He showed up on time, was always in the mood, could go on for hours, and paid for everything so that I never had to as I did with other lovers, who would usually expect to go Dutch on dates, drinks or hotel rooms. He entertained me with stories about the old-world poker club in Paris where he learned his craft, and about the colourful characters who played at his tables from Morocco to Martinique.

Although Marc was steady, gallant, even tender at times, he never closed his eyes when we kissed. There was a formality about him that made me feel I could never bring up fantasies or kinks. Not once did he ask me about my personal life. I often wondered whether he even knew I was married or had a child, or if he simply found it irrelevant. In that way, he was almost professional in his approach to sex.

I didn't mind. I was learning about what I wanted in my lovers, paying attention to how I felt after spending time with each one. I enjoyed the thoughtfulness and intimacy of Charlie, the warmth and intensity of Rick, the competence and consistency of Marc. I appreciated how all of them desired me yet expressed respect for me, even found my boundaries sexy.

The occasional injection of novelty was nice to have, but not necessary. I was no longer prepared to stake my time and energy on just any random Tinder date for the sake of variety. Every experience had to be exceptional and unusual. Every lover had to be absolutely worth the time I spent away from my family.

*

By mutual agreement, the sessions Marcus and I had with Noam came to an end that same autumn. Marcus had grown comfortable expressing his feelings and needs, trusting that I valued them and would always consider them first. Waiting for an appointment at the therapist's office no longer felt necessary when we could check in with each other any time we wanted, over morning coffee or an evening glass of wine.

The presence of regular lovers in the background – Charlie, then Rick, followed by Marc – no longer felt like a threat. A light-hearted familiarity had crept into our exchanges about dates and dating. Marcus had begun to explore his own kinks, which are not mine to share. I reassured him that it would take much more than sexual exploration, with or without me, to erode his place in my life as a good man, a good father and a good husband. I knew we were ready to move on from therapy when Marcus told me about the way he'd come to see things.

'I've started to think of us as being in a bubble, you and me,' he began. 'What happens inside our bubble is within our sphere of responsibility. What you do outside our bubble – with other people, with dates, even with work or friends – is beyond my control. So why should I waste my energy trying to control what's outside our bubble, when I have something right here that I can put my effort into?'

We came to call it bubble theory. The more intention we

put into our bubble – the more attention, consideration, joy, pleasure – the stronger it became. We were free to choose what we did outside our bubble and with whom, as we kept on working on our own. But we had to be careful with what we brought back, whether it was a bad energy, a bad mood, or trouble.

'If we can do that, then what we do outside the bubble – be it with friends, colleagues or even lovers – doesn't harm or detract from it,' Marcus finished.

Bubble time! became a secret code, an affirmation, a cheerful refrain we sang out when we closed the door to our daughter's bedroom after tucking her in, or while breaking out the gin and tonic on a Friday night. *I can't wait for bubble time*, we'd say in the thick of crunch time at work, or on a particularly hairy Monday. *Bubble time*, we'd murmur, snuggling into each other with satisfying ease at the end of a long week.

Our final appointment with Noam felt, in a way, like graduation. After so many tumultuous months, it was a good place to be. We agreed that we could come back for a session any time we felt at odds, stuck, or needed support. We settled into a comfortable rhythm in our open marriage, where everything finally started to feel . . . normal.

Familiar. Even easy.

Then, in the winter before everything changed, I met Robert.

12

What happens if you fall in love?

It was the eyebrows that got me: thick and dark, framing wide hazel eyes set above high cheekbones in a narrow, elfin face.

I studied the lines of text below the Tinder profile photos. *Robert, 33, photographer. Loves pub quizzes, live music and local knowledge.* The bio was thin, but the brows were compelling.

I fired the first shot. *You must get compliments on your eyebrows all the time. They're amazing*, I wrote.

Why, thank you! came the reply. *They've had a rough day and appreciate the compliment. They each have their own ego and could use a boost every now and then.*

I offered his eyebrows a cuddle and a cup of tea. *Aren't you incredibly charming and quite forward*, he replied. *I haven't even asked about your man yet! Is he the real flesh-and-blood type, or just someone you've made up to start a conversation?*

After almost twelve years of marriage he's mostly real, or at least he was the last time I checked.

I see, he said. *And what are you looking for from the single, impressionable Irish guys you find on Tinder?*

Casual fun, I replied. *Interesting times with interesting people.*

His answer came quickly. *I have a feeling we're a reaction waiting to happen*, he messaged. *I have a thing for writers. Words woo me in wonderful ways, although I'm terrible at spelling.*

And I have a thing for Irish accents, I said, *but doesn't everyone?*

Mine's quite mild, but I'm sure you'll like it. May I have your number?

It happened so fast, it was almost too good to be true: a cute, charismatic Irish photographer who seemed into me, judging from the way messages pinged back and forth between us on WhatsApp. Three days later, as I cycled to Checkpoint Charlie, the cosy neighbourhood bar where we agreed to meet, I thought: *Maybe he won't even show up. Maybe he's not even real.*

I was delighted to find him there in the flesh, perched on a bar stool with a half-drained pint. His hazel eyes were even more startling in person: bright, sparkly, framed with long lashes that turned up at the corners, giving them something of a permanent twinkle.

Robert turned out to be engaging and gregarious, with the merry warmth and knack for storytelling that seems universally acknowledged to be possessed by the Irish. Our chemistry was instant, our conversation spirited. We were well past the three-hour mark when I decided I wanted to kiss him. My demure days were far behind me; all I needed was an opening.

As if reading my mind, Robert said: 'I just never know when to make the next move. Then I end up missing the moment and messing up the whole date.'

'I have a hard time believing that,' I said, looking right at him. 'You're very charming.'

'It was the eyes,' he confessed to me later. 'You gave me *this look* and I suddenly realized, *Oh! This is it! She wants you to kiss her, Robert, go on, kiss her!*'

Robert was right. The reaction that was waiting to happen found its release then, in the form of a long, deep, open-mouthed kiss that lit a delicious spark of curiosity. I wanted to find out if there was more, and what that more might be like. So when he asked, 'Would you like to come over to my place?' my answer was an unequivocal yes.

We met on a Monday. By Friday, we were on our second date. I invited him to De School for a night of dancing, which nearly turned into a disaster.

Over the past year, I'd befriended an Australian mum named Emma. We'd met at a neighbourhood café and ended up chatting for hours, work and laptops forgotten. We discovered we were two of a kind: dark-haired and curvy, working mothers who juggled parenting duties with hedonistic pleasures, and we shared an affinity for fancy cocktails and club nights. Since Emma had split from her husband and started dating again, we'd matched with many of the same men on dating apps; trading Tinder warnings over nachos and margaritas sealed our friendship.

After Elise moved back to Canada, Emma had grown into the role of my best friend and partner in crime. I was already inside the club with her when I received a call from Robert. The infamously strict door staff had barred him from entering. He sounded beside himself with mortification.

'What is it?' said Emma. 'Where is he?' I filled her in on the situation.

We pondered the possibilities in silence. 'We could go somewhere else,' I said, thinking fast and naming another club in the far reaches of Amsterdam Nieuw-West. 'Spielraum is on. We can find last-minute tickets on TicketSwap.'

Emma wrinkled her nose. 'I hate that place. Not a fan of Spielraum, either.'

'I know.' I didn't want to plead, but Emma got it. She gave a deep sigh. 'Fine. Let's get our coats.'

Outside we rescued Robert, who was all nervous laughter and Irish charm turned up to 200 per cent to compensate for his rookie mistake, and piled into an Uber.

After we got into the club, Emma pulled me aside. 'I'm third-wheeling really hard here!' she hissed. 'I'm going home.'

'Emma,' I said, mortified. 'I'm sorry!'

'You two are all over each other. Seriously.'

'But –'

'Stay. Really, stay. But you owe me. Big time.'

With a hug and 'Bye, lovebirds!' she was gone.

Left to our own devices, Robert and I ended up on a plush couch in a secluded corner, partially hidden from dancing bodies and pulsating lights. Robert pushed aside the deep V of my plunging red lace bodysuit, bent down and sucked on my nipples until I came. If the person sitting next to us heard anything between the booming bass and Robert's hand over my mouth, they didn't let on.

'I think I'm going to let you lead me into all sorts of dangerous and delicious situations,' he said.

Everything about me seemed new and exciting to Robert, and his enthusiasm reeled me in. I liked how eager and willing he was: curious, animated and up for everything. I'd never kissed a man who wanted so much to be lost in a kiss.

I remember thinking: *He wants to fall in love, this one.*

Every lover has their own personal boundaries of intimacy: unspoken rules about things better left alone, unasked and unexplored. Subtle signs are littered everywhere: in the way they kiss goodbye, or the haste with which they get up to shower after sex, or how they speak (or don't speak) of particular events or figures in their lives. It's why some people can feel like you've known them forever after just one evening, and why others can still feel like strangers after six months of dating.

I had learned that by paying attention to these clues, I could figure out my place in someone's life quickly enough: how they wanted to engage with me, the level of familiarity they were comfortable with, and how close they were willing to let me in – or not. I could then conduct myself appropriately and reciprocate in kind.

The open book was rare, which made Robert quite a find. He was a whimsical pop-up whose pages blew open in the wind, revealing a hundred little doors and windows that were a delight to peek into. Free of guile or game, Robert had deft, instinctive ways of making me feel welcome in his world, as though I could let my guard down and be fully myself around him, too.

It wasn't long before Robert began to confide in me about Diana, a woman he'd met on a farm in Australia and fallen for. When he talked about her, it wasn't to play mind games or to put me in my place as a casual fling. Robert simply wore his heart on his sleeve that way, and it seemed his heart belonged on the other side of the world with Diana. I liked getting to know him better and readjusted my initial assessment of him. He didn't want to fall in love; he already was.

I saw Robert infrequently, whenever I could slip him into my juggling act of work and family, parties and dates, writing classes and travel. But, like me, Robert was a whirlwind. He always had something going on, whether it was sewing a pair of tiny pants for a friend's newborn baby or creating new, original still-life photographs for his solo exhibition.

Robert invited me to his studio, where under the hot bright gaze of his lights, bits of plastic he'd salvaged from the trash came alive with his obsessive prodding and poking before being immortalized by his camera. I enjoyed dropping in on whatever project he was magicking, and often left enchanted and energized, as though I was one of the objects he infused with his effervescence and transformed into art.

Whenever Robert was creating, there was an air of the mad scientist about him, with his dark curls sticking up every which way, randomly-on-purpose mismatched socks, and colourful printed shirts adorned with an assortment of clips, clamps and strips of tape. But there was also a bit of the child who animated his toys with a vivid imagination, a flair for the dramatic, and an honest belief in magic.

Robert's best friend transformed her house into a gallery for his second solo exhibition. On opening night, everyone I met – from his mentors and colleagues to the family and friends who flew in from Dublin for the occasion – seemed to adore Robert, drawing me even deeper into his world. Wine overflowed and laughter rang late into the night. In the wee hours, Robert and I slipped upstairs to the guest bedroom where he bent me over, pulled up my dress, and pushed my panties aside. Urgent and breathless, we fucked deliriously in the dark before falling asleep on top of the winter coats piled high on the bed.

Robert entered my orbit as others drifted in and out of it. Rick flung himself into a new relationship with an alarming but not unexpected intensity, and Marc was called away to glitzy casinos in exotic places, but I hardly had time to be broken up about their departure. There was just too much going on, too much I still wanted to experience and explore.

Dating was a revolving door with new people streaming in and out all the time, and Robert was just one of many. In Rotterdam I met Marlies and Jos, a sexy Dutch couple with whom I exchanged kisses in a three-way make-out that made the bartender's eyes pop out on to the countertop. I went on my first date with a woman: Carolien, a bisexual young mother whose angelic face and cascade of dark-blonde curls made me feel like a nervous sixteen-year-old.

Life was full and rich. My marriage was solid and secure. I was a very busy woman.

But in March 2020, all of that ground to a halt.

*

When news broke of the first wave of pandemic deaths in Europe, I was still shaking off the fatigue and exhilaration of my first mother–daughter holiday and a perk of my Instagram side gig, a sponsored girls-only skiing trip in Austria. Only twenty-four hours after our flight back to Amsterdam, authorities closed down Alpine ski resorts following an outbreak in Tyrol. We made it back just in time.

The Netherlands shut down the day before our daughter turned seven. Uncertain and fearful, we decided to cancel the birthday party we'd planned and binned the treats we'd made for her to take to school. I cried at the dining table when we broke the news to her, and again after I put her to bed.

Schools, shops, cafés, restaurants, bars and clubs shut down. Marcus's daily commute to his office in Rotterdam was replaced by a never-ending black hole of all-day video calls. Normalcy was cancelled overnight.

Nobody knew anything for sure, least of all how long this would last. 'We'll be dancing again by July,' I remember Emma saying. In a matter of weeks, she revised her fearless forecast to September. Putting our lives on hold until then seemed impossible. If we had only known.

Within the first few days of the pandemic, Marcus and I switched into crisis mode and kicked into gear as a team. We cobbled together a makeshift schedule that included math and sports with Marcus, and reading and writing (all in Dutch, thanks to a link provided by school administrators) and violin practice with me. Unfettered by the pace of her peers, our daughter tore through everything on our haphazard curriculum. The constant scramble to come up with more fell to me while Marcus waged his daily battle with corporate panic over Zoom.

Yet that first lockdown held its own strange beauty, magnifying minute domestic pleasures. Liberated from the morning rush and daily school run, I relished our leisurely sleep-ins, cuddling our daughter while the cat curled up, heavy and warm, on our legs. Marcus baked fresh *pan de sal* for breakfast, the yeasty smell of the neighbourhood bakeries of our Filipino childhood filling our home with nostalgia and comfort. We sowed seeds in cardboard take-out containers and watched them grow on the windowsills, pushing their delicate green heads up into the early spring sunshine.

Above all, my body took to the enforced downtime like a desert caravan to water. Like the rest of the planet, I was overdue for a reset. I wasn't even aware I'd been running myself into the ground until the lockdown forced me to rest.

Marcus was my rock: his logic and practicality, his steady presence and calm reassurance. With him, the unknown seemed less a fearsome chasm than a bridge we could traverse together, hand in hand and step by step. The crisis only confirmed that we were the perfect partners for each other and made a great team. There was no one else I'd rather be stuck at home with, even if it was for the indefinite future.

Together, one day at a time, we adjusted.

*

'You want to WHAT?' Marcus exclaimed.

'I want to start seeing Robert again,' I repeated.

'You and I haven't had sex since this whole clusterfuck began. Now you want to go and have sex with someone else?' he asked, incredulous. 'How do you have the energy for this? Where's the energy for *our* sex life?'

'I don't *have* energy,' I said. 'It's all going into this hamster wheel of home schooling – sorry, *distance learning* – and risk management and figuring out what we can do and not do and God knows whatever else. Do *you* have energy for our sex life?'

'No, I'm exhausted!'

'We both are,' I said. 'Look, Marcus, I know what I'm asking is not an easy thing. But if this is going to go on for as long as they say it is, I need to put some things back in place so I can start functioning normally again. I can't power through this the way you can. I can't go on like this forever.'

'I need to think about it,' Marcus said at last. 'Can I think about it?'

'Take your time,' I said.

The next morning, Marcus came to me with his answer while our child was busy with schoolwork. The speed at which Marcus could now resolve challenging questions surprised and amazed me. The trust we had built through the years was serving us well, making difficult conversations easier.

Though they were fewer and further between, Marcus's

own adventures – and the moments of intense intimacy we'd shared – had filtered into that foundation of trust. He told me he couldn't judge me for what I'd asked of him, because he knew first-hand how energizing and life-affirming such experiences – and connections – could be.

The roots of empathy go deeper and yield more abundance than the desire to please or the fear of loss. Marcus saw I was struggling and wanted me to be happy, but that wasn't the only reason he consented to my seeing Robert again. He was saying yes to this simply because he understood.

Bringing up my needs had been less disruptive than cathartic for both of us. Our talk allowed Marcus to release some of his own frustrations and opened up an opportunity for him to reflect on what he needed to get through this. It still took me by surprise when he thanked me for conversations such as these.

Marcus made it clear that our bubble needed attention, too. Without the usual resources we relied on – our child's school routine and the occasional sleepover, the light-hearted romance of date nights, or the sense of freedom and release we found in the club – the pandemic made it that much harder to nurture our marriage. We were both running on empty. If one of us could bring energy back into our bubble, ultimately it would benefit our relationship and our family.

'It's not fair for me to demand energy from you for our sex life, when I don't have it myself,' Marcus said. 'But if all of this has shown me anything, it's that the fundamentals of who we are as a couple are strong. So do what you need to do. Normalize your social life. Reclaim some energy. Then, when things settle down a bit, let's build up our bubble again.'

*

Space cake.

Robert and I agreed that our return to physical contact would benefit from a slice of space cake, if only because I'd never tried it and he enjoyed it. Besides, there was nothing else to do, nowhere to go. Why not fill the hours with something new?

At first glance, Boerenjongens in Oud-West looks like an old-world pharmacy with glass-fronted wooden cabinets and assistants in crisp white lab coats. But it dispenses cures of a different kind, including what is said to be the most delicious space cake in all of Amsterdam: a rich chocolate brownie baked with generous portions of marijuana-infused butter, handled by white-gloved hands and wrapped up in a shiny white box with gold trim.

Robert and I met at sundown by the canal in front of Boerenjongens to procure our treat. 'It would be good to see the world before we cocoon ourselves,' he said. By the time we arrived at Robert's apartment and sliced into the faintly herbal-smelling chocolate square, I was nervous and trembling, my heart pounding with anticipation and risk.

Our first kiss in the kitchen – our first kiss in months – was ravenous and lingering, the deep open wetness of Robert's mouth shocking in its foreignness. Had our senses been so deprived? It was as if I'd never kissed him before, or anyone else, for that matter.

My restless nights of vivid dreams filled with fantasies of enmeshed bodies; Robert's craving for touch and my need for release; his loneliness and my anxiety; the fear of death and the lure of the forbidden; our fragile trust and sense of safety. All these were fuel to the fire of the kisses that followed. Shedding our clothes and kicking them aside, we made it as far as the living room before Robert pulled me down on to the carpet, taking what I was only too eager to give.

Then the space cake kicked in, making a funhouse mirror of time, looping the seconds into spirals, peeling apart the layers of the minutes, warping the edges of the hours so that they blended into one another and never seemed to end. In those boundless hours, I had been gifted the liberty to think of no one but myself: permission granted by my husband, my lover and myself.

With Robert, I could be selfish, greedy and demanding. 'You're insatiable,' he said long after we made it to the bedroom, when the most intense peaks had ebbed into tingling ripples. 'By now most women would have said: *Enough!*'

Most men too, I thought. Whenever he seemed spent, Robert would dig deep and find more to give – a fresh burst of energy, a hand around my throat, a teeth-clenching grip that blossomed into a bruise on my shoulder – surprising me with his eagerness to please and lavish attention to my pleasure.

'I don't want it to end,' I remember him saying somewhere in between gasps and cries, between ragged breaths and slippery sweat, between mouthfuls of moist rich chocolate and the subtle grassy flavour of butter melting on to my tongue.

Whoever they were, they were right, I remember thinking, *about the brownie.*

Towards the end of the evening, when we were both exhausted, Robert made a remark that stayed with me. 'What we have exists in its own bubble, and it works very well in its own bubble. Don't you think so?'

Bubble! I thought. *Do you and I have a bubble now, too?*

Instead, I said, 'It's a very nice bubble.'

*

WHAT HAPPENS IF YOU FALL IN LOVE?

The relentless routine of life in lockdown continued. My freelance copywriting work dried up overnight, making me a full-time, stay-at-home mother once more. For the first time in years I was as routine-bound, overwhelmed and hyper-focused on my daughter as I had been in the early days after her birth. But now, the baby was a bright, inquisitive child to educate and entertain, with nowhere for us to go.

It was a period of intensive parenting. I dug deep to find my inner Pinterest mom and scoured the internet for colouring pages, craft projects, reading material in Filipino, anything and everything to keep our child engaged and occupied. We baked, gardened, drew, made up games to play, wrote letters to her schoolfriends and delivered them by bicycle. She was learning how to read, and I devised new locations for her to practise in every day: a pillow fort, a tent made of blankets, in the bathtub, on the balcony, under the dining table. Her favourite spot was in our bed, snuggled against me, listening to my belly gurgling as it rose and fell with my breath.

After she finished her improvised lesson plan and went off to play on her own, I would close the bedroom door, crawl into bed, plug into the internet, and succumb to anxiety. The news cycle sent me into a tailspin of fear and frustration, even more so when I thought of my mother and sister in the Philippines. Some afternoons I cried while doomscrolling on my phone, but mostly my brain shut down. Sleep was the easiest way to block out all the confusion and reset my emotional equilibrium. I craved the first few moments of peace after waking up, when my mind was blank and free from worry.

Meanwhile, Marcus wrestled with corporate absurdities like the ice-cream supply in Eastern Europe, on never-ending Zoom calls that drained his energy. Some evenings he crawled into bed and laid his head on my lap, stressed and frazzled. I would cradle him and stroke his hair, listening as he poured out the frustrations of the day. My husband needed mothering, too.

Throughout the week, I belonged to my family. But for a few hours each weekend, I was off the hook. I could stop being a mother and a wife, and just be myself, or whoever I was when I didn't have a function to perform. No matter how hard the week had been, I knew that once I hopped on my bike, I was only twelve minutes away from freedom.

My weekly evening at Robert's became my escape, no longer a carefree luxury, but a lifeline. In an unwitting mirror of the code I shared with Marcus, Robert began calling them bubble nights as well.

The exertion and euphoria of those nights replaced the lost delirium of the dance floor, silencing the roar of anxiety, bringing me back to my senses. Before daybreak, I would steal out of his bedroom, pedal home with stiff thighs and aching legs, crawl into bed with Marcus for a few hours of sleep, and wake up feeling reborn.

Replenished, I had more to give. People, relationships and the world seemed to be falling apart all around me, but our little unit held. I began to flourish, even as so much of what we had once called normal life remained frozen.

I had a secret source of playfulness, joy and energy, and his name was Robert.

*

Between Robert's elegantly backrolled joints, the bottles of natural wine I'd grown to love, and the occasional lick of a fingertip dabbed into a bag of MDMA – a pinch compared to what I'd been used to before the clubs shut down – nights in the bubble could get hazy.

We filled breathless pauses with fantasies and confessions, dreams and indiscretions, half-knowing that the finer points of our rambling conversations could fade in the morning light. I regaled Robert with episodes from my catalogue of lovers and misadventures; he told me about his attraction to Jane, a glowing, moon-faced girl from his circle of friends, who I recalled meeting briefly at his exhibition.

Robert always spoke of Diana. The pandemic had turned Australia from an improbable fantasy into an impenetrable fortress, making Diana – and whatever hope he nurtured of rekindling their holiday romance – into a distant dream. Ever the optimist, I was confident that as soon as borders re-opened, he would be on the first plane to Australia. I only wanted to enjoy him, and this, for a little while before he flew away, possibly even for good.

Each night in the bubble was a little different, with an element of whimsy that I loved. One evening I was Robert's doll, a sexy plaything to adorn with the lingerie I'd brought over. 'Boys like to play with dolls, too. Oh, open-toed stilettos! Deepa, how did you *know*?' he'd cried, picking through my overnight bag and pulling out one outfit after the other.

Another night, I was his hairdresser. With barber shops closed for nearly three months, his hair had started sprouting unruly wings on both sides. 'I look like Robin Williams in *Good Will Hunting*,' he said mournfully, showing me a clip on YouTube. I giggled at the likeness, then offered to bring over my scissors. It turned out that Robert's painful insecurity about his hair and his paralysing hatred of haircuts was the first real vulnerability he revealed to me. 'This means I really trust you now,' he said.

No other woman had ever cut his hair, except Diana. And no barber would ever wear a flouncy black miniskirt, assless panties, lacy thigh-highs and stilettos to give him a trim.

I was careful with my scissors and comb, trying to be as soothing and gentle as I could as he squirmed and fretted beneath my touch. I sighed in relief when he preened in front of the hallway mirror and pronounced his satisfaction with the result.

'I've been keeping you at arm's length a little bit on purpose,' he said as we lay together, limbs tangled and gleaming with sweat, in the warm light of his bedroom lamp.

'Oh,' I said. It didn't seem that way; I'd just assumed he had a lot going on, like I did. 'Why is that?'

'We have no future together, Deepa. This is the longest time I've been with someone without falling in love.'

'What do you think it would look like if you *weren't* keeping your distance from me?' I asked him.

'I hadn't considered it,' he replied, taking a swig from a can of beer and placing it on his bedside table. 'It's not really an option, is it? You said it would never go there.'

'It's not,' I said mildly. 'I just wonder.'

'I'd want you to be around more,' he said slowly. 'We'd see each other more often, maybe three or four times a week. We'd be a lot more involved. I'd want you to be with me in my ups and downs. But could you do that, Deepa? Could you bend the rules so that you could sleep over? Could you wake up with me the next morning?'

'No. I can't do any of that. It's a lot of responsibility. More than I can handle, or wish to at this point.'

'I would just never be the priority,' Robert said.

He wasn't wrong. But in the dreamy haze of the bubble, it didn't seem to matter.

*

It was the haircut that rang alarm bells for Marcus, sending him into a flare-up of jealousy that I'd almost forgotten he was capable of.

'You're jealous because I offered to cut his hair?' I found this ridiculous, and I felt trapped and controlled. 'Do you realize we spend all our time together now? Both you and I are home 24/7, and we're together more than ever, except for those few hours a week! Do you want to own those hours, too?' I demanded. 'How much of my time and energy do you want? When will it ever be enough?'

'I understand your need to gain energy back from being around people, and that you need to feel free of responsibility every now and then. But *this*, I did not sign up for,' Marcus said. 'This feels like you're a couple, like something you'd do for a boyfriend. So what are you?'

'He was starting to look like a mad scientist! I thought I could do it, so I did. That's all it is!'

'Is it really?' Marcus asked. 'Where is this going, Deepa?'

'Nowhere,' I said. 'It's going nowhere.'

Where could it go? Robert longed to be a father someday; that much was clear from the way he doted on children, sewed clothes for his friends' babies, and spoke about his own father, who had passed away several years before. The kind of love Robert wanted – the kind of woman he needed – was someone who would make him the father he wanted to become, who would be the mother to the children he dreamed of having.

That was never going to be me.

So, whatever this was, it was temporary. It would end one day, though it wasn't clear when or how. Until then, I just wanted to enjoy it for what it was, for as long as I could.

*

The world caught its breath as spring warmed into summer. Schools and daycares reopened; playdates between children were allowed again. Open-air socializing was deemed safe, and Amsterdammers jostled for tables at the makeshift terraces that sprang up on sidewalks all over the city. A mood of relief and cautious optimism set in as we shook off our collective cabin fever. The Dutch government encouraged lonely singles to find *knuffelmaatjes* – cuddle mates, a euphemism for friends with benefits. Underground raves were happening again.

A measure of normalcy returned; with it came time and energy for my marriage. With our daughter back at school and reunited with her friends, Marcus and I rushed to spend every moment of child-free time together. We welcomed every invitation for a playdate with grateful enthusiasm, then sped off to the park to share a joint or a cold bottle of Viognier in the sunshine. We lay next to each other in the grass within neatly spray-painted circles that were exactly 1.5 metres apart, which would have felt absurd if not for our sheer relief to be outside again, and together once more – not as Mama and Papa, but as Marcus and Deepa. With the return of our intimacy, Marcus's jealousy abated, just as we both knew it would.

I reconnected with Charlie, my comet from the galaxy of Nijmegen, who agreed that technology was good for some things after all, and that video calls were a terrific replacement for the two-hour train ride between Nijmegen and Amsterdam.

'Why is he keeping his distance?' Charlie asked after I'd caught him up on Robert over FaceTime. 'What's so bad about falling in love with you? You're awesome.'

'Charlie, I have a family,' I said.

'Yes, but he already knows that. And he's *still* seeing you.'

'We just don't have a future together,' I said, repeating Robert's words to me.

Charlie hadn't lost his knack for asking questions that made me stop and reassess my perspective. He simply replied: 'So? Do you need one?'

My conversation with Charlie was the first real pause, a nudge towards reflection instead of constant action and reaction. For the first time, I allowed myself to think about falling in love with Robert.

I realized I no longer believed that romantic love was the only way to love. I loved different people in different ways; I even had a kind of love for Rui and Charlie, though it might be better described as platonic. Being in an open marriage had shifted my understanding, seeding the definition of another kind of love in my mind.

Perhaps love was, in its purest and simplest form, a kind of recognition: a profound appreciation of what made someone worth loving, free of the need to hold on to them. I didn't need to build a life with someone or have a future with them to do that.

I thought I might be capable of loving Robert in a way

that was open, not possessive, neither asking for nor expecting anything from him, without reshuffling the existing commitments of my life. But his idea of love was goal-oriented, with a particular purpose and trajectory. We were too different in that sense.

On my next night in the bubble, dreamy and verbose thanks to a fingertip lick of MDMA dust, I attempted to share my newfound insight with Robert. 'I think you have a very specific definition of love,' I said.

'Ohhh . . . kay? What does that mean?' he asked.

We were curled up in bed, with our legs folded and leaning against each other.

'Falling in love has: One. Purpose. Only,' I said, poking the top of his knee with my index finger, marking it as the goal. 'You want a family.'

'Is it that obvious?'

'Oh yeah,' I said. 'The only kind of love that you want, that's worth it to you, is a love that will get you there. To marriage and wife and kids. But I see things differently.'

I circled my finger around his kneecap, lightly touching his leg in half a dozen places. 'For me, love can look like and be so many other things. All of this can be love, too. And this, and this, and this.'

Now well and truly afloat in clouds of blah-blah-blah, I went on: 'I think I already love you a little bit. And I don't need anything from you, I suppose, except to be around you and know that you think I'm special.'

For a heartbeat, I felt his shock.

'But you are, Deepa!' he said. 'You're the most unique personality I've ever come across. I had this whole thing with Diana, and this attraction to Jane. Then you came along with your own – what do I even call it? Your own gravity and atmosphere. You're a disturbance in my continuum.'

The clouds that had sent me floating down this stream of consciousness were already starting to drift away. 'Oh, Robert, don't worry about it,' I said. 'I mean, what's the worst that can happen?'

*

Aren't you afraid of falling in love?

People who ask me this question tend to be sceptics. They tend to have a pretty set idea of how love and relationships ought to work. They often want to be proven right and believe they eventually will be.

You think it's all fun and games now, they say, wagging the proverbial finger at my salacious escapades, my open marriage. *Wait till you fall in love. Then it'll be a disaster. Then maybe you'll come to your senses and stop risking a perfectly good thing for all this nonsense. You'll see.*

What is so disastrous about falling in love?

Falling in love, and the whole concept of romantic love, is loaded with meaning. Depending on the culture we are born into and where we are in life, falling in love triggers a sequence of behaviours and actions that society expects us to take after what is essentially a chemical reaction between two people. For example, falling in love in your teens carries a different set of expectations than doing so in your twenties.

For someone in my position – happily married with a young child – falling in love spells disaster. This is textbook midlife crisis: falling in love with someone new will make me want to leave my husband, wrecking my family in the process. The underlying assumption is that ultimately I will want to – *have* to – choose.

But what if I don't have to?

The morning after my talk with Robert, my first thought upon waking was: *Fuck. Did I break the bubble?*

When I recounted my spacey ramblings to Emma, she laughed like a benevolent Mother Superior counselling a confuzzled Fräulein Maria after her ballroom whirl with Captain von Trapp. 'Oh, Deepa, Deepa, Deepa,' she said. If we'd been speaking in person, I'm positive she would have patted my head, or hand, or both. 'You can't love someone just a little bit.'

Emotional safety was a key feature of the bubble. It was what allowed Robert and I to fully let go and enjoy each other as much as we did. Those boundaries had been stretched, through my own doing, to the edge of unexplored territory. A sense of safety had to be restored if these nights with Robert were to continue.

I would have to be more responsible with my words, more firm with my boundaries, possibly withdraw for a while until stability had been re-established. What I didn't realize then was that I had moved the goalposts for the relationship – and for Robert – without even knowing it.

For a moment I felt embarrassed, almost vulnerable, but I dusted myself off. It was all going to be fine. I hadn't fallen in love with Robert yet. I was still the breezy, sexy woman who sailed in and out of men's lives and bedrooms on her own wave of energy and magnetism – as he'd put it himself, with her own gravity and atmosphere.

Wasn't I?

*

When the pressure of the lockdown eased, so did the urgency of my nights with Robert. I spent more time with my family, he with his friends. The attraction between Robert and Jane took off, and they started sleeping together. It was just as well: young, single and childless, Jane seemed more appropriate and far more available than I could ever be. She was girlfriend material, which I was not.

But when Robert's ancient diesel van was sentenced to the scrapyard by the city government, it was me and not Jane he called with his crazy idea.

'You want to film a funeral for your car,' I repeated.

'Beverly,' Robert supplied.

'Your car is called Beverly.'

'Maybe it's a stupid idea,' he said, back-pedalling.

'But is it fun?' I said. 'Fun is a great reason to do things! Let's go!'

Half an hour later I was outside Robert's house in the rain, using my iPhone to film him in his improvised priest's costume – a blue velvet bathrobe, scarf draped like a liturgical stole around his neck, and jaunty white sailor's cap. Before leaving the house, I had even scooped up peony petals that had fallen from a vase on my desk.

'Beverly loved peonies,' he said, accepting them with great solemnity. He scattered them on her hood as I fed him lines from the eulogy he'd scripted, while trying to keep my cold, rain-wet hands steady. We didn't realize it then, but Beverly's funeral sealed a mutual confidence: that Robert could trust me with his ideas, no matter how crazy, and I could trust him with mine.

I reciprocated by telling him about a Dutch word I had stumbled upon in a pandemic lexicon and become fascinated with: *huidhonger*, literally skin hunger, or the longing for physical contact while in quarantine. He seized upon it, transforming it into a sketch in his leather-bound notebook, which snowballed into several days together in his studio wrestling with plastic, posing for portraits, and being inducted into his exacting perfectionism.

I had worked as a producer while living in Singapore and knew how to move around a set. 'You get it,' Robert said. 'You just get it.' No longer a silent observer, I was promoted to model, muse and co-conspirator.

Our creative partnership was born. Without the unexpected alchemy we found together in the studio, Robert and I might have drifted apart at this point. But that shared moment of recognition – *wait, this is good, and this is rare* – brought us closer. From then on, Robert and I were almost always scheming together, whether for a night of debauchery in the bubble or a photography project in the studio.

I found that I could write again, dusting off old essays and starting new ones. *Life is just an exchange of energy*, I thought to myself. Robert gave so much of himself during nights in the bubble; the energy he gave me, I channelled into my marriage, my family and my writing.

Studio time with Robert brought me into contact with more people from his world. The wide, knowing grins of his fellow photographers when I met them made me realize that everyone in Robert's life knew about me, but hardly anybody in my life knew about him.

'Robert, who have you told about me?' I asked him.

'Everyone,' he said, with a look that said: *Duh*. 'Why do you look so surprised? You don't want to be someone's dirty little secret, do you?'

Up until then, Marcus and I had been discreet about our open marriage. Aside from the one-liner disclosures on our Tinder profiles and a handful of close friends we trusted not to judge us, no one knew about our dating adventures.

Robert's words had a profound impact on me. Was I treating *him* like *my* dirty little secret? Was that fair? Why was I still living in shame for my choices, and not simply living? Was I going to hide forever?

As the borders of our bubble expanded beyond the privacy of Robert's apartment, he wanted to know how we should conduct ourselves out in the open.

'What if we bump into people who know you two are married? Should we come up with a story or distance ourselves from each other? Maybe a hand signal?' he asked me.

The absurdity of skulking around in public struck me then. It felt sleazy and farcical. It wasn't what I wanted for myself or for Robert. Not when I already cared about him. Not when we were becoming this close. Why should someone like him be banished to the shadows?

'There shouldn't have to be,' I said. 'If we're out together and someone asks how we know each other, we should just tell the truth. Yes, we're seeing one another. Yes, we're here together.'

'Thank you,' he said. 'That makes me feel valued. Special.'

'Good,' I said. 'Because you are.'

I was at Robert's one evening, half-listening to him as he chattered on about Jane. Privately I believed what he did with her was no one's business but their own, but I thought it important to feel we could continue being open with each other about the people in our lives, the way he had been with me about Diana.

'The two of you couldn't be more different,' Robert was saying, 'almost total opposites in every way! I mean, for one thing she's like Snow White, and you're, like, my dark Asian princess.'

I froze, blindsided. What had I just heard?

Dark? Asian? Princess?

In my shock, I registered him prattling on without a care in the world, face animated and eyes bright, not realizing what he'd just said. I immediately tried to rationalize it to myself: *He doesn't mean anything by it. It's a good thing. Right?*

'I'm not your princess, Robert,' I managed, words that sounded weak and hollow, sidestepping the true source of the swirling storm of feelings in me. Caught in an internal conflict I hadn't anticipated, I was angry at him and disgusted at myself for trying to automatically smooth things over to keep the peace.

'Oh, of course you're not!' he cried, pulling me to him. 'You're a strong independent woman. I'm so sorry!'

It was only when I reached home that the tremendous weight of Robert's words hit me, and my anger boiled over. I wasn't upset that he had called me a princess: it was that he'd exoticized me with a single careless remark. Was that all I was to him? An exotic collectible? A novelty? I thought I'd become good at filtering out the box-tickers and the fetishists, the kinds of men who made such insensitive comments. How had I been so stupid as to let one sneak in close enough to hurt me?

I called him out on it. Robert was mortified, responding immediately with a lengthy, stammering voice message asking for my forgiveness. Seeing the string of notifications and missed calls on my phone, I realized I had no obligation to make him feel better or to educate him.

We didn't have to work this out. I wasn't his girlfriend. We weren't in a relationship.

I could simply walk.

This isn't a conversation I want to have over WhatsApp, Robert, I said, when I finally regained the composure to reply to his messages. *So why don't you come over to my studio and let's talk.*

When Robert arrived, he was subdued, baseball cap pulled low over his forehead, eyes hidden behind sunglasses. We sat out on the deck, where the bright June sun glinted off the waters of the Marnixkade as an early summer procession of boats and swans floated past.

I listened, arms folded across my chest, as he spoke haltingly about his upbringing as a white, private-schooled male in Dublin, practically wringing his hands in distress. Perhaps no one had ever challenged him to confront both his privilege and discomfort in this way before. But he was doing it.

'I'm so deeply sorry that I've hurt you,' Robert apologized. 'As if my offensive comment wasn't enough, the most insensitive thing I've done was to compare you and Jane. I shouldn't be making any kind of comparison in the first place. Both of you are unique and special in your own way. Neither of you deserved what I said.'

I sensed his sincerity; I could tell he was torn up by the damage his flippant remark had caused. 'I don't want to feel that you're attracted to me because I'm some exotic creature,' I said. 'I don't want to wonder if that's the only reason you're with me at all.' To my horror, tears began to fall as I spoke. I hastily wiped them away.

'No, Deepa, no!' he said. 'That's the last thing I want you to think. I'm attracted to you because of who you are. I've always been drawn to women who are "alternative", if you want to call it that, but you really live it. You think, and conduct your relationships, and live your life differently from anyone I've ever met. That's what I truly am attracted to about you. Please, *please* don't let this one stupid, senseless remark make you believe anything else.'

I stayed silent.

'Deepa, you and I both know this is going to end someday,' he plunged on. 'But if it's going to end, I hope it's going to be on a day when we're both ready for it, and grateful for the time we've had. Not like this. Not because of something ignorant that I've said.'

Across the deck, I saw a tear sliding down his cheek from underneath the corner of his sunglasses.

'You're a beautiful woman, and you're very special to me. If I lost you now, I'd be devastated,' Robert said. 'Deepa, I'm not ready for this to end.'

It was then I realized: neither was I.

*

Decades from now, we're going to look back on 2020, shake our heads, and say to ourselves: *What the heck were we thinking?* Who knows why we binged on *Tiger King* and Korean dramas, became experts on fermentation and virology, baked sourdough loaves and banana bread, fell into black holes on Clubhouse and Discord, or filled our shopping carts and homes with things we didn't want or need?

In the best of times, I believed I could have seen what was coming from a mile away. But in a time of brain fog, debilitating anxiety, information overload and never-ending risk assessment, I didn't have the clarity to see it unfolding, nor the will to deal with it. Cognitive abilities under fire and emotional bandwidth stretched to the limit, I was in survival mode, as we all were.

I believed I was safe. Marcus and I had stayed tethered to each other in a time of crisis; our intimacy was flourishing, our commitment secure. Robert was safely occupied: pining for Diana, his holiday romance, and seeing Jane, who was (at least as far as I knew) textbook girlfriend material. Dreamy and sensual as they were, the few hours I spent with Robert each week posed no threat to a marriage that had been to hell and back.

Love crept in while I was busy trying to stay alive, while I was focused on keeping me and my family safe and sane. It was easier – *so* much easier – not to look at it too closely. By the time I did, it had taken on a life of its own and could not be pulled back.

*

Robert told me he loved me for the first time in front of an audience of more than eighty naked, fornicating strangers on Zoom.

In a surreal slice of pandemic bizarreness, we were at an online play party hosted by a queer-friendly, sex-positive rave community based in London. A tenner gave us a password-protected login to a Zoom call, where we were presented with a digital code of conduct and entered into a compact of mutual voyeurism and exhibitionism.

Robert and I watched, rapt and turned on, as people in various states of dress and undress flirted, flogged and fucked from within the forced isolation of their kitchens, bedrooms and toilets.

In exchange, we allowed strangers to watch us have sex in Robert's living room. True to his perfectionist nature as a photographer, Robert had rearranged his furniture into a DIY porn set, complete with lamps meticulously angled to achieve flattering lighting. He'd gone all out, buying us both sexy new outfits and sex toys. He had even baked space cake.

With our audio muted, no one heard his declaration of love but me. Despite the dance music that was being cast from an apartment in London, boomeranging around the room from his Sonos speakers, every word rang clear and sealed itself in my memory.

'I don't want this to get weird, Deepa,' he said, as if a Zoom sex party wasn't already peak pandemic weirdness. 'But the truth is, I do love you.'

When he said the words, I expected to panic. Where were the alarm bells, the sirens going off in my head? There were none. All I felt was a wonder that made my heart float and everything go quiet. His words were only a confirmation of what I had already sensed all along.

Overcome, I did not say them back; I didn't feel that he expected me to or would be disappointed if I didn't. Yet there was something else. In the tender silence that followed, a tiny voice in me whispered: *Marcus*.

I wonder what I might have been trying to tell myself then. That despite all I had said to Robert about love and falling in love, I couldn't say the words 'I love you' to him until I had admitted the fact of it to Marcus? That Marcus should know first? Looking back now, I realize that even in this most intimate and revealing of moments between Robert and myself, Marcus was there, rooted in the deepest part of me – and perhaps he would always be.

Robert's love was unexpected and beautiful. Like him, it was open-hearted and unrestrained, colourful and a little reckless. I saw it every time he looked at me; I heard it whenever he told me how much he adored me, how I challenged him and made him feel special. I felt it in our nights together, which only seemed to get better over time; in his respect for my boundaries and acceptance of his place in my hierarchy of priorities; in his ability to lose himself so completely in the time we shared, limited as it was by where I was in life and the commitments I chose to honour.

I'd thought embarking on an open marriage would be mostly about self-discovery and the excitement of sexual exploration. What I'd grown to cherish was the freedom to meet extraordinary people who were lovable in so many different ways, to appreciate them, and grow in intimacy with them, liberated from the expectations of what society decreed as normal and necessary in a relationship. Robert was one of those people, with so much about him to love.

Robert or I could have ended it then. It would have been logical and reasonable – *Hey, this wasn't the deal. It's been great, but I'm out.* But neither of us were playing by logic; it wasn't a logical time. The world had been turned upside down. All the rules didn't seem to apply. We lived in a state of constant flux. All I could do – all I did do – was hold on to the few things that I knew for sure.

I knew for sure that Robert and I were good together. In the deep intimacy and playful energy of our nights, parts of myself expanded and continued to grow. My sexual self found a safe space for all her wildness and curiosity; my creative self, who was just being born, had found a partner and co-conspirator.

I also knew that whatever Robert and I had was time-bound and impermanent. His deepest desire was for a family of his own, but he felt he wasn't ready yet. I wanted him to have everything he wanted in life. I wanted him to be happy. No matter how close we became, or how good we were together, I would never be the woman who could give him what he wanted. I wanted to be no one else's wife and life partner but Marcus's, and no one else's mother but my child's. These were roles I had chosen for life.

In opening myself to love, I accepted – or perhaps imposed on myself – the unspoken condition that I had to be ready, if the situation changed or if Robert wanted it, to let him go. Whatever this was with Robert, it wouldn't last forever, and we both knew it.

The sense that we were living on borrowed time – that this could end at any moment – charged our time together with a sweet urgency, urging us to enjoy it to the fullest while we had it.

So I fell in love.

It wasn't a disaster.

13

So does it really work?

What began as a temporary escape from the pressure of lockdown solidified into a parallel existence. As my evenings with Robert became a weekly fixture of my pandemic life, my asthma inhaler was the first to move in, claiming a spot on his bedside table. Not long after, a toothbrush, moisturizer, deodorant and a half-empty bottle of Greek olive blossom cologne took up residence on his bathroom shelf.

One thing at a time; a gradual acclimatization. Wasn't that how Marcus and I had reached this new terrain in the first place?

Since I'd dated Charlie, Rick and Marc, Marcus had grown more at ease with me seeing one person with some regularity. But the problem with me seeing Robert wasn't frequency: it was intensity.

In the best of times, Marcus would have considerable emotional capital to draw on so we could talk about a new connection calmly, as we'd done so often over morning coffee or an after-bedtime glass of wine. But 2020 was far from the best of times, and he was nearly tapped out.

'I'm not in a good space, Deepa!' he burst out when I came home from Robert's one evening. 'I'm tired, I'm stressed, I haven't been able to work out, and I'm not eating healthily. I know there's a lot I can do to feel better about myself, but I don't want to be the drained husband competing for your attention.'

'You don't have to compete,' I said. 'I'm sorry. I don't

want you to feel that way.' In my journal the next morning, I jotted down the changes I resolved to make. *Initiate more sex with Marcus. Reach out to Robert less (let him initiate plans). Support Marcus in getting enough exercise and rest. No more MDMA with Robert.* But it was easier said than done.

Robert's revelation was an escalation. After he'd confessed the depth of his feelings for me, I found it harder to pull away from him, and more drawn to the idea of doing things together. It dawned on me that I was caught up in the intoxicating thrill that polyamorous discourse calls new relationship energy, or NRE.

And Marcus could feel it.

The necessary rigour of emotional housekeeping and our readiness to tackle new situations and difficult conversations had been decimated by pandemic fatigue. We agreed that going back to Noam's office would give us the support we needed.

Returning to therapy for the first time in over a year, I was confronted with what was written in black and white in Noam's client dossier. 'Emotional bonds with others are not part of your contract,' he reminded me.

Before we could renegotiate this agreement, Marcus needed his anxiety and fear to be heard, so he could feel safe in our relationship again. I, in turn, needed to relearn how to listen amidst the noise of months of pandemic survival mode, inextricable from my intensifying feelings for Robert. For a while it felt like we were talking in circles, but sometimes the right words need time to fall into place.

Stepping out of Noam's office, we found a bench on a tree-shaded square where we could steady ourselves and navigate our way back to calm. It was then, in the gathering twilight, with the muted rhythms of the city around us, that Marcus found the words to name his fear.

'I know you don't want to replace me. I believe you when you say you don't want to leave me for Robert. That's not what I'm afraid of,' he said. 'You know what you want and don't want at the moment. But what about six months, a year, three years from now?'

'What I'm really afraid of is . . . what if Robert becomes a part of our life indefinitely? What happens if he sticks around long enough for you to change your mind?' he continued. 'How do I know you won't outgrow our relationship and grow into a relationship with him – not now, but someday?'

Then I understood. The most frightening thing about the future is that it is unknown. None of us can guarantee it.

For Marcus, Robert taking up more and more of my time and attention was scary, full stop. The fear of me leaving him – not today, but in some not-too-distant future – was real and present in his world, even if it wasn't so much as a whisper of a possibility in mine.

'I get it. It's really fucking scary, because the future comes with no assurances,' I said. 'Neither you nor I know what we'll want a year from now, or in five years or ten. I can't say what will happen. And neither can you. How do I know *you* won't meet someone and fall in love and want to leave *me*?'

'This is already here,' he said. 'But I see your point.'

'What I do know for sure is that I want to stay married to you and I don't want to ever grow out of it,' I replied. 'Think about it: everything we set our minds to, and worked on with intention, and committed to doing together, has unfolded the way *we* wanted it to. Hasn't it? Moving to Europe. Starting a family. Buying our house. Getting to where we are in our careers. Even choosing to be together after being able to explore other options.'

'Intention,' Marcus repeated. I could see this sinking in.

'My intention is to be your partner for the rest of your life. Nothing has changed that. And I know that if I put effort towards that, it will work out the way we say it will. Because we want it to. Because we say so.'

A tram clanged its bell as it rattled past, filling a silence that had grown thoughtful. I could feel Marcus listening intently.

'You fear that I'll outgrow us and grow into a relationship with someone else. As if that would be so easy,' I said. 'Don't you realize that you're part of me now, after all this time, after all this life we've made together? Like trees whose roots have grown so entwined underground . . . wait, who wrote that?'

'Kahlil Gibran, *The Prophet*?' he supplied, a smile on his lips for the first time since we'd left Noam's office. 'My mom gave me that book. I quoted it to her when we fought once. I said to her, "Your children are not your children." Man, she threw a *fit*.'

We laughed together, the first breath of ease in a charged evening.

'Whoever said that, that's how I feel about us,' I said. 'Our roots have grown together. And they've grown deep. They won't come undone just like that. Tearing us apart would hurt me as deeply as it would hurt you. I would lose a part of me if I lost you. I'm not about to let that happen.'

When Marcus reached over to pull me into a tight

embrace, I knew what I'd said had landed. Acknowledging fear and listening to it was a first and necessary step. Sometimes, being heard is enough to defuse its power.

I'd expected a protracted struggle over multiple sessions with Noam, but Marcus's fear and insecurity seemed to dissipate almost overnight. He didn't ask me to choose, or demand that I shut down my relationship with Robert. He didn't want to control me or impose new rules.

It turns out that one thing almost four years of navigating change gives you is the ability to navigate even more change. This new emotional landscape looked unfamiliar and its atmosphere felt different, but Marcus and I had a working understanding of how to traverse it. In career parlance, we had enough relevant experience and transferable skills – along with trust in ourselves and each other – to venture forth, hand in hand.

Experience had taught us that moments of discomfort were temporary and would pass, and that our relationship was bigger and stronger than any of them. We knew all the best ways for us to reconnect after new adventures with other people. We knew how this worked, even if we didn't know exactly what it would be like now that I was falling in love with someone else.

I suppose it must be something like having a second child. Even if they are an entirely different creature from the first one, you're not going in completely lost as a parent, the way you did the first time. You just sort of know what to do.

Marcus and I weren't ready for this, but in a way we also were. We were no longer the same Marcus or Deepa we'd been at the start of our crazy experiment. As a unit, our marriage had deepened in security and intimacy; as individuals, we had grown in pluck and maturity. We could reach into the toolbox Amanda had helped us furnish almost four years ago, pick out the tools we needed for a particular situation – whether it was dealing with jealousy or renegotiating boundaries – and wield them with greater mastery than we had at the outset.

Seeking support for a difficult conversation we couldn't handle on our own had enabled us to listen to each other and recognize each other's needs once more. It enabled me to give Marcus the attention and reassurance he needed, until he felt secure enough to give me even greater freedom and trust in return. Above all, we were doing this together – as a team, the way we had promised to face life.

If my marriage has taught me anything, it is that commitment is saying to one another: *This has come into my life, but I won't let it take me away from you.* It means saying: *Yes, this person and this relationship is worth the work of having them in my life. This is work, but I will do the work with you.*

Long before marriage, parenthood and non-monogamy, a wise friend told me: *Life is hard, so choose the things that are worth the work.* I chose Marcus; every time the choice comes up, Marcus chooses me. I know how lucky I am to have found a love that is willing to grow and expand with me through all of life's changes, whether chosen or circumstantial. A love that sees me, simply, as worth the work. This is why I choose him for life and will never give up this love for any other.

And because we've rewritten the rules of our marriage, I will never have to.

*

SO DOES IT REALLY WORK?

As we drifted from summer into autumn, we learned to live in sprints of normalcy between reopenings and lockdowns. The flux of pandemic restrictions adjusted the scope of our optimism and appetite for life like light through the aperture of a lens.

To be clear, what was generally considered a lockdown in the Netherlands was never as restrictive or strictly enforced as in other countries. The Dutch government focused on keeping the economy and healthcare afloat; for all else, it emphasized personal responsibility and social awareness. It made the public aware of their civic duty to uphold the pandemic restrictions, but was far too practical-minded to expend resources on compelling every single citizen to follow every single rule to the letter.

The Dutch police had better things to do, leaving it to the *handhaving* – non-armed municipal enforcement officers who keep the peace in public spaces – to stroll around parks with their thumbs in their belt loops reminding people to keep 1.5 metres apart, to shut down house parties, or to hand out the occasional fine. It seemed very few people I knew, us included, ever had to live in total isolation, or worry about the *handhaving* knocking on the door to check if two people had come over for dinner instead of one. Instead, we struggled to keep tabs on the closing times of bars and restaurants or the number of houseguests you could have, which seemed to change from week to week.

As a result, it wasn't difficult to form social bubbles, nurture and maintain a few close friendships, or even date. And so, ironically, it was in these conditions – when social connections had to be less exuberantly random and more consciously chosen – that Marcus found the resources to cope with my growing closeness with Robert. Some adjustments were easy to welcome, and others were . . . well, a little less so.

*

As newly-weds in Singapore, fresh out of a long-distance relationship, Marcus and I had been inseparable. Our interests, activities, social circles and emotional lives were enmeshed, inextricable from one another. Over a decade later, we understood that being married meant we were each other's first port of call for things that we wanted to do, and so we did a lot of things together – but we didn't have to do *everything* together.

Non-monogamy had created breathing room in our relationship. Marcus filled that space with his own interests: drawing, painting and martial arts. But what he enjoyed most was cooking for people. I was the extreme extrovert who thrived in groups, but Marcus had always preferred one-on-one connections – and, conveniently, Dutch pandemic restrictions always allowed one houseguest. So while I was at Robert's, he would invite a colleague or friend over for drinks or dinner.

After Marcus and I moved to Amsterdam, the work of friendship maintenance – seeking out new acquaintances and nurturing relationships with them – fell to me. Meeting another expat couple, for example, I would often joke, 'Have your people get in touch with my people,' for we all knew that the husbands would leave it to the wives to make plans for the next brunch or dinner.

With me otherwise engaged elsewhere, Marcus took responsibility for cultivating new friendships and building his own support network. He began to reach out to Dutch parents in our daughter's class – which, as the more fluent Dutch speaker in the marriage, I usually did, coordinating playdates and school outings – and developed those relationships, too.

Bit by bit, during the hours that I was away, Marcus built a social life independent of our marriage and an emotional life that didn't revolve around his identity as my husband. This was how he met Zenya.

Permanently swathed in voluminous, earth-toned garments, Zenya was a desert nomad trapped in the body of an Amsterdam urbanite. I met her at a dinner party for female creatives, where she rhapsodized about Morocco with such passion that by dessert I was sold on booking a family holiday to Marrakesh. A photographer and art director with a minimalist style and perpetually sun-kissed complexion, Zenya might have been easy to dismiss as a pretentious aesthete. But I was hooked by the extraordinary range of her laughter, which ran from infectious schoolgirl giggles to silvery peals of head-thrown-back delight in the course of a single meal. People who are unafraid to laugh with such depth and candour are my kind of people.

I might have met Zenya first, but it was she and Marcus who hit it off. Within minutes of their introduction at a house party, where all three of us were guests of a mutual friend, they discovered their shared affinity for martial arts. They agreed to meet up at the Westerpark for a Saturday skirmish: he would teach her *arnis de mano*, a Filipino style of combat that used two hardwood sticks, and she would demonstrate what she knew of kung fu using a staff, à la David Carradine.

I'll never forget how incredulous Marcus sounded when Zenya showed up at the park: he in his scruffy workout gear, she with her tall wooden staff, sleek gelled topknot, flowing sand-coloured wrap coat, and oversized gold hoop earrings. 'I was like: is she serious about doing kung fu in that outfit? With those earrings?' he told me, shaking his head. But by the end of their sweaty stick-fighting session, Zenya had impressed him with her natural athletic grace and won him over with her light-hearted Zen calm.

I have many fine qualities as a partner, but athleticism isn't among them. Zenya became the sporting buddy to Marcus that I could never be. They played basketball and went kayaking. They cooked for each other and traded recipes. Her sensitivity for aesthetics complemented Marcus's love for art. And because she yawned and made for home and bed at promptly ten o'clock every night, their evenings always ended with Marcus smiling and well rested.

'Zenya again? Are you sure there's nothing going on between those two?' Robert wondered. It was an easy assumption to make, but I assured him that the connection between Zenya and Marcus was as fraternal as that of Rui and I.

In any other marriage, especially in the culture I come from, a closeness like theirs would be met with possessiveness, suspicion, even hostility. An attractive single woman and a married man could never be trusted to spend this much time together. But our trust was impeccable, and so was my trust in Zenya. I became grateful for her friendship and her sunny, serene presence in Marcus's life. In fact, I still am.

Pandemic dating functioned like an extension of the one-houseguest policy: if it was safe enough to invite one person over for dinner, it was probably also safe enough to meet one person for a date. With bars and clubs closed, the city's parks were filled with cautiously courting couples exchanging awkward first-date questions and clutching coffee cups on long walks. Marcus joined their ranks, going on a few dates with women he met on dating apps: a single mother with entire weekends to herself, an ex-colleague who surfaced on Happn, an aspiring rope bunny who wanted to explore *shibari*.

My personal theory is that he appealed to women as a safe choice: a work-from-home dad with a wife, child, mortgage and steady employment was less likely to be indiscriminately partying and more likely to be responsibly socializing than, say, a single 24-year-old fuckboy living off pizza in student housing.

We always talked about his dates before he went on them, and I always felt reassured that Marcus was doing his due diligence. Initiating a Covid conversation with someone and enquiring into their social life and habits wasn't that different from having a safer-sex discussion and asking about their sexual and testing history.

Because more women were being cautious and opting to meet for long walks instead of casual hook-ups, Marcus had more opportunity to engage his dates in conversation and impress them with how easy-going, smart and interesting he was, qualities I've always loved about him. Those measured, intentional dates built his confidence and self-image until he started to appreciate those qualities about himself as well.

Except for my evenings with Robert, the pandemic shut down my carefree carousel of casual hook-ups. The opposite happened to Marcus: when the world slowed down, he finally found his groove. 'I guess I'm just a late bloomer,' he said. I couldn't begrudge him that – not when my relationship with Robert was blooming, too.

When it comes to change, I've always been a quick spark, while Marcus is more of a long fuse. But even a slow start picks up momentum eventually, and when it does, you'd better be holding on for the ride.

*

One Sunday morning after a date, Marcus padded into the living room, where our daughter was absorbed in a Netflix cartoon series. By the glazed look in his eyes as he made coffee, I could tell it had been an intense night.

'How was your evening?' I ventured.

Cradling a coffee cup in his hands, he took a deep breath. 'I – I'm still processing it,' he said finally. 'It . . . it wasn't what I expected.'

At that point I should have stopped and given him the time he needed to knit himself together, but curiosity nudged me to override the signs of a potential misstep.

My curiosity tends to do that.

'I'm going to take a shower,' I announced. 'You wanna come and tell me about it in there?'

Still unmoored, not quite all there, he replied, 'Sure, let's do that.' Together we went into the bathroom, that blessed sanctuary of apartment-dwelling parents, and locked the door. The first blast of hot water hit my head and shoulders when Marcus revealed: 'She ghosted me.'

'What?'

Last night was meant to have been his second date with a woman he'd had a sexual spark with, a 26-year-old lawyer from another Dutch city with whom the first walk in the park had turned into an all-nighter. She expressed interest in meeting a second time and even toyed with the idea of inviting me along. The logistics of a threesome when two participants are full-time parents were too complex to navigate, so they agreed to meet without me.

Backpack full of sexy goodies, hotel room booked for the night, Marcus was excited and had big plans. But she didn't show up. Ignored his calls and texts. Blocked him on WhatsApp. Ugh.

'Human beings can be such *assholes*!' I say, stamping my foot in the shower. 'I'm so sorry, babe, that sucks! Why didn't you tell me right away? We would have been happy to have you home.'

'Wait. So first, I was pissed . . .'

'Obviously!'

'But then I figured, I have the night off with an empty hotel room to myself, so . . .' A pissed-off Marcus is a determined Marcus – and a determined Marcus gets results. I could see where this was going, and pictured Marcus on his phone, rifling through his modest but well-vetted little black book to save his night. Things were about to get interesting.

'Did you find someone else?' I ask.

He did. She was Russian, a writer of erotica who used a pseudonym to meet strangers online and gather material for her stories. I couldn't have picked a better replacement myself. By the end of my shower, it was he, not she, who was hog-tied in bed – and he discovered, for the first time, that he loved it.

'Well, you really turned that around!' I said, washing out the last of my conditioner. 'That sounds epic.' Congratulating him and meaning it, I recognized the feeling of elation at Marcus's rescued night as compersion.

Flashes of this happiness had come more naturally to me, and earlier in our open marriage, than to Marcus. But they were becoming more frequent for both of us. Most recently, Marcus had admired the portraits I'd collaborated on with Robert. 'I understand why this gives you energy,' he said. 'Go for it.' Later, he told me he wondered: *Am I feeling compersion?*

Standing in the shower as Marcus told me about his date, I realized I was actually happy that his sexual boundaries had been pushed. I was pleased, even a little proud, that the intensity of his night caused new cracks in the armour of shame and guilt that had long guarded his experience of sex and desire; that he had tried new things, felt new pleasures, and learned something new about himself. I knew what that was like. How could I not want it for him, too?

'Wait,' he said. 'I'm not done yet.' There was *more*?

His face obscured by condensation, Marcus proceeded to enumerate the night's sins to me through the foggy shower door, as if seeking absolution. I felt duty-bound to hear him to the end. I couldn't make him stop now. I'd asked for this, hadn't I?

The Russian writer of erotica announced she had to leave at 10 p.m. 'But we're having so much fun,' Marcus pointed out. 'Are you sure I can't convince you to stay any longer?'

'I'll stay,' she said, 'if you make it interesting for me.'

My eyes widened. *Crack that whip, woman!* I thought. *I'm stealing that one.*

Challenge accepted. Back he went on his phone, receiving either silence or polite declines from people who already had plans for the night.

'I thought, this is it,' he said, perched on the edge of the bathtub, looking at me in the mirror as I towelled my hair dry. 'She'll leave at ten, and that'll be the end of my night. I had my fun. I can be happy with that.'

At ten minutes before ten, two women showed up. Two plus two makes four.

A foursome. My husband had a foursome.

To hear him tell it, it was a four-hour erotic extravaganza, masterfully staged by this Russian writer, also apparently a budding director. She marshalled them into tableau after tableau involving various permutations of body parts, ropes, blindfolds, gags, Polaroids and a remote-controlled bullet vibrator (I didn't even know we had one?).

By this time, we'd left the bathroom and I was sitting on the bed in my bathrobe, the remnants of a smile still frozen at the corners of my mouth, less . . . enthusiastic than I'd been a moment ago, as Marcus rambled on and on about this *woman*, the first he had ever allowed to sexually dominate him.

His reaction wasn't a huge surprise. Logically, I understood that flipping the switch on the sexual power dynamic would have a tremendous erotic impact. I knew before he did that this would drive him wild. But all of a sudden, I wasn't quite operating on a logical level.

Feelings can be messy that way. So are humans. And relationships.

I struggled to keep my grasp on reality. *This is really good for him, Deepa, you asked for this, don't make it about you, just listen, look how excited he is, don't shit on his excitement, this is part of his growth!*

Just then his voice floated into the stream of noise in my

head. As if from far away, I heard him say: 'She was just *pure feminine sexual energy* –'

Pure. Feminine. Sexual. Energy.

Hearing those four words, I lost it. I burst into tears.

Marcus became a deer in the headlights. Then it hit him. *Oh shit.*

Immediately I tried to backtrack, retrieve my previous enthusiasm, sort out my feelings, articulate them, and hold space for his experiences – all at the same time. The part of me that felt happy for him was still there, but another part of me had muscled in: one that wondered why he had never invited me to play that role in our sexual life.

I sniffled through stop–start sentences until I finally grasped the stinging heart of the matter. 'If she's pure sexual feminine energy, then *what am I*?' I asked. As soon as I said it out loud, I understood that it wasn't entirely fair, but my wounded ego had already spoken. I also understood that it didn't serve anyone for my ego to be pandered to; all it wanted was to be heard.

And Marcus listened.

He took my hand, apologized, and as I struggled to rein in a full-blown Claire Danes ugly cry, I realized something. Because he hadn't had enough time to make sense of his experiences, he'd unloaded a torrent of graphic detail and crossed one of our boundaries: *broad strokes only*.

Retracing our steps, we quickly found the point in the conversation when it started to feel *not okay*, when I could have stopped him and said: *Right, I think I've heard enough* or *Let's talk about this another time.* That was my responsibility. But what had been more important to me in the moment:

satisfying my curiosity? Staying in character as the cool, supportive, sexually liberated wife?

Sometimes what you want in the moment doesn't become clear until much later, by which time you've gone hurtling down one road or another.

If being in an open marriage has taught me anything, it is that moments are just moments. Caught early enough, they can still be undone. We had caught this one just in time.

Being in an open marriage doesn't make me immune to feelings, either. I had not reached some kind of lofty peak of enlightenment and Buddha-like detachment, where I would never suffer wounds to my ego, or envy, or even jealousy. What I was doing, however, was investing in managing my feelings so that they didn't derail me or prevent Marcus from having expansive experiences that I believed were worth having.

Then the doorbell rang.

'Fuck,' I said. 'Emma's here.'

'Fuck!' Marcus said. 'Is the Sinterklaas thing today?'

Sinterklaas, the feast of Saint Nicholas, is the highlight of the year for children in the Netherlands. Though Sint's birthday is celebrated on December 5th, the weeks leading up to it are studded with Sinterklaas-themed events designed to whip children into a frenzy, with small gifts, chocolate and gingerbread in various addictive forms such as round *kruidnoten* and *speculaas* cookies.

I'd forgotten. I'd bought tickets for a Sinterklaas scavenger hunt at the Zaanse Schans, a postcard-perfect strip of windmills a twenty-minute drive out of Amsterdam, and invited my best friend Emma and her six-year-old daughter to join us. Oh, joy.

Emma could see something was up as soon as I opened the door. 'Hiiiiiiii . . . guys,' she said, registering my tear-stained face and Marcus looking both sheepish and tense behind me.

I greeted Emma and her daughter a little too brightly, addressing the small human hiding behind Emma's legs. 'Oh, wow, someone's dressed up in her Piet suit!' Piet is Sint's beloved helper, whose multicoloured satin pageboy outfit is a staple of Dutch children's wardrobes. 'Guess who else is dressed up as Piet today?'

'Is it Marcus?' Emma joked, looking concerned when neither of us laughed.

'Uh, you guys . . .' Emma whispered as her satin-clad child bounded into the living room in search of mine. 'Is everything okay?'

'Big night. Long story,' I said, stuffing my feet into my boots. 'I'll tell you later. Let's get this show on the road.'

'If you two need to sort things out . . . we don't have to go.'

'What do you mean, we don't have to go? Of course we have to go!' I hissed. 'We've been selling them the whole song and dance of Sint's secret *speculaas* factory all week! They're sitting there *dressed as Piet*. We can't cancel now!'

'It'll be fine,' Marcus said, backing me up. 'Really.'

'I could take the girls –' Emma offered. Though she was a hero for suggesting this, I cut her off.

'You don't drive! How would you get there? No, no, no, Marcus will drive, you'll sit in the back with the girls, and everyone will get their Sinterklaas magic as planned. Okay?'

I hustled all of us – children and adults – into our coats, out the door, into the car, and off to the Zaanse Museum for a sugar-fuelled scavenger hunt.

As we tailed the girls through the Dutch equivalent of

Willy Wonka's chocolate factory, I filled Emma in on the highlights. She winced when I got to *pure feminine sexual energy*. 'Oooh,' she said, wrinkling her nose. 'Your husband is many wonderful things, but that was not his finest moment.'

I felt oddly vindicated. 'Trust me, he knows,' I said.

In the blur of churning biscuit machines, sugar-crazed children and bewildered parents, I stopped to catch my breath. A ghosting lover, a surprise foursome, a Russian vortex of *pure feminine sexual energy*. It was a lot to tack on to parenting, but this was the life I'd chosen in all its glory and chaos.

Marcus caught my eye and took my hand: a fleeting moment of reconnection in all the madness, just enough to bring me back to what truly mattered.

By some Sinterklaas miracle, both girls completed their mission before either of them had a meltdown. We brought them home, little joyous faces buried in their goodie bags, the cinnamon-sugary scent of crushed *kruidnoten* filling the car.

Later that night, Marcus and I put our daughter to bed, collapsed on the couch and held each other, simply breathing in the quiet relief of making it through a manic day. We poured two glasses of wine, made new agreements – *I should wait until you're fully recovered, I should ask if it's okay to go on telling you* – and sealed them with kisses.

So, does it really work?

Yes. *This* is how it works.

I often find myself having to convince people of the health and happiness of my open marriage. When I say, *Yes, it works for us*, or that we're happy, people tend to demand proof in a way that they never do when I simply say that I am married. But why do we assume that monogamy means happy, perfect and conflict-free? Does it, really?

The sceptics tend to make one or more of the following assumptions: that neither Marcus nor I are being honest. That I am a skilful manipulator who is holding my husband emotional hostage somehow. That he is not a thinking, intelligent, fully functional adult. That he is spineless and can't make his own decisions about what is good for him or not.

Is it so hard to believe that we can be happy in a situation that you've never found yourself in? Or do we believe that if something doesn't work 100 per cent of the time, it doesn't work at all? That if we're not happy 100 per cent of the time, we're not happy at all?

Every relationship requires some level of compromise; we choose what we compromise on to make it work. Making it work is a self-renewing process. We will never fully reach a point of perfection where it all operates flawlessly, like magic, for the rest of our lives. Inevitably, some new bend in the road will emerge, and we will turn to each other and ask: So how does this work *now*?

We get flashes of brilliance and joy, and flashes of bliss and adventure. We get moments of intimacy and connection, and moments of tension and space. Some days are harder, and some days are better. Because we've gotten used to them over time, the intensity of difficult moments has softened from visceral threat to tolerable, even negligible discomfort.

Then the moment passes, the shadows lift, and all is light again.

*

December brought a dozen red roses in celebration of our first date at Checkpoint Charlie. 'Happy Robert met Deepa day!' he greeted me first thing in the morning. Later that evening, he gave me a handwritten letter that read: *Happy anniversary, my darling. We both know it won't always be this way, but I will be forever grateful that I know you and love you as much as I do.*

Robert's excitement to celebrate what he insisted on calling our first anniversary made me cry. I was never going to be a normal girlfriend, but he loved and wanted me in his life all the same. And what was normal anyway?

When Robert left to spend Christmas in Dublin with his family, he asked me to take care of his plants and handed me a set of keys to his apartment. 'You can write there, too, if you like,' he said, knowing how I hated the cold in my shared studio.

In return, I bought him new flannel sheets and remade his bed, stocked his refrigerator with groceries, and left handwritten sticky notes around the place welcoming him home.

Robert never asked for his keys back.

Our hopes that 2021 would be different were dashed shortly after the New Year. For the first time since the Second World War, the Netherlands imposed the *avondklok* (evening clock), a nationwide curfew from 9 p.m. to 4 a.m. daily, which was to last from January to April.

Nightlife had already been shut down for months. But the curfew cut me off with even greater severity from the parts of myself that blossomed in the hours between sunset and sunrise, and from all the possibilities the night once held.

I had barely enough time to consider what this might mean for my evenings with Robert when Marcus remarked, 'I guess you'll be coming home from Robert's before nine p.m., then.'

'I'm sorry, what?' I said incredulously. 'Do you expect me to leave after bedtime, cycle there, then cycle back as soon as I arrive?'

'Okay, then I guess you can leave here before bedtime,' he said with a shrug.

'You can't be serious. That's not even enough time to sit down for dinner together!'

The no-sleepover rule had been Marcus's idea when we first began. Waking up together was too intimate and special, he said; we should save that for each other. But the *avondklok* forced Marcus to put his money where his mouth was. Having returned to dating, only with connections he had vetted well and trusted, he now realized he would have to end his nights out early as well.

So . . . this seems like a slow burn. We might get there much later in the night. Is that okay? he texted me from a date's house a few days after the curfew was announced.

Sure, love. The night is yours to enjoy, I replied absently. At a minute before 9 p.m., it hit me. *Wait! Did you make it out before the curfew? Or are you sleeping over there?*

I'm still having dinner, came the reply.

I see, I said.

Sometimes Marcus had to experience a situation himself to develop empathy for it. It took waking up next to someone himself to realize that it wasn't as damaging to our bond as he had feared it might be.

The next time I left for Robert's, I said, 'I would love to be able to sleep in a bit and not have to drag myself home at four a.m. as soon as the curfew ends. Is that all right?'

Marcus's reply: 'You've been seeing Robert for over a year now. There's no need to be so pedantic about the rules.'

SO DOES IT REALLY WORK?

My days of slithering home at dawn were over.

The curfew helped us talk about sleepovers to our daughter. At the age of seven, she had already slept over at friends' houses and knew about the *avondklok* from school, where the pandemic and the constantly changing restrictions were a frequent topic. She thought nothing of it the first time I told her that Papa was sleeping over elsewhere. *Of course* he couldn't be caught cycling home after 9 p.m. *Of course* nobody wanted to be caught by the *handhaving* or pay a fine. It all checked out; it simply felt normal to her.

When the *avondklok* was lifted some three months later, sleepovers felt normal to us, too. We never looked back.

Renegotiating our boundaries felt less like waging a kitchen-table battle and calling a truce. It had become more like moving into a dance, in which the only way to keep flowing to the same rhythm was to listen intently and hold each other close. It felt less like following rules or asking for permission, and more like staying in sync.

In recontracting our agreements, we discovered this simple truth: the rules are whatever you say they are. Rewriting them is so much more powerful and life-affirming if you do so together.

The first time I woke up in Robert's bed at nine in the morning felt like a milestone. Robert and I would never celebrate the markers that 'normal' relationships assumed as standard, aspired to and worked towards. We would never meet the parents, move in together, go apartment hunting or share long holidays with each other's friends or family. We would never announce our engagement, send out wedding invitations, go on honeymoon, buy a home, or shop for soft, tiny garments for a baby.

But now we could go out for freshly baked croissants together, masks strapped on, arm in arm, to the bakery around the corner. We could argue about whose turn it was to put the coffee on. We could watch the first rays of spring sunshine creep into the uppermost corner of Robert's bedroom window, signalling the end of a long winter.

We would never do the big things together. But these small joys, magnified by the strangeness of our times and the unusual compact we had entered into, were the milestones and measures of our relationship, with a fullness all their own.

For now, and for a long time, they would be enough.

Because all of our lives and social circles had shrunk so dramatically, the pandemic enabled me to be present in both relationships to a degree that I wanted to, and that was comfortable – or acceptable – to both Marcus and Robert. It wouldn't always be that way.

Eventually, Marcus would be called back into the office and to the social life he had built for himself in the hours of my absence. Robert would be pulled to new opportunities for work and travel. My natural curiosity and appetite for novel experiences would revive itself, although never back to pre-pandemic levels. My daughter, on the threshold of her pre-teen years, would need more.

Love isn't a pie, where a bigger slice for someone means a smaller slice for someone else, but resources are finite: time, attention, energy.

At this moment, Robert's needs from a relationship fit perfectly against the slice of time, attention and energy I could offer him. But someday this would change, and we both knew it. He accepted his place in my life, but being third priority wouldn't satisfy him forever, no matter how skilfully I negotiated with Marcus to expand the limits of what I could give him. That wouldn't be a personal shortcoming of Robert's, but would only be natural and fair.

Robert accepted the realities of my being married with a child; one day I would have to deal with the realities of his being younger, single and childless. He operated free from the commitments and responsibilities or constraints on time and energy that I did. He could easily roll a date with someone new into a three-day romp in bed, which I could never do, or pack up his life and leave for a different city in a week if he wished.

The day awaited when I would be unable to be present for all the adventures he was at liberty to have on his own. If he desired more from me, I would be unable to give it to him. I couldn't be everywhere all at once, and that was no character flaw or personal failing of mine, either. It was simply the reality. Until that day came, we could fling ourselves deeply into the pleasure of what we had while we had it.

Our bubble gave us so much to enjoy. Spontaneous poetry readings in bed. Recording sessions late at night, where I narrated my essays and he captured my voice, trimming it just so for me to mail out to a small email list that I started. Nerdy made-up games involving his primary-school dictionary (most of which I won). Shoots at the studio, transforming the ideas and discoveries we shared with each other into photographs: my pearl necklace draped across an elaborate web he constructed from white sewing thread; a delicate dried hydrangea I found on the street; a translucent pink plastic bag I picked up on the beach because it reminded me of the work he'd made for his solo show, back when we barely knew each other and had no idea of what was to come.

*

As we emerged from the throes of our first pandemic winter, just before our girl's eighth birthday, Marcus asked me if I loved Robert. Perhaps he asked because he already knew and was prepared to hear the answer.

'I do,' I replied. 'It's not the kind of love we have, or the kind of falling in love we did when we were young. It's not the kind of falling in love we did with each other, and not the kind of love I have for you. But yes, I do love him.'

The revelation was an iceberg. We had been approaching it, the tip just visible, shimmering above the horizon, but now we had hit it full on. Our ship hadn't gone down, it was stronger than that, but it was shaken. It would need time and energy to right the ship and bring it back on course.

In the days that followed, a subtle strain surfaced in the space between Marcus and I when we were in the same room together. It was different from the discomfort, jealousy or even hostility after my dates, all of which already felt so long ago, and Marcus a different person. This was not quite awkwardness or tension, but something softer.

A few times I caught Marcus looking at me with that softness in his eyes: loss, perhaps, or sadness. He never told me what it was; I trusted that if it was too much for him to handle on his own, he would say.

In the meantime, we were swept up in the preparations for our daughter's eighth birthday. Since enrolling in after-school cooking classes, she'd made it clear that she wanted a cooking-themed party. We had children's aprons and chocolate eggs to order, loot bags to fill, and a chocolate caramel birthday cake in the shape of a number 8 to pick up and transport.

Marcus and I relied on these mundane tasks to soothe us, reaching a shared understanding that required no words. Turning towards the family we had made, we found each other on steady ground, surrounded by the laughter of my daughter and her friends, buoyed by the comforting warmth and tender delights of the life we had created together.

The truth of my love for Robert changed nothing about us. Marcus and I still loved each other and wanted to be together all our lives. It didn't make us love each other less. Pretending or denying it might have made us more comfortable, but it also would have minimized the level of the effort we needed to put into our marriage to keep it alive, vibrant and capable of holding its own against the intensity of a new love.

Like a light that had switched on in the background, this new love with Robert threw my marriage with Marcus into high contrast and sharp detail.

It wasn't that I now had something to compare my marriage to: it was that everything I loved about Marcus and myself, everything that made him irreplaceable to me and made us special to each other, suddenly seemed more vivid and intense. Our deep comfort in each other, our familiar compatibility, our physical affection, and the lifelong project and shared joy of raising our daughter together.

Our promise to always be honest with ourselves and each other had allowed us to face the truth of my love for Robert with recognition: an unflinching willingness to look at difficult things together, to have tough but necessary conversations, while somehow managing to be kind to ourselves and each other. It wasn't easy. But we had done it before, and we knew we could always seek support if we needed it.

From recognition, we moved into intention: a deliberate choice to navigate this new path together. In the weeks to come, I felt both of us pulling for our marriage. Our desire to spend time with each other intensified, accompanied by a heightened awareness of how important that time was.

From intention, we moved into action: making time for more of what we love about each other, what we love together, and what marks our relationship as special and unique. Instead of seeing something new as a threat and eliminating it, we chose to recognize the beauty in it and create something bigger instead.

Instead of scarcity, abundance. Instead of fear, love.

More laughter. More joy. More dreams. More plans for the future. More sleepy cuddles in bed with our daughter, more chest-expanding pride in her growth, more silly faces and gap-toothed smiles and misshapen pancakes on Sunday mornings. More late-night conversations and bubble baths and delicious meals cooked with love. More adventures as a family, whenever and wherever we could have them: at a shimmering turquoise lake in Luxembourg; along the pale, wild northern coast of Holland; in a forest cabin with a crackling fire; wintry walks among icy puddles and snowy bogs in North Brabant.

More adventures, just the two of us, carefully planned, made precious by their rarity. An evening of records and wine with close friends that melted into a night of pleasure shared among four bodies. A wedding anniversary, our lucky thirteenth, spent at an empty hotel on the Keizersgracht, and a midnight ramble through the deserted, rain-wet streets of what was surely the most beautiful city in the world, the one we now called home.

More of everything we loved about each other. More of what we loved together. To be honest, this part isn't hard. This part doesn't feel like work. It just feels like . . . us.

I have found that love has room for all of this, and for so much more.

*

When the world expanded again in the spring, I expected it to burst the bubble Robert and I had created. Normal life would bring him fresh options: new faces, distractions, places to go and people to meet. He might go back on Tinder or, more likely, charm the pants off someone in a pub. Amsterdam was full of beautiful, eligible, single women who could make him a priority in a way I never could. *Then he won't need me any more*, I thought. Part of me was always aware that the love of his life might be waiting just around the corner and could arrive at any time. 'You could meet the girl of your dreams tomorrow, while shopping at the Albert Heijn,' I teased him, though perhaps more to remind myself than anyone else.

'That's never going to happen,' he retorted. 'I shop at the Lidl!'

It turned out he had no patience for dating apps. Neither did he hit bars or parties to meet women, as I had expected him to.

To my surprise, the bubble held.

The world opening up again brought us more things to

enjoy together. Now I was Robert's girlfriend not only within the four walls of his apartment, within a fantasy that we both shared, but in the real world: at bars and restaurants, on summer boat rides and lazy lie-downs at the park with our friends, on Taco Tuesdays at his best friend's house and, most surprising of all, in Marcus's world.

We had talked about this meeting many times, and agreed it was long overdue.

'It feels absurd not to have met him yet, when he's so clearly a part of your life,' Marcus had said.

We'd pictured beers at our neighbourhood bar, at the park or on the side of some canal somewhere, preferably in the sunshine, feet dangling over the water. We hadn't pictured it like this at all, unfolding awkwardly on the street next to a double-parked van that held a guitar, firewood and photography gear. But that was how it happened.

Life is funny, strange and wonderful that way.

Robert and I were to drive down to Drenthe on our first official holiday together: two nights in a lakeside teepee at a campsite three hours by car from Amsterdam.

'I guess it's fine, if it's just one night,' Marcus said the first time I asked him.

One night! I saw Robert gulp and blink when he heard this, but in a mighty effort to respect Marcus's boundaries, he just rolled with it. 'Okay, then,' he said, 'one night it is.'

Marcus eventually realized he was being ridiculous and conceded to a two-night trip. And now, seeing me struggle with my bags – I was an inexperienced camper and hadn't learned how to pack light – he turned to me and said: 'Do you want me to help you bring your stuff downstairs?'

'Are you sure?' I said, raising an eyebrow.

SO DOES IT REALLY WORK?

He shrugged and said, 'Sure, why not.'

Marcus is coming downstairs to help me with my bags, I texted Robert, but of course he never looked at his phone. Instead, he hopped out of the driver's seat when he saw Marcus carrying my bags out the front door.

You could have warned me, said his eyebrows.

You could have checked your phone, my eyebrows said back.

Robert popped open the rear doors of the van so that Marcus could load my bags into the back, sidestepping bicycles that whizzed past him on the street. Then the men in my life exchanged wide smiles, nervous laughter and tight-gripped handshakes for the very first time.

Having never imagined that this moment would ever come to pass, I watched, secretly thrilled, awed at the life I had made that somehow made this possible.

It's really happening, I remember thinking to myself. *Wild.*

Robert said, 'Finally, a face to the name,' boggling my mind as to how he'd never once searched for Marcus on social media in all the time we'd been together.

Marcus said, 'Take care of her,' because he was protective of me that way.

Mentions of a long-overdue beer were made, or perhaps coffee, followed by rapid head-bobbing and more nervous laughter. I loved them both for it.

Before I got into the van, I hugged Marcus, whispering, 'Thank you. I love you.'

He hugged me back. 'This is so awkward. I love you, too. Have fun. I got this.'

14

What do you tell your daughter?

I always thought I would have a second child.

For this reason, I hung on to as many of my daughter's baby things as I could. Clothes, books, toys, even my maternity outfits – I stuffed them all into a giant closet in her room, into every possible nook and cranny that could hold them, stretching the storage capacity of our 86-square-metre Amsterdam apartment to its absolute maximum. It reached the point where I was fishing baby shoes out of winter boots and finding baby socks wedged in between the laundry detergent and fabric softener.

The closer I got to forty, the more certain I became: I didn't want another child. The decision was one I came to after many quiet nights and searching conversations with Marcus, when we would dance towards the possibility then scurry away from it.

Let's make another one, we would say to each other teasingly and with affection, during moments when we felt close to one another, or were caught up in intense adoration for our little girl. But during the pandemic, *Let's make another one* became *God, aren't you glad we didn't have another one?*

Marcus and I agreed that life was full enough with just the three of us, and that our family didn't need another child to feel perfect and complete. We felt a definite shift into another phase of life: each of us in our careers, our daughter into her pre-teen years. I had been fully present for her baby- and toddlerhood, savoured every drop of sweetness and joy those tender years had yielded. I'd never felt biologically compelled, as some of my friends had, to get pregnant again (and again).

In the Filipino Catholic culture, where large families are the norm, only children are seen as objects of pity, and their parents as selfish for violating the laws of nature and depriving them of potential God-sent siblings. But I felt at peace with our choice, along with a tinge of pride for not caving into societal pressure to keep producing more children.

The decision was made. Our daughter was it. Now all I had to do was dispose of the baby clothes, toys, bottles, monitor, strollers (plural), crib, bedding, high chair, and everything from age nought to seven that I had thought I would use again someday. I wasn't a disciplined declutterer to begin with, but I'd put it off for so long that it had grown into a mammoth task, both in physical bulk and emotional weight. I didn't want to face it.

It was Robert who came up with the idea of turning the objects of her childhood into still lifes. 'If you like, we can bring them into the studio and take pictures of them,' he offered. 'That way, you can keep the pictures and look back at the memories any time. Then it makes it easier to let the actual stuff go.' I loved the idea, and I loved him for suggesting it.

Robert built a set by cutting large shapes out of plywood and painted them in bright, powdery-soft pastels. We enlisted his stylist friend Kiki to help arrange the clothes and toys into artful layouts against the backdrops.

'It feels like you should come by the studio,' I said to Marcus as we pawed through vacuum bags stuffed with baby clothes, labelled with ages written on masking tape with black marker – *50 to 54 cm, 62 to 68 cm, 1 y, 2 y, 4 y summer, 4 y winter* – our eyes misting over forgotten bath toys and chewed-up board books, laughing-crying as we sorted through all the years together. 'This isn't just my shoot. These are *our* memories, our daughter, our life.'

'I think you're right,' he replied.

That was how, on a rainy October morning a few weeks shy of my fortieth birthday, Marcus and Robert met for the second time. Seven bags stuffed full of baby clothes and toys were too much for me to carry on my bike, so Marcus drove me to Robert's studio and brought them in.

They greeted each other amiably, shaking hands and exchanging smiles that felt casual and natural, not forced or fake. I showed Marcus where to deposit the bags, then set about making coffee.

This meeting was less tentative than the first time, for there was enough to keep all three of us busy. If either of them was nervous, they didn't show it. I made a conscious effort to stay equidistant between my two loves, never too close to one or the other for too long. I hoped it would help them both feel at ease if I showed no marked favour, distributing my presence as equally as I could.

Sipping from his mug, Marcus watched Robert do his thing: rigging and testing, focusing and firing, cable-snaking and light-making. Then he had to hightail it back home for a 9 a.m. conference call. Before he left, he went over to Robert, clapped him on the shoulder and said, 'Thank you for doing this. I really appreciate it.'

'You're welcome, Marcus,' Robert replied. 'It's my pleasure.'

In that exchange I felt a flash of genuine good regard

between them, something tenuous but sincere between two open-hearted men. It was one of those moments when my heart lit with a wild flash of elation, gratitude and incredulity at my own life.

*

In the process of deciding what to shoot, toss or give away, as I waded through a sea of reusable cloth diapers, fleece zip-up sleep sacks and one too many toddler-sized straw hats with animal ears, I unearthed a treasure I'd almost completely forgotten about.

When I was twenty-eight weeks pregnant, my sister hosted a baby shower for me back home in Manila. As the hat-themed brunch drew to a close, she handed out a stack of blank greeting cards, each labelled with a number from four to eighteen. Then she asked the guests to write down advice for my unborn daughter, according to the age printed on each card. The long table fell into a thoughtful silence as my girlfriends scribbled down words of wisdom, their feathered fascinators and floppy brims bobbing up and down as they wrote.

When people ask me, 'What does your daughter know? What do you tell her?' I think of that stack of notecards. Each contains a message crafted with a specific age in mind, to be handed over at the right time, not to be rushed or given all at once. In the same way, though the reality of how this marriage works surrounds our daughter and implicitly shapes her everyday life, the explicit truth of our choices is broken down into small, manageable chunks, with the intention to release them thoughtfully, and with care, over the span of her life.

What our daughter knows – and what we have chosen to tell her – depends on how old she is and what she understands at that age. What she knew at three was different from what she knew at six, which is different from what she knows at nine, which will be different from what she will know at twelve, eighteen or twenty-four.

She was three years old when Marcus and I first started swiping on Tinder. At that age, she had no sense of minutes, hours or days, unless it was her birthday, Sinterklaas or Christmas. Because she was a champion sleeper, she was oblivious to anything we did after bedtime. Most of my dates took place between her sleeping and waking, unless it was a lunchtime quickie or afternoon delight while she was in school, which I stopped doing as I began to prioritize deeper, more fulfilling connections. In that way, our dating life remained conveniently out of her sight.

As with most toddlers, she had only a tenuous understanding of anyone or anything that wasn't concrete and immediate, right there in front of her. We never brought lovers home, and I didn't know how long I'd be dating any of them anyway, so we never saw the point in mentioning anyone to her by name.

As she grew, so did her sense of awareness. I suppose we were lucky that she tended towards dreaminess and solitude, rather than boundless energy and unstoppable curiosity. She was four the first time she asked where I or Marcus were going. We chose to be selective about details: Mama's going out to dinner, Papa's going out for a drink. By that time, I was dating more regularly – Charlie, Rick, Marc – and felt comfortable saying that I was going to visit a friend.

She was also four when she had her first sleepover with

her then best friend, Elise's daughter. After their family moved away, another little girl who lived a few doors down from us became her new best friend and sleepover buddy, from whom she was inseparable. Sleepovers enabled Marcus and I to stay out all night every few months, which was great for partying together.

Our daughter's working knowledge of sleepovers – you can sleep at a friend's house, and it's fun – helped us explain and normalize our sleepovers to her: first, when the pandemic curfew made them practical; then later, when they became a regular feature of my relationship with Robert.

This is the principle I've since come to rely on: meet her where she is, understand what she understands, then build on that a little bit at a time.

'Bye, *mahal*. I'm sleeping over at Robert's,' I said to her as I kissed her goodbye.

It was the first time I had mentioned a lover to her by name.

'Okay, Mama,' she said. 'Have fun. See you tomorrow.'

'See you tomorrow, my love.'

*

One of the concepts Marcus and I established with our daughter early on was that of different kinds of time.

Between the ages of two to about four, she went through a phase of intense attachment to Marcus and intense jealousy of me. Many of our holiday photos in this period are of me holding her in my arms while she reaches out screaming for the man behind the camera. She would literally push me away whenever I moved to take her from Marcus's arms; untangle our fingers if she saw us holding hands; and fix me with a sulky side-eye if I dared tag along on her Saturday morning market date with Papa.

When she became more verbal, she initially expressed mild resistance to our dates. 'Why do you have to go out without me?' she asked.

'This is Mama and Papa time,' we said, trying to explain why a babysitter would come over so that we could step out for wine, dinner or a movie after she went to bed. 'That's important.'

'Why?'

'Well, there's different kinds of time,' I said. 'There's you and Papa time, when you and Papa do something special together, just the two of you.'

Silence, as our four-year-old pondered this. 'Like when we go to the market?'

'Exactly!' I said. 'Then there's you and Mama time, when you and I do something special together, just the two of us. Like going to violin, or going to the park on Wednesdays after school. Then there's Mama–Papa–you time, when all three of us do fun things together. Like . . .'

'Breakfast in bed!' she piped up. She was starting to get it.

'Yes! Or riding an airplane, or going on holiday,' I said. 'So when Mama and Papa go out, that's Mama and Papa time, where we do something special together, just the two of us.'

'Okay,' she said, wiggling in impatience. This was a long explanation, but a necessary one.

'And then there's Mama time for Mama. Papa time for Papa. And you time for you. That's when we all get time to ourselves to do things we like, without each other. Like when Papa went surfing in Portugal. Or when Mama goes to have coffee with Emma. Or when you play at a friend's house, or have quiet time in the bath, or watch *Pokémon*.

'All of those times are equally important,' I finished. 'So, do you understand, sweetheart? Is it okay if we have Mama and Papa time?'

'Mmm, I guess it's okay,' she says. 'I like all those times.'

'Me too,' I said.

'I like the way you explained that,' Marcus told me later. 'I think it's great.'

This concept of time is one we fall back upon again and again. When I go out, it's Mama time; sleepovers at Robert's fall into that category. Then it's her and Marcus's time. She gets to order sushi and pick a movie to watch with Papa, then sleep next to him in the big bed. I can assure you: she spends more time choosing the movie than mourning my absence. Marcus once asked her how she feels about me being away on Friday nights. 'It's okay, if Mama is happy,' she replied. 'Can we watch *Hotel Transylvania 2* again?' When I see this special time between father and daughter, and the strength of their bond, I think: *She has something I never had.*

Recently, she pouted about Marcus going out late. I had to remind her that Papa having his own time was important to him. 'How would you feel if Papa or I told you that you shouldn't have so much time to yourself?' I asked her. 'It wouldn't feel nice, right?'

'No,' she said. 'I guess not.'

'It wouldn't feel nice if Papa says to me, *Hey, you've had enough Mama time*, or you say to me, *I think you've had enough Mama time*,' I continued. 'That's because you are the only person who knows best how much "you time" you need.

Where you *do* have a say is in the time you spend with each of us.' I paused for emphasis.

'Listen. You can always, always say to us: *Hey, I need more Mama-and-me time* or *I need more Papa-and-me time*. Does that sound fair?'

'Okay,' she agreed. 'Fair.'

'So, let's see. In the last few weeks, do you feel like you've had enough time with each of us, or with the three of us all together?'

She tipped her head to one side, considering. 'I think so,' she said after a pause. Then she nodded. 'Actually, yeah.'

'Will you tell me or Papa if you feel like you're not getting enough of any of those kinds of time?'

'Sure,' she said. 'That's easy.'

'Perfect.' I pulled her close, gave her a big kiss on the top of her head, and felt her snuggle into my arm.

As she grows, I want her box of tools to grow too, just as ours did when we expanded our relationship. This is one that I'm happy to give her: an easy way to ask for more of our time, and an agreement that we will always listen. With her teenage years approaching, I have a feeling we're going to need it.

*

As parents know, the curiosities and obsessions of young children are written all over them. What our daughter knew at age nine about falling in love, sex, relationships or boyfriends (and girlfriends) is no mystery to me.

'Do you know that boy goats pee on the ground and dunk their foreheads in it?' she announced once, reading aloud from her favourite book of animal facts. 'Then the girl goat comes to him, smells the pee, and –' she fluttered her eyelids like Daisy Duck '– they fall in *love*!'

There's a young nine and there's a mature nine. At her age, I was the latter: already boy-crazy and writing very secret, very bad love poems in a padlocked diary. Being a young nine, none of that makes sense to her yet, so to announce that Robert is my boyfriend serves no purpose. If he had to, say, pick her up from school or join us for dinner every Friday night, it might make sense to explain it. But the decision to not make him part of our family life is a mutual choice among Marcus, myself and Robert, because it feels best for all of us.

Robert has maintained what I would describe as a respectful distance. I am a courier for his small, sweet gifts: scraps of fabric for her papier-mâché mouse house (after a popular Dutch children's book called *Het Muizenhuis*, about a pair of mice named Sam and Julia), which she and Marcus like to work on together; an illustrated book of Irish myths and legends, peppered with Celtic names that I murdered when I read them to her at bedtime; a plastic-wrapped packet of stickers.

One cold afternoon, Marcus and I took our daughter and her best friend on a long walk through the park. As the girls raced ahead of us, Marcus confessed an irrational stab of jealousy at Robert's gifts. It was understandable: he's almost more protective of their father–daughter bond than he is of our marriage. The gifts, which seemed thoughtful to me, were threatening if he chose to see them as the first steps of an interloper encroaching on his territory as the man in our little girl's life.

It took us one lap around the park to talk it through. Marcus broke it down, doing the work, grasping that he can never be replaced as her father, just as mine was never replaced by any of my mother's loves.

'I want our daughter to know and feel that she is loved by many people,' he said.

The first time Robert met my daughter was when he agreed to take care of our plants and cat while we went to Greece for a summer holiday. Marcus and I decided that Robert could come over so I could brief him on what needed to be done. He'd never been in our house before.

When he arrived, she was playing with her *muizenhuis*, which was installed in a corner of the living room. 'Sweetheart, this is Robert,' I said.

'Hi!' Robert piped up. 'I've heard so much about you.'

'Hi,' she murmured, eyes fixed on the unfolding of some unspoken, mouse-sized narrative.

'How are you?'

'Fine,' she said.

'Robert is going to take care of our kitty while we're in Greece,' I told her. 'He was the one who gave you the fabric for the *muizenhuis*, remember?'

'Fabric?' she asked, looking up.

'The one which you made into socks for Sam and a dress for Julia,' I reminded her.

'Ohhhhh, yeah,' she said, brightening.

'Would you like to show Robert what you made? You could give him a tour of the *muizenhuis*, too.'

'Okay,' she said. Robert inched closer so she could point out all the rooms to him as he oohed and aahed over every tiny design feature, asking all the right questions. 'Wonderful,' he enthused, his Irish charm filling each pronouncement with a mellifluous warmth. 'Brilliant. Very clever! Did you make that yourself? Oh, look at those little chairs! Fair play, that's very well done.'

He thanked her for showing him around, and she went back to playing. I gave him the grand tour of our (human-sized) house, finishing with the plants he was to water on the balcony. As he headed out the door, he called, 'Bye, honey! It was lovely to meet you.'

'Bye!' she called back.

Before, Robert was only a name I said from time to time, attached to a place where I slept over once a week. Now, it is attached to a face, an infrequent presence, and a list of facts that continues to grow in drips and dots.

She knows Robert is a photographer, likes to sew, and hails from Ireland (which we've looked at together in her illustrated atlas). Later, she will come to know that his favourite insect is a butterfly (a question she asked him herself); that he drives a black van and owns a tent for camping; and that his neighbour's cat is a fat calico named Boef, who likes to saunter into his garden and sit in the plant box on his balcony like a prince on a throne.

*

My daughter observes and absorbs things in her own quiet way, even if she may not be as inquisitive as other children. She knows I'm a writer and has seen me working on my book on my laptop at home. 'Is your book a *roman*?' she asked me once, using the Dutch word for fiction.

'No, sweetheart. It's about real life. It's about my life,

mostly about me and Papa actually, and a little bit about our family.'

She nodded. 'I've seen Papa's name in it.'

She was the first person I told the first time an agent asked me for my full manuscript. From then on, I shared every milestone with her, explaining each part of the process as it happened: from signing with an agent to submitting to editors, going to auction to meeting publishers in London. I wanted her to understand what I'd accomplished, but more importantly, I wanted her to be part of my joy.

Securing a book deal with a major publisher made the prospect of going public with our story finally, irrevocably real. Up until this point, the dynamics of our marriage were hidden in plain sight, familiar yet unnamed. All that remained was to make the implicit explicit. I figured we had about a year for the concept to fully sink in before the book came out. Then the words 'open marriage' would be all around her.

When I was learning Dutch, my teacher told me about a student who built his vocabulary by sticking Post-its with Dutch words for common household objects all around his apartment. Maybe telling her would be like this, I thought: sticking a new word on something she already knows.

The excitement around the book deal piqued her long-slumbering curiosity. 'She asked me again today what your book was about,' Marcus said to me one morning over coffee.

'I feel like the time is now,' I said. All I needed was an opening.

I think back to the way I formed an understanding of my world as a child: a gradual unfolding that developed over time.

What you grow up with is what you believe is normal,

until you become old enough to realize that not every family operates as yours does. For example, all throughout my childhood I assumed it was normal to have just one parent. My childhood best friend had both a father and a mother, but my nine-year-old self just thought it was more complicated that way, how she played them off against each other, running to her papa when her mama refused her something she wanted.

It's so much easier just having to ask Mom, I thought then. It was only much later when I realized the multiple implications of being raised by a mother who was widowed young, an understanding that continued to deepen into adulthood, when I became a mother myself.

When I was a little girl, certain people were present in our family's life in varying degrees. There was the constellation of women who always seemed to be at our house after my father's death. There were aunts I came to see as auxiliary grandmothers: Lola N., who taught me how to sew, and Lola E., who always brought my mother's favourite treats from her hometown – *kesong puti*, homemade cottage cheese, and *sinukmani*, sticky-sweet brown rice cooked in coconut milk, wrapped up in glossy banana leaves for the long bus ride to the city. There were my mother's friends: Tita M., who worked in a tall shiny building in the Makati financial district, and Tita Y., whose birthday was a day before Mom's.

Making the connection between their presence and their significance came much later. I was in my early teens when I learned that Tita M. had been one of the two witnesses at my parents' spontaneous City Hall wedding. I was in college when I asked: *How are we related to Lola N.? To Lola E.?* (They were both my mother's aunts by marriage.) And I was already a mother when Mom told me that Tita Y. was the one who swept in and took over the arrangements for Dad's wake, funeral and burial, down to the words engraved on his tombstone. It was only recently that I realized those women were there to hold my mother – and our family – in the depths of her grief.

I trust that in the same way, when our daughter is ready to know more, she will ask. I trust that the significance of Robert will become apparent to her someday.

Oh, she will say to herself with a dawning understanding. *Mama sleeps over at Robert's place. Oh*, that's *what she was doing there*. She'll figure it out, a little bit on her own and a little bit with my help, just as I did. Then it will be normal to her, because I've never hidden it. The way Marcus accepts this without tension or rancour will tell her it's normal, too – if not in the wider world, then at least in our family.

Until then: she's a child. Explicit sexual details have no place in a child's life. Children should never be put in a position to deal with sexual content before they are mature enough to process it. If monogamous parents aren't expected to share details of their sexual lives with their children, why should I?

For now, I have only to deal with the simplest of questions. 'How was it?' she typically asks on Saturday morning when I walk in from Robert's.

'It was good!'

Or she might ask, 'Did you have fun?' the same way I ask her if she had fun at a birthday party at a friend's house. 'Yes, I did,' is my truthful, if vague reply.

'What did you do last night?' she asked another time.

'We built a bee hotel!' I replied, showing her photographic

evidence on my phone, thanking my lucky stars that Robert is the type who always has a project on the go.

*

After my book is sold at auction, a *studiedag* – teachers away studying, children off from school – gives me the opening I am looking for. With Marcus at the office, she and I have the whole day together, just us girls, which feels special; so does a slow morning, plenty of reading time on the couch, and a late lunch in our pyjamas – delights usually reserved for Sunday slipped into a boring old Tuesday.

We have just conspired to polish off the last slice of cake in the refrigerator; I'm brewing a pot of chamomile tea. There's nowhere we have to be, nothing we have to do. This is exactly what I wanted, so I could take the time and care this conversation needed.

I've lined up a few talking points in my head and cleared them with Marcus, but I don't know exactly how to begin with a ten-year-old.

I take a deep breath. I will just have to wing it.

'So, I heard your friends want to know what the book is about,' I begin, setting the pot on the table with a pair of small Turkish tea glasses. This is true. A few parents from school have congratulated me on my book deal; one of them let on that their child had asked ours what the book was about, and was surprised that she didn't know.

'Sort of,' she says. 'It's more like . . . *bruh, I can't believe you don't know what your mom is writing about!*'

'Well, if you want to tell them, let's start with what you do know,' I say. Together, we tick the facts off on our fingers: the book isn't fiction; it's mostly about me and Papa; and she is in it.

'It's a kind of book called a memoir,' I say, pouring tea into both glasses. 'A memoir is a book about real-life things that happen to real people. Not, like, from the day they're born until the day they die, but about a certain part of their life that's interesting.'

'Like, if you lived in Japan for three years, it could just be about that time?' she asks, reaching for her glass. Her current set of obsessions include sushi and manga, and extend to all things *kawaii* and Japanese.

'Exactly,' I say. 'So the reason publishers are interested in my book – in my memoir – is because Papa and I have an open marriage.'

It is the first time I say the words to her out loud.

I wonder if her heart has also started beating a bit faster, like mine.

'An open marriage means Papa and I are married, and we love each other, and we know we're going to be together for life,' I say. 'Papa and I have also agreed that we can see other people and have other special people in our lives.' I take a gulp of tea, too fast and too hot.

Across the table, her slender fingers rest on the sides of her glass, waiting for it to cool.

'Not a lot of people have open marriages. But lots of people ask me questions about being in an open marriage, so I decided to write down the answers. And that's why the title of my book is called *Ask Me How It Works*.'

'Ohhh,' she says, and I see puzzle pieces coming together in her eyes. Perhaps she has glimpsed the words somewhere: in an email on my laptop screen, printed on a draft, on the silver Mylar balloon that Emma sent to congratulate me on the book deal.

'Take your class, for example. There are what – twenty? Twenty-one kids,' I say, and she nods. 'Most of them have one mama and one papa, and their mama and papa have agreed that they will only have each other in their lives. But there are a few families doing something different. Like –' I name a boy in her class. 'He has two papas. And the kids next door who moved away? They had two mamas.'

'I remember,' she says.

'Sometimes, when something is different, and not a lot of people are doing it, it makes others curious. Sometimes it's hard for them to understand, and they might not say nice things about it,' I say. 'You know your friends best. You know who will understand, and who might not.

'No matter what you decide to tell them, the most important thing is that *you* know, and the three of *us* know, that Papa and I love you very much. That we love each other very much. And that even if we do things a bit differently, our family loves each other very much, and that we're happy.'

It is only at the end of this entire speech that I realize I've been holding my breath.

Ever so slowly, she takes her first sip of tea and puts down her glass. Then she says: 'My brain has a lot of information now.' What she means is clear. *Ease up, slow down.*

Both of us welcome a pause, sipping our tea and scraping the last licks of icing off our cake plates. As the silence continues, my tenuous relief at having muddled through the most important bits with what I hope is minimal awkwardness turns into a flicker of anxiety. Why does she *still* have no questions?

'Umm, sweetheart,' I begin again. 'Is it – is it clear to you what an open marriage is?'

'I think so,' she says, before flooring me with her next statement. 'We're not the only family in class with an open marriage.'

What?

So unprepared am I for this that for a beat I panic: have I botched it up? Does she have it all wrong? 'No, darling, his parents have a *same-sex* marriage,' I try to correct her. 'That's not the same as an open marriage.'

The look she gives me holds the genesis of a sassy teenage eyeroll. 'I don't mean him,' she says. 'I mean –' She names two other classmates, and I am gobsmacked.

'Are you sure? How do you know?'

Apparently, one just said it outright: 'My parents have an open marriage.' (The fact that my daughter had zero inclination to ask exactly what that meant is, well, consistent.) Another time, she overheard a group of boys talking during their lunch break. 'My parents prefer a closed marriage,' said one of them.

'My parents prefer something else,' replied another.

'Oooooh,' chorused the whole group before breaking into laughter, then drifting away to start a game of football.

Welcome to Amsterdam! I thought to myself. How funny that I'd been fretting about how to broach the topic of an open marriage, when my daughter had already heard about it from her friends. And how perfect that we'd made our lives here, in a community where three kids out of twenty-one – and perhaps more that we didn't know of – had parents who'd chosen to live as we did and be open with their children, too.

Knowing my daughter won't feel alone makes *me* feel less alone.

It makes me feel as though somehow, at last, we belong.

*

The process of writing this book has been a catalyst for conversation and a deepening of intimacy in my closest relationships. Marcus and I spent many evenings going over the events as I wrote about them, seeing them and each other with wiser, more compassionate eyes.

After I completed my first draft, I handed copies to Marcus and Robert, Emma and my sister. More than being my earliest critics, they read through the lenses of their relationships with me as husband and boyfriend, best friend and sister. It will be the same for her: she will read it as a daughter first, then as partner, wife or mother, if she chooses to become one.

Now that I can speak openly to her about the book, I find that I can also refer to the dynamics of our open marriage more directly, nudging the abstract towards the concrete, one soft touch at a time.

One afternoon I tell her that I'm working on the book again, this time with edits from my publisher.

'Are there any suggestions you don't agree with?' she asks.

'Well, let's see. In my book each chapter doesn't start with a number, but a question. So we're thinking about changing some of the questions, or putting them on their own page,' I explain. 'I'm not sure about that yet.'

'Like what kind of questions?'

'Mmm, questions people ask me all the time, when they want to know why –'

'– why you chose to have an open marriage,' she says, finishing my thought for me. Her words both lift my heart and fill me with relief.

'Right! For example, one chapter is called: *Are you ever jealous?*' I continue, watching her face closely – for a hiccup, a stumbling block, some warning sign that I'm going too far and ought to pull back. 'Like, people want to know if I'm ever jealous of Papa going out with other people. Or if Papa is ever jealous of Robert.'

'Ahh,' she says, her brows lifting. 'So will you take your editor's suggestion?'

'I have to try it out and see,' I say. A mixture of relief and pride blooms in my chest, a subtle warmth spreading through me. She just gets it; there is no need to push on or say more.

By the time she is mature enough to read this book, it is my hope that we'll have had years to establish trust, openness and honesty. Until then, Marcus and I will build up her background of implicit knowledge like paint on canvas: in broad sweeps and light strokes, allowing time to elapse between layers, letting impressions solidify before adding new ones.

This is the work of a lifetime, and I chose the perfect partner for it.

*

What else do I know that she knows?

She knows that Mama and Papa argue, but that people who love one another can disagree sometimes because they see things differently. She knows that we always talk it over, and that we love each other. She knows that if and when we fight, it's not her fault, and she must never think that. She knows that we love her no matter what; that we are proud of her; that we consider ourselves lucky to be her mama and papa.

I also know that there's no way to know everything she knows.

For now, that will be enough, until it isn't. Then we'll figure it out all over again.

Someday, I hope she will know that she can ask and tell me anything. That being the way you are, liking the things you like, loving the way you want to love, is okay. That trying new things to understand yourself better is okay, too. That being smart about risks doesn't have to mean living in fear, and that making mistakes doesn't have to mean living in shame. That people who truly love you will always want you to grow, be more and more of yourself, and be free.

Epilogue

Are you happier this way?

A celebration.

It began as a joke during the pandemic, when all the music festivals we had hoped for were called off one by one for the second summer in a row. 'My fortieth birthday is going to be festival-themed!' I quipped to friends. 'Every room in the house will be a different stage. Come dressed for the festival that you had tickets for but got cancelled.' The joke gathered steam throughout late summer until it started to sound like a good idea.

I sent out the first round of invitations on WhatsApp, then two rounds of postponements as we became statistics in the Delta outbreak of 2021. Our daughter was the first to come down with a fever, a sore throat and the sniffles. By the third day she was her chirpy self again, but as per quarantine guidelines at the time, we waited until the following week to send her back to school.

A day after she got sick, Marcus fell ill with what looked like full-blown man flu. With a sinking heart, I realized Covid was coming for me next, if I didn't already have it.

'Should we try to isolate?' Marcus asked. 'Maybe you won't get it.'

'It's worth a try,' I said glumly.

For the next few days Marcus and our daughter slept in our bedroom and I on the couch. He handled their food and disinfected the bathroom after they used it; we both masked up whenever he entered the living room. In an attempt at levity, we dubbed our respective sides of the apartment the north and south wing.

In the next few days of my attempted isolation, it was Robert who came to the door with an air mattress ('Might be more comfortable than the couch?' he suggested) and a week's worth of groceries, along with my favourite chocolate-covered croissants, a bouquet of flowers and a bottle of Pinot Grigio. At night he sent me voice messages reading funny excerpts from a new poetry book that had just arrived in the post.

Because we are a family that thrives on hugs and kisses, the loss of physical contact in isolation limbo felt jarring, bizarre and futile. Sleepless nights and anxious days shredded what was left of my immune system until I succumbed to Covid two days shy of my fortieth birthday.

It took me a month to fully recover. I rescheduled the party to the end of November, before the government declared a second winter lockdown.

*

I often thought that turning forty would feel like I was turning into my mother. But I had become someone different – different from my mother, from the other women around me, and from whom I imagined I might become.

To me, forty was my mother's age. In my child's mind, Mom at forty was the ultimate symbol of womanhood. This meant polished scarlet fingernails, delicate earlobes adorned with South Sea pearls, and black hair swept back into a sleek, elegant bun. It meant the lingering scent of Estée Lauder perfume, a decadent dash of red Chanel lipstick, the buttery sheen of Ferragamo loafers — textures and scents that not only smelled of luxury and success, but also hinted at the ownership of one's destiny and the autonomy to choose one's pleasures.

At forty, my mother was at the height of her feminine power. In our house, she called the shots, made the decisions, paid the bills. She didn't subscribe to gender roles or bow to expectations of domesticity. While the other mothers cooked, cleaned, and gossiped together while waiting for the school gates to open, Mom spread her wings.

As an investment consultant and commodities trader, she flew to Europe in tweed coats and silk scarves; as the one-time owner of a gold mine, she trampled through the jungles of Agusan Valley with an all-male entourage of engineers, geologists, and local Manobo tribesmen who worked for her.

My mother was not like the other mothers. Neither am I.

Now, in my forties, I am a published author, a Filipina-Indian immigrant living in the Netherlands, and a polyamorous woman with a husband and boyfriend. In my marriage of seventeen years, of which eight have been consensually non-monogamous, I've held the roles of wife, mother (eleven years), sexual adventurer (the better part of eight years), and girlfriend (going on five years).

If you had asked me at twenty, then again at thirty, if I ever pictured myself like this at forty, I would have thought you were crazy. In my wildest imagination I would not have dreamed this combination of identities was possible, or that I would be living it.

I am in an unusual position compared to my peers, who are mostly in the 'married with two or three kids' zone of life. From where I am, I see very few moms like me. We stick out like sore thumbs. I suppose this makes it easier for us to spot each other, like Khalil and his aliens.

I find myself possessed of a confidence that is more than just skin deep. It comes from having messed up and cleaned up; being vocal about my boundaries, desires and needs; and trusting that the people in my life will love me anyway. It comes from being intimately acquainted with my own quirks, weaknesses and limitations so that I can help those I love navigate around them. It comes from knowing that I bring enough to the table to make me a partner worth having – whether for a night, a season or a lifetime.

It also comes from the courage to have tough conversations, the willingness to listen, and the ability to say and hear *no*. At the beginning of my open marriage, that meant saying to Marcus: *I need an outlet for my desire for intense experiences, sexual variety and adventure. I know that's hard to give. What can I/we do to make that easier for you? What do you need from me in return?* (I'm oversimplifying. Adulting conversations are never that easy.)

When I lost my taste for casual sex and began wanting deeper, more fulfilling connections, I had to advocate for my own needs and desires once more, by saying: *I've had casual experiences that have left me feeling unfulfilled and unsafe. Can I see certain people more regularly? What do you need for that to feel safer for you?*

Contemplating a more emotionally intimate relationship with Robert, I stated my boundaries: *I can't sleep over, or spend as much time with you as you might need or want. I can't move in with you, buy a house with you, marry you or bear your children. Knowing all that, I see a lot is still possible for us. Do you want to explore that with me?*

Maybe the best part of all this is that adventure has become experience, and experience has become instinct. From where I sit, all the tough conversations, mistakes and learnings have helped me shape a life where I can navigate sex, intimacy and relationships by the internal compass I've spent years learning to trust, free of internal conflict, guilt or shame. Flying on my instincts and seeing them proven true feels more deeply satisfying than any orgasm.

A huge and valuable part of being myself at this age is liking it this way.

*

On the night of the party, I remember my phone pinging with snapshots of our friends' negative self-tests, one pink stripe on each of them.

I remember unboxing a treasure trove of pink, blue and orange silk sarees – bought on a breakneck sprint through Gariahat Market with a gaggle of Indian aunts, worn to a wedding in Kolkata, then stashed away for years – and draping them over our bed, their golden fringe and embroidered paisley gleaming in the light of the white pillar candles on the windowsill. Pearlescent balloons trailed curly tails of silver from the ceiling.

Marcus and I filled our bathtub with 200 red, blue and yellow plastic balls to make it a ball pit for adults, which turned out to be a hit. Before leaving for a sleepover, our daughter gave us permission to use her bedroom as a chillout spot, strictly no drinking and dancing allowed. We switched on the fairy lights in her reading nook as the first guests arrived to find *adobo* and *lumpia* on banana leaves spread out on the dining table, and rum, whisky and gin at my writing-desk-turned-bar.

Our home swelled with guests, conversation, laughter. Looking at the people I had gathered over a decade in Amsterdam, each with their own story of how they came into my life and I into theirs, I saw years of incremental effort ripening to fruition. I couldn't help but think: *This is a long way from the time when my closest friend in the world was a stranger I met on Craigslist.*

The simple realization – *I have a house full of friends* – made my heart feel full.

I allowed myself a moment to relish this fullness; after all, tonight was a celebration.

Presiding over the kitchen, Marcus brought a magnificent slow-roast pork belly out of the oven to *oohs* and *aahs*. My friends – many of whom had gotten to know Marcus well over the years, until I thought of them as our friends – aimed their phones at the satisfying crunch of the crackling as he sliced into it with a knife. He was basking in the glow of appreciation for his cooking when Robert arrived with a cloud of pastel balloons and a rainbow cape he'd sewn himself, made for joyous twirling.

This was no longer a rushed handshake on the street in front of a double-parked van. Neither was it a harried drop-off with bags full of props and clothes at Robert's photography studio. They busied themselves for a few minutes – Robert with his balloons, Marcus with his food – before greeting each other with grins and claps on the back, gestures that revealed familiarity and respect.

Both had been given ample time to ready themselves for this moment, when they would occupy the same space and inhabit their respective roles among an audience that knew the facts of our relationship – a public debut, in a way, of how it works. That preparation, together with the implicit acceptance of the people around us, helped create comfort and ease between them that night. Dancing bodies closed any gaps that might be awkward. Music and laughter filled any silences that might be uncomfortable.

Knowing that Marcus felt secure in the home we shared and among the friends we had made throughout our married life, I attended to Robert. He needed a project to occupy him so I assigned him to the bar, where his years of experience bartending at an Irish pub served him well. Needing friends to anchor him, he gravitated towards Emma, who he had met several times, and was delighted when his favourite stylist and dear friend Kiki turned up straight from a shoot, ready to party.

Deep into the night, Marcus and Robert shared a beer on the balcony, exchanged pleasantries and words that remained between the two of them. Much later, Robert told me he felt welcome in our home. Everyone knew who he was in my life, a role legitimized by his presence alongside Marcus.

I floated between Marcus and Robert throughout the evening, sharing kisses and embraces with one while the other was occupied with people, dancing, drinking. Nothing was flaunted; nothing felt forced. Everything flowed like wine in the warm glow of candlelight.

It wouldn't be the last time they shared space to celebrate and support me. As I made more of my writing public, there would be readings, panels, parties where I showed up as someone I never thought I'd be: a polyamorous woman with two partners.

Here is my husband. Here is my boyfriend.
Here we are.
Here I am.

*

I'm no longer just in an open marriage; I am polyamorous. I know that now. I am capable of romantic love for more than one person; receptive to the challenges of navigating more than one romantic relationship; and deeply fulfilled by doing so.

Being polyamorous, to me, means managing intangible essentials like feelings and needs – my own and, to varying degrees, the feelings and needs of the people I love, depending on how much responsibility I assume for them – alongside the finite resources of time and energy. Becoming a parent radically shifted my perception of both; so has becoming polyamorous.

I feel more *myself* this way. I have worked hard to understand how I am different, and accept it. Now that I do, I love this about me.

Marcus and Robert accept this about me, too. Both of them make me feel loved, wanted and cherished for who I am. Neither of them is polyamorous the way I am, and I don't expect them to be.

I am a hinge between two men who have agreed to slightly different forms of non-monogamy with me. 'I can't do what you do,' Marcus says of the complexity of managing a second relationship; he is happy with his occasional casual adventures. Robert isn't dating anyone at the moment; neither am I. Someday, when one or both of us will feel like doing so, we will have to figure out how it works for us.

When Marcus and I were together long-distance, it was easy to define our relationship by the amount of time we spent apart. Hours and days went by fast enough, because we had busy enough lives to fill them. After a few weeks, the time apart would catch up to one or both of us, suddenly becoming coloured with meaning – *Why am I alone on a Friday night again? Until when are we going to do this? If he can stand being away from me this long, does he really love me? Does he really want to be with me?*

The emotional charge in these questions came from some underlying feeling that something was wrong with the relationship, or with me. Time together would resolve these doubts, filling me with enough love, reassurance and optimism to fuel me through the next separation.

After some years, the amount of time we had spent apart became proof of our devotion and commitment, and of my worthiness and lovability. *We've been long-distance for four years*, I'd say with pride, secretly basking in the impressed reactions of those who were listening.

In the current form of our marriage, the hours we spend apart have become, to me, simply blocks of time, neutralized of their emotional or moral charge. Because I believe space is healthy, and trust that we can ask each other for more time together if we need it, I accept these hours apart as a feature of our relationship. And because I believe my husband is an intrinsically good man, I trust that what he does when we are apart – what he chooses to do with that time – is ultimately good for him.

Hours Marcus spends dancing his heart out, or expanding his sexual boundaries, or learning more about himself in the mirror of a new connection, are the same – as worthy – to me as any other activity that wives are expected to excuse our husbands for, like spending countless hours at the gym or playing video games or dirt biking or golf.

The hours we spend apart mean nothing about our relationship, or me.

The hours we spend together are what matters. Not absence, but presence.

I think this helped me with any mom guilt I might have struggled with at the beginning, when the pursuit of pleasure – satisfying my needs for adventure, exploration and self-expression through the vehicle of sex – took me away from home and family.

I know now that my worth as a wife and mother is not judged by the hours of my absence, but the quality of my presence.

Wherever I am, whoever I'm with, I choose to say: *Here I am. I'm all in.*

*

Long after the guests leave and the music fades, all that remains of that night are the Instax snapshots I find in odd places: in the tub, on the fridge, propped up against books, stashed in drawers. I select a handful to give away to friends; the rest I keep for myself, for the pleasure of remembering.

Of all these photos, it is one of the three of us together, grinning and clutching beers – Robert in his jaunty sailor hat, Marcus in his black linen shirt, me in gold shorts and fluffy white bunny ears lined with pink satin, standing in between them – that I treasure most.

This moment is a slice of time in the life I never knew I

wanted, sealed in paper and emulsion, preserved in memory and meaning. In this picture, it all works. But this picture may look very different tomorrow; it probably already does.

So if at some point in the future you run into me on the street, bump into me at a party, or pick up this book and feel the stirrings of curiosity, go ahead.

Ask me how it works.

Resources

Stealthing is non-consensual condom removal and is punishable as a sexual offence under Dutch law: https://stealthing.nl/en. If you live in the Netherlands and have experienced stealthing or any form of sexual assault, contact the Centrum Seksueel Geweld, or Sexual Assault Centre, within seven days. Call (or ask your doctor to call) their free, anonymous hotline at 0800-0188: https://centrumseksueelgeweld.nl

To consult with a fully licensed, English-speaking psychotherapist in Amsterdam, I am happy to recommend Dr Onno de Boer: http://www.expattherapy.nl

If you are interested in non-violent communication for individuals, couples or organizations in the Randstad area, reach out to Cara Crisler of Crisler Coaching. Let her know I sent you: https://crislercoaching.com

Acknowledgements

To embark on a non-monogamous marriage by choice and to have written and published a book are immense privileges. I am grateful for every act of kindness and generosity, every opportunity and advantage granted to me that led me here and made this all possible.

To our parents, especially Mom. You came from nothing and employed every bit of character, determination, hard work, street smarts, and heart at your disposal to give us the best possible start in life. For this, our education, and our blueprint for loving, I can never thank you enough.

To Ate, the best sister I could ask for.

To Uncle H., for my earliest experiences of a world beyond the Philippines, and an extended family I've cherished all my life.

To Colegio de Sta. Rosa – I'm sorry I didn't quite turn out as you'd hoped, but you have my gratitude, particularly to Sr Tess Bautista A R, for writing off my final year of tuition.

To the Ateneo de Manila University, the Office of Admission and Aid, and the Ateneo de Manila University Alumni Association of California.

To Doreen Fernandez, for believing in me and for always keeping your office door open.

To Maya and Lille, my first editors at *Seventeen*. To all the bosses who took a chance on me and helped me grow creatively in so many different ways: Surajit, Dino, Lilian and James, and Natalie.

To my mentor, coach and friend Nina Siegal, for seeing the book in an essay no one would publish. Your questions pushed me to look deeper; your encouragement taught me to trust my instincts. Thank you for keeping me moving forward, 'like a shark'.

To Jo Unwin, for saving me from the slush pile when I was just about to give up. You saw me, and my life changed. And to wonder girl Daisy Arendell and Donna Greaves at JULA, thank you.

To my dream team at Viking: Harriet Bourton, you Superwoman, I've loved every minute of working with you. To Jane Gentle, Kayla Fuller, Ruth Johnstone and the UK and international sales teams, Rosey Battle, Meredith Benson and Chris Bentham, cover design wizard. To Preena Gadher: I'll never forget how you ran up to me that day at the Penguin offices and made me feel so welcome. Natalie Wall, Sarah-Jane Forder, Sarah Barlow and Emma Adams, thanks for your precision and care.

To Kate Burton and César Castañeda Gámez at C&W; Deborah Schneider at Gelfman & Schneider; Abby Singer at Casarotto Ramsay; Alexandra Hummel and the Hanserblau team; Melle van Loenen, Francis Wehkamp, and everyone at Park Uitgevers.

To the London Writers' Salon, for making Writers' Hour such a magical place that I kept coming back to write, even when I didn't want to write any more.

To Cinelle Barnes, for your warmth and insight. To Asha Indralingam and Ana P. Santos – I can't call you beta readers because you are both hella alpha. To Sarah Gallucci and my classmates in Catapult's Writing Real Sex class; creative doulas Emma Rice and Eva Visser Plaza; Joelle Fraser, for your Thirty-Minute Memoir class at Creative Nonfiction, where this book was born; Martyn Jones, for cleaning up my first pages; Lilly Dancyger, for your eyes on my query letter; and Alexandra Penrhyn Lowe, for our writerly chats.

To Titia Melessen, for sharing your knowledge of the Dutch law on sexual crimes; Atty. Hershel Dimagiba-Co, for briefing me on the Family Code of the Philippines; Grace Velasco, for writing the definitive Simple Girl Index. Grace, you are missed.

To Morgan and Shari, for convening the Professionals in Sex Society (PISS), giving us perverts a place to share, have fun, and thrive. To Nina, Maxi, Josh, Rebecca and Morgan (again!) for inviting me to read at Nina.V, Body Electric, Schmutz Cinema, Come Alive, and the Felix Meritis Institute. To Jokin at Creative Mornings Amsterdam – I should have warmed up the audience before launching into the butt-plug story cold at 8.30 a.m., but thanks for having me.

To our dear friends in Amsterdam and Manila, who listened and understood, hosted our girl on playdates and sleepovers, and supported our marriage and family. To the Poly Moms, who have no time for this.

To 'Thomas' and 'Charlie', for your friendship; to 'Rui', my home in Paris.

To 'Emma', me-in-another-body, for your magnificence, wisdom and expansive heart.

To my Robert: darling co-schemer, creative partner, and Distraction Police. Without you there would be no book.

ACKNOWLEDGEMENTS

Who could have imagined how far we'd come? Thank you for coming along on this crazy ride with me.

To my Googly: my husband, life partner, rock and safe place. Without you there would be no story. What a life we've made together. Thank you for making it with me.

And finally, to my daughter: Little Mango, Cinnamon Stick, our Girlby. Having you rewrote my story and gave me the courage to tell it. I am so lucky and proud to be your mama.

husband? H
you tell each
ou afraid of t
appens if yo
does it real
do you tell yo
Are you happ
What's it like
start? Was y